OPERATIONS OF 1st CANADIAN CORPS
HOLLAND   APRIL-MAY 1945

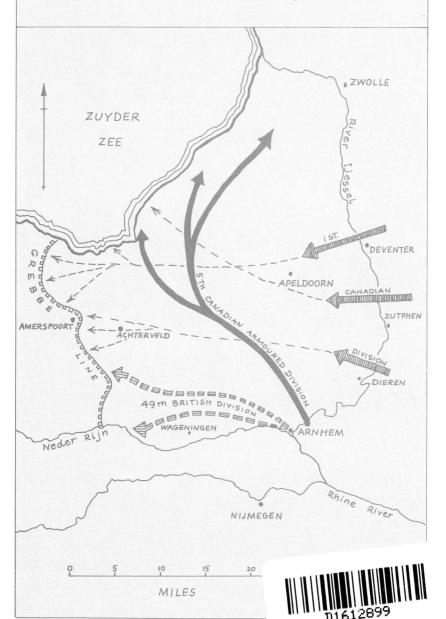

ZWOLLE

ZUYDER

ZEE

River Ijssel

1 ST.

DEVENTER

GREBBE

APELDOORN

CANADIAN

ZUTPHEN

AMERSFOORT

ACHTERVELD

5TH CANADIAN ARMOURED DIVISION

DIVISION

LINE

DIEREN

49th BRITISH DIVISION

WAGENINGEN

ARNHEM

Neder Rijn

NIJMEGEN

Rhine River

0   5   10   15   20

MILES

To Doug and Mary with my love

George Kitching Apr '86

Mud and Green Fields

THE MEMOIRS OF
MAJOR GENERAL GEORGE KITCHING

WITH AN INTRODUCTION BY
COLONEL CHARLES P. STACEY

Among the soldiers this is muttered. . .
that here you maintain several factions
and. . . that you are disputing with your
generals. One would have lingering wars,
with little cost; another would fly swift,
but wanteth wings; a third man thinks,
without expense at all, by guileful fair
words peace may be obtained.

SHAKESPEARE
HENRY VI ACT 1

BATTLELINE BOOKS
1986

These memoirs are dedicated to the men and women
of the Canadian Army and the British Army
with whom I served.

In peace there's nothing so becomes a man
as modest stillness and humility

SHAKESPEARE
HENRY V ACT 3

ISBN 0-920849-02-4

First Printing 1986
Canadians At War Series

Published by
BATTLELINE BOOKS
20076 46A Avenue
Langley, B.C.
Canada V3A 6J3

Contents

MAPS

Foreword

by
Colonel Charles P. Stacey
Soldier Author & Historian

Few Canadian soldiers, and fewer Canadian generals, have written accounts of their experiences in the Second World War. Fortunately, George Kitching is an exception, and he has an exceptional story to tell. During his wartime career he served in every rank from subaltern to major general, and in most of the theatres where the Canadian Army fought.

He was one of the first Canadians to go overseas in 1939. He was the senior staff officer of the 1st Canadian Division during the fighting in Sicily, the army's first protracted campaign. After further service on the Italian mainland as a brigade commander, he commanded the 4th Canadian Armoured Division in the Battle of Normandy, and in the final stages of the war he was Chief of Staff of the 1st Canadian Corps in Italy and the Netherlands. He was an actor in great events and an associate of great personalities, and his account of what he saw is an important addition to history.

As a senior officer of the postwar Canadian Army, General Kitching witnessed its development into a force much respected by our NATO allies, and its subsequent emasculation by Messrs. Hellyer and (after Kitching's retirement) Trudeau. His frank comments on these matters are a contribution to public education.

When General Kitching retired from the service, he took with him the goodwill and good wishes of a vast number of friends. It is a pleasure and an honour to introduce his memoirs to the public.

Preface

The following pages tell the story of my 35 years as an officer in the Armed Services of Canada and Britain. In the 1930's I was fortunate enough to have served with a British regiment in India and, as a platoon and company commander, participated in a number of extensive manoeuvres involving as many as twenty thousand men. In addition, during that same period, I took special courses on all the new weapons and equipment being introduced into the British Army. It was valuable experience for any young officer.

When World War II broke out in September 1939 I was in Canada and joined the Royal Canadian Regiment as a 2nd Lieutenant. Four years later I was commanding a brigade in Italy and six months after that, an armoured division in Normandy. Cedit for this rapid promotion must go, in part, to my early military training which brought me to the attention of Major-General Pearkes in 1941 and Brigadier Simonds a year later.

My account of the years from 1939 to 1945, dealing mainly with my personal experiences and the theatres of war in which I served, is not intended as a complete historical record. That has been left to the historians. But as a senior officer I met a number of very important people whose actions and opinions greatly interested and frequently surprised me.

With the exception of the conscription issue and their treatment of General McNaughton, I had a healthy respect for the government's handling of matters concerning the Armed Forces. This stayed with me until 1965 when my feelings changed.

How is it that, in a democracy like ours, politicans can continue to mislead the people for so long about the condition of the Armed Forces? They hide behind the veil of secrecy and the loyalty of serving officers who are not permitted to air their problems publicly. It seems strange, also, that our society should be so apathetic and uncaring.

If social programmes are cut, adverse reaction is instant. On the other hand, defence expenditures can be reduced with barely a murmur of complaint. It is not inspiring for those in the Armed Forces to serve a disinterested public yet it appears to take a major disaster or a war to get their attention.

It has always seemed to me that the national pride of a country is reflected in the condition of her Armed Forces. When they are subjected to neglect national pride also suffers. Our armed forces have been neglected and ignored for too long. They need reorganization, new equipment and a greater sense of purpose. Perhaps what they need most is the encouragement of our political leaders and the support of a well informed and proud public.

George Kitching
Christmas 1985

Acknowledgements

I would like to thank Mrs. Gloria Orr who typed the first draft from my handwritten manuscript, and Mrs. Kitty Tolhurst who gave the many later drafts a professional look. Both were cheerful, helpful and encouraging.

Renny Englebert, who helped me to reduce my earlier drafts to more manageable proportions, spent many hours with me, checking my syntax and the continuity of my story. It was a pleasure to work with him.

I have had a lot of help from friends here in Victoria, but the support I have had from my wife, Audrey, has been my greatest encouragement.

Prologue

Brigadier Chris Vokes, commander of the 2nd Canadian Infantry Brigade was getting impatient.

"The trouble with these bloody Gippos" he grumbled, "is that they are all up front and no behind—they don't seem to have any backsides."

We were in a department store in Cairo and were trying to outfit ourselves as civilians; Chris was trying on his third pair of grey slacks as he expounded in colourful English on the physical differences between Canadians and Egyptians.

It was true; the waists were alright and so were the legs but there was no room for what our tailors call the "buttocks." We each finally settled for a pair of the least uncomfortable slacks; then, after buying white cotton bush-jackets climbed into our staff car and headed back to Shepheard's Hotel. It was the 8th May 1943.

We had been in Egypt with General Guy Simonds for several days, planning, in great secrecy, the operations of our 1st Canadian Division for the assault on the island of Sicily scheduled for July. Having completed all arrangements we were now to return to England in two parties. Guy Simonds would fly by R.A.F. plane accompanied by Lieut.-Colonel Geoff Walsh, our Engineer Commander, and Major A.B. Knight, the deputy head of administration of the Division.

Brigadier Chris Vokes, Lieut.-Colonel Jake Eaman, our Signals chief, and I (I was a Lieut.-Colonel and head of the Operations Staff) were to become civilians and travel by civil aircraft of Imperial Air ways. Since all our plans had already been cabled by secret means to our staff in England there was no reason for us to carry any documents or maps. Guy Simonds' party would take all our military uniforms with them in their aircraft; we were to be civilians and cautioned that we were not to reveal our Canadian identity to anyone; it must not be known that the Canadian Army was in any way interested in Mediterranean operations. Hence our visit to the department store and our very uncomfortable grey slacks.

Early the next morning we were driven to the airport dressed in our recently purchased clothing and trying to look as "civilian" as possible. We were soon airborne and after a short flight touched down for an hour at the much destroyed airfield at El Adem. This airfield and the small group of huts which made up the village of the same name had been the centre of much bitter fighting in Cyrenaica and it showed. Smashed vehicles. tanks and aircraft littered the whole countryside which was uninviting in the first place since it was flat desert with scrub growth struggling to stay alive.

After takeoff from El Adem we flew into Algiers at about 6:00 p.m. and were told to go to the St. George Hotel where we would find accommodation for the night. We were now Mr. Vokes, Mr. Eaman and Mr. Kitching. If questioned we were to say we were "shipwrecked mariners." In case of trouble we should always carry our Canadian identity cards but we were not to reveal our identity to anyone except an official.

Chris and I had a bath and then sauntered out of the hotel to look for a suitable bistro. We thought we could find one with the usual sidewalk seating so that we could ogle the girls as they promenaded past. Alas, we couldn't find a sidewalk cafe that looked inviting and furthermore, and perhaps more important, the girls didn't seem to be out that evening.

Instead we entered a building that advertised an upstairs bar. It was full of naval officers from a variety of Allied navies and we would obviously be at home in our new disguise as "shipwrecked mariners."

All went well at first; we sidled up to the bar and propped it up as we consumed what passed for Scotch whisky when a Royal Naval Captain, who was rather the worse for drink, strolled over to us and asked if we were shipwrecked. "Yes," replied Chris curtly as he turned back to the bar. The Captain seemed happy for a while but then approached us again. "What ship?" he enquired. "Go away," replied Chris who was getting a little angry by this time. "What ship?" the Captain repeated himself. "Go away—it's none of your business." Chris was very angry, "and if you don't understand that perhaps you will understand this," and he let loose a string of four letter words to imply "Go away and get lost."

Normally anyone receiving a blast of that magnitude from Chris Vokes would go off and shoot himself or at least resign his commission, but our gallant captain, buoyed with quantities of liquor, was not to be deterred. Muttering about 'spies' he went downstairs and reappeared accompanied by a Sergeant of the British Military Police. Pointing an accusing finger at us he ordered the sergeant to take us away and put us in irons. Fortunately, the sergeant realized that our hero had been into the sauce so he turned his back on him and spoke quietly to us. Chris asked the sergeant if there was an officer of the Military Police to whom we could identify ourselves. The sergeant went off for a few minutes and returned with a Captain of the Military Police to whom Chris told our real identity. Soon all was well although we didn't feel we should remain in that particular bar and returned to the hotel.

In the morning we were taken to the airport and climbed aboard our Imperial Airways aircraft for what we hoped would be the final hop to England. By this time we had worn our bushshirts and uncomfortable trousers for 24 hours and felt we needed a change even if it would be back into good old battledress.

Soon after takeoff we were informed that we would be landing in Lisbon where there would be a short stop to take on additional passengers. We were to remain on board the aircraft.

On landing at Lisbon, two of our tires blew out which did slight damage to the undercarriage. Shortly after the plane came to a halt an individual from the British Embassy came aboard. After talking with the captain of the aircraft, he announced that we would probably have to remain in Lisbon for two or three nights until the aircraft could be repaired or another one brought in to replace it. He told us which hotel we were to stay at, gave us each three pounds sterling and a ride in an embassy car to the hotel. The money was to last us for three days.

He knew our correct identity because after we had left the plane he took us aside and cautioned us. Lisbon, he said, was a hotbed of German spies since Portugal was the only neutral country in Europe except for Sweden and Switzerland. We were to be careful when walking in the streets, in fact it would be better if we took our walks and exercise very early in the morning and remain in the hotel for the rest of the day. If we went into the hotel bar, we must be particularly careful because a number of the girls who frequented it were known agents of the Germans.

Chris Vokes and I shared a large room overlooking a small but attractive square. Jake Eaman had a smaller room on the same floor.

The British official told us to change our money into Portugese Escudos at the hotel. We found to our horror that a Scotch and soda cost the equivalent of ten shillings so that with our pocket money of one pound a day, we would be limited to only two drinks a day. It was a bleak outlook.

What was really concerning each of us at that time was the condition of our one and only bush-jacket. We had sent our military clothing back to London in General Simonds' aircraft so that all we had were toothbrushes and razors. We were beginning to look a little like ship-wrecked sailors and smelled almost as bad. We decided to have our two whiskies, then have dinner after which we would wash our bush-jackets and underwear and hang them up to dry on the balcony off the bedroom. Fortunately May is a warm and lovely month in Lisbon and by 5:00 a.m. our laundry was reasonably dry. This was the time for our exercise so we left the hotel and headed up the hill past what is now the Ritz Hotel. Lisbon is a beautiful city and I think we saw it at its best with the early morning sun highlighting the infinite variety of colours in parks and city squares. We were thoroughly enjoying ourselves, the sun was helping to dry our slightly damp bush-jackets and all was right with the world. We decided to rest a while on one of the park seats. This was our first mistake because within two minutes we were surrounded by little shoe shine boys anxious to get to work on us. We had already agreed that we would not spend any of our escudos on unnecessary items as it would limit our daily whisky allowance. We told the boys we did not want a shine and that they should buzz off.

At this point both Chris and I had long moustaches. His was large, blond and brushed upwards; mine was long, dark and rather wispy. I had a lot of dark hair, Chris had very little—in fact he looked very much like a marshal of the Russian Army whose name was well known at that time. Marshal Budyonny's armies had recently inflicted a defeat on the Germans so his photograph was shown in every newspaper including those in Lisbon.

The shoe shine boys did not buzz off as requested, instead they became very curious and started to ask our nationality.

"English?" "No!"

"German?" "No! No! Buzz off."

"Russki?" "Yah—Russki," exploded Chris as he raised his clenched fist in salute. The youngsters were fascinated and returned his salute jumping around shouting "Russki! Russki!" We quickly resumed our walk.

One or two of the boys ran along beside us for a while but fortunately local citizens who needed a shoe shine soon attracted them elsewhere. We returned to the hotel and a welcome breakfast.

That evening we went to the hotel bar. Shortly after ordering our Scotch and soda, Chris Vokes gave me a nudge that almost knocked me off my stool. "Look," he hissed in a whisper that could be heard two blocks away, "one of the girls has just come in." Sure enough, a dark-haired beauty had just taken a seat in the window. I could see her reflection in the mirror behind the bar. Up to that moment we had about three feet between us as we sat facing the barman. We closed ranks. We didn't want anything to come between us. If we were going to be attacked it would be on our flanks and not through the centre. We waited expectantly and were quite disappointed when the girl got up and left.

"Don't forget, George," whispered Chris in a hoarse rumble, "We can't afford to give 'em a drink—just beat 'em off if they come at us." He had no sooner said this than we saw the girl returning accompanied by another equally attractive young lady. Instead of going to the table she had just vacated, they both headed straight for us. We sat shoulder to shoulder, clutching our whiskies and hoping for the worst. "Here they come, don't look at them." Chris was quite hoarse by this time. We stared straight ahead, following their course in the mirror. They bracketed us, one coming up on each side. "You Engleesh?" asked the girl on my side. "No. No spik Engleesh," I replied in a loud voice that I hoped Chris would hear, "Me Swedish." We had not thought much about our nationality in case were were assaulted and I hoped Chris would settle for being a Swede for the evening. I needn't have worried because at that moment the girl on his side was tip-toeing with her fingers along his left forearm which was bared by the short sleeve of his bush-jacket. As her fingers caressed his arm she was saying in the sexiest voice she could muster, "I only love men who have blond hairy arms." This was like a red rag to a bull because Chris was quite sensitive about the amount of hair on his arms. With a quick movement of his left arm that would have felled an ox he sent her reeling along the bar. "Bugger off," he roared in most unSwedish language.

That was the end of their amorous approaches. The only other remark Chris made before we ordered our second drink was that it was lucky he had his first drink in his right hand or he might have spilled it as he waved her away!

We went for another long walk early the next morning and were amused to see thousands of British five pound notes for sale at quite ridiculous prices. These were forgeries made in Germany as part of the economic war that was then being waged with an intensity that equalled the great land battles.

Not much happened the third day of our stay until early evening when our friend from the British Embassy surfaced again to tell us that we would be flying to the U.K. the next day. We would be picked up at the hotel at 9:00 a.m.

On arrival at the airport we were surprised to hear that we would be flying in a two-engined Dakota of a Dutch airline that flew daily from Bristol to Lisbon and return. It was called "De Fliegende Hollander" or the Flying Dutchman. For some reason the Germans allowed these planes free passage on most occasions and we assumed that this was because they brought from England every day a great many copies of the daily newspapers which were then picked up by the German Embassy. Possibly they formed the basis of Lord Haw-Haw's accurate statements when he broadcast from Berlin each day.

We had been told that at the airport we would pass the large office of the German airline Lufthansa and would be scrutinised very closely by their staff, many of whom were members of Himmler's Secret Police.

Sure enough, there must have been twelve or fifteen Lufthansa 'employees' waiting for us and it gave me a funny feeling to think that here were a number of the enemy playing a cat and mouse game with us and we could do nothing about it. I hoped Chris wouldn't give them his famous clenched-fist Budyonny salute! Certainly neither Chris nor I looked like normal civilians. We were tanned, in almost perfect physical shape and wearing 'civilian' clothes that no self-respecting civilian would wear because by this time even our ill-fitting grey slacks were very much in need of a 'clean and press.'

Our pilot was a very well-known Dutchman named Parmenter. He had taken part in many long distance air races between the U.K. and Australia before the war. We did not know the identity of any of the other passengers and were surprised to note that the windows had all been securely covered by plywood and the lights were left on throughout the flight. It gave us a strange feeling.

The distance for a peace-time flight from Lisbon to Bristol was about 800 miles—or about four and a half hours flying in a Dakota. However, we were cooped up in the Flying Dutchman for a period of about 8½ hours which indicated that the captain gave the German radars and fighter aircraft at Brest a wide berth to avoid them. We landed safely in Bristol and were soon bound for London by train but two days later the same Dakota flown by Parmenter on the flight from Lisbon to Bristol was intercepted and shot down by German fighters. There were no survivors and amongst those killed was the celebrated British actor, Leslie Howard.

I began to think that I must have a charmed life. Not only had we missed a watery grave by a narrow margin on this occasion but, only two weeks before, General Salmon had finally decided to leave me in London when he was to fly to Cairo. He and all other passengers were killed when his plane crashed shortly after take-off.

But that is another story.

1

Early Days

Shameen is an island on the Pearl River only a stone's throw from the great city of Canton in South China. Originally a mud-flat, used as a breakwater to protect the vast number of junks and sampans that anchored along the old city waterfront, it was ceded in 1875 by the Emperor of China to the British and French as an international trading settlement. From that time its appearance changed dramatically. Large numbers of Chinese were employed in dredging the exposed foreshore, building a sea wall and bringing in hundreds of tons of fill. By 1900 the island—one mile long and half a mile wide—was a level twelve feet above the surrounding river. Modern houses and warehouses were built, the island soon became a flourishing trading centre, three quarters of it under British Administration and the remainder either French, German or Portugese.

It was there that I was born on the 19th of September 1910. My father, George Charlesworth Kitching, was the Manager of A.S. Watsons Ltd., a company dealing in a wide variety of merchandise including pharmaceuticals, liquor and soft drinks. He and my mother lived in the house adjoining the Watson's warehouse and factory. It was in this house that my older brother Hugh and I were born. We had a very happy childhood and many friends amongst the thirty other children who lived on the Island. My father and mother made the most of the somewhat restricted facilities available. They both enjoyed life and made sure we enjoyed it with them. Picnics were the order of the day and they would take us with them to the golf course at Tung Shan and the lakes in the White Cloud Mountains; on other occasions my father would row us all up river to visit friends. We were a happy family although the first World War began to affect us even in far off Shameen..

When the War broke out in 1914 my father immediately volunteered for service; however, as he was then 36 years old he was requested to remain on Shameen and command the volunteer company that was raised to assist the Royal Navy in protecting the island. Dad had never been a regular soldier, although he would have been a very good one, but he had volunteered in 1901 during the Boxer Rebellion when the Dowager Empress of China had encouraged large numbers of her people to drive the Europeans out of the country. Most of the action had taken place in North China around the cities of Peking and Tientsin and Dad took part in the operations in the latter city. During the period when my father was in command of the Shameen Volunteers the ''enemy'' was not so much the Germans as the Chinese War Lords who were then on the rampage throughout the country following the Revolution that had established a Republic in 1912. A War Lord would move into a city, squeeze as much money as he could out of it and then depart only to be replaced by another. Sometimes there would be fighting and I can distinctly remember seeing one of the War Lords enter the city in triumph one week and then seeing his headless body being carried out in the next. The authorities on Shameen were concerned that one or other of the War Lords would try to gain asylum on the island. It was to prevent this that the Royal Navy and the Volunteers surrounded the island with barbed wire and sandbagged machine-gun posts.

In view of the unsettled state of China my parents decided that my mother would take my brother and me to Canada. So in early 1916 we sailed from Hong Kong to Tokyo and from there took a Japanese ship to Vancouver and then the ferry to Victoria. We rented a house on Rupert Street between Humboldt and Beacon Hill Park. To Hugh and me the Park and the shoreline on its western limits were a paradise. In 1916 the Park was largely wild and unspoiled and we used it to the full accompanied by a number of other children who lived in the area. We stayed in Victoria for about 9 months during which we visited Toronto. Whilst there my mother tried to arrange passage for us all to England; however, the unrestricted submarine warfare in the Atlantic was reaching its height and women and children were not permitted to travel on any ship. We returned to Victoria and, after a couple of months, to Shameen.

Back in China Hugh and I went north to school in Wei-Hai-Wei on the Shantung peninsula. This was a boarding school with about 80 boys of whom twenty were the sons of Russian families who had fled from the Revolution. Although I have many happy memories of my year at the school I can also remember that I was very homesick and extremely glad to get back to Shameen. Just before leaving the school we were told that the Great War was over and that a peace treaty would ensure that there would be no more wars! That was in November 1981.

From my parents' point of view the end of the war meant that we could now travel by ship to England and the decision was taken that my mother, Hugh and I would go there in 1919. We were to go to school there, my mother would remain with us, and my father would take a long leave and join us as soon as he could.

In England we stayed at my mother's family home, The Grange in Somersham, Huntingdonshire. Her father and mother were still alive and well—he was David Rowe, originally from Lincolnshire; she was Elizabeth Jane Kett, a well known family from Norfolk. The Grange was a nice old house with lovely gardens, many out buildings and twenty-five acres of fields in which we youngsters played to our hearts content.

Schooling was a problem. Hugh had his name down to enter Winchester; however he failed the entrance examinations in spite of the earnest coaching by a local parson, the Reverend Septimus Didimus Brace. The next choice was Cranleigh School which agreed to take both of us but not before 1922. In the interim we went to the Royal Grammar School in Lancaster. Academically this was a very good school although at the age of ten I am afraid I didn't really learn a lot. The majority of the boys at the school were day-boys who lived in the vicinity and who came and went each day. However, there were about 80 boarders, 20 of whom lived in Storey House under the wing of a wonderful and kindly lady, Mrs. Thompson. Hugh and I were lucky enough to be put in her care.

In 1921 my father came back on extended leave from China and he and my mother had planned a series of family outings which occupied our complete summer. Those months with them both more than made up for their long absences; and Hugh and I agreed many years later that those months with them in 1921, and later in 1925 when we were reunited again, were the happiest in our young lives.

My father's family were originally from Sussex and Kent in southeast England but, like many others of Saxon origin, they moved north after the Norman invasion; all the good jobs and benefits were being given only to those of Norman blood. In the north they headed for the rugged Pennine hills where, for a while, they became "Petit Baronnes" and then sank into hardworking obscurity. One emerged in the middle of the 18th century to fight with Clive in India but perhaps this very English family received its biggest jolt when my great grandfather married an Irish lady Catherine O'Neill in 1824. I'm sure she brought a sparkle and a sense of humour to the family which after many generations in the fastness of the Pennine moors might have become a little dour.

Unfortunately one of her sons, Samuel, who was my grandfather, had perhaps too much of the Irish in him because he became very fond of gambling on the horses. This failing, assisted by quantities of alcohol, caused many financial problems. Only the strong character of my grandmother held the family together; her firmness and guidance were dominating influences on my father in his early youth.

Later in his life he became a shrewd business man, somewhat stubborn at times but very fair and honest in his dealings with other people although I often felt that he was inclined to favour the underdog. But, above all, he enjoyed laughter and had a happy sense of humour. I like to think I inherited his sense of fairness along with his sense of humour. Both sides of mother's family contained their share of rebels. Her father's family were Rowe's and Wraxhalls, originally from Lincolnshire, who were strong puritan supporters of Cromwell in his struggle against Charles I. Her mother was a Kett from Norfolk. One of her ancestors raised a rebellion against Henry VIII for the way he was handing over the wealth of the monasteries to his friends instead of distributing it amongst the poor. Kett was defeated in battle by a mercenary force of Germans sent by the King; he was later hanged from the tower of Norwich Cathedral. The Rowe's have been farmers for generations in the fenlands of East Anglia; they worked hard but, in season, found time to enjoy riding to hounds and shooting their share of partridge and pheasant. From them I have inherited their love of the countryside and their distrust of autocratic Establishments.

In 1922 Hugh went to Cranleigh and I joined him there the following year. Cranleigh had a quite different environment to Lancaster and a quite different character. Lancaster was an ancient school founded in the 15th century during the Wars of the Roses. To show its loyalty the school crest which we wore on blue caps was the Red Rose of Lancaster. The purpose of the school was to educate as many students as possible for either commerce or the university and it had a very high academic record. The number of boys attaining Higher Certificate and Matriculation was far higher than most schools—certainly far higher than Cranleigh. In appearance Lancaster was sombre—a vast building of grey stone surrounded by a wall which enclosed very little in the way of sports facilities. Sports were not considered important there. Cranleigh was the exact opposite. It was of red brick and stood well back from the road in about 200 acres of playing fields, parks and a nine hole golf course. It was a comparatively new school, having been founded in 1865 by the Anglican Church to provide young men for the Colonial and Civil services, the Armed Forces and the many missions that had been established by the Church in the fast expanding Empire of the 19th century. Competitive sports were a big part of life at Cranleigh then and it was better known for the quality of its rugby football players than for its standard of learning. The Headmaster was the Reverend H. A. Rhodes—a somewhat ascetic churchman with eyes that seemed to bore right through you.

On arrival I was placed in Form II B—there was nothing lower. And since I was by far the youngest boy at the school I remained in that Form for two terms instead of one. The Form master was Mr. Gower—the man who coached and ran our famous rugby football teams. He was an acknowledged genius in that field but that was the limit of his knowledge. However, he had been in the R.C.M.P. in Canada, a miner in South Africa, a bushwhacker in Australia and had played rugby for Wales. What more could you wish for in a teacher of geography? I learned about the Kaffirs in the Kalihari Desert, the aboriginies at Lake Yama Yama and the difference between Saskatchewan and Saskatoon. All very useful information.

The school was divided into six Houses named after various points of the compass and each House had about 45 boys varying in age from 14 to 18 or 19. I was in West House with my brother Hugh—thank goodness—because, being only 12 years old, I was the youngest boy and not very big. I was homesick and wept each night for my first two or three weeks when Hugh was a great comfort. I progressed regularly through the different grades or Forms, always a little younger than those around me but I enjoyed life and made a number of friends as I climbed the ladder of success. On our holidays Hugh and I would spend part of the time with an aunt in Lancaster and a part at the Grange in Somersham. We would always try to be in Somersham for the summer holidays to enjoy the country life there and also to work on one of the farms owned by the family. When I was 13 I was allowed to work for a couple of weeks during harvesting. My job was to lead a cart, when it was loaded, from the fields to the thrashing machines and then take the empty cart back to the fields for reloading. These carts were four wheeler "wains" and very large, each pulled by two hugh Shire horses. They are magnificent animals with powerful legs and chests capable of hauling the heaviest of loads. My two Shires were brother and sister named "Prince" and "Queen." Both were brown with white feet and white blaze on each forehead. When loaded I would lead them from the front by a length of rope but when returning empty I would climb up and sit on one of their backs. I was a knight looking for some damsel to rescue or some dragon to kill.

Unfortunately, on one occasion I must have let my imagination run away with me. I coaxed Prince and Queen from a walk to a trot, then to a canter and the next thing I knew we were going at a full gallop, pounding along the two rutted farm road with the empty hay wain swaying behind me. I quickly ceased being a knight and became a terrified boy. I was scared stiff and at one time thought I would jump off the back of "Prince" but one look to the rear convinced me that if I jumped I would probably be run over by one of the wheels of the behemoth behind me.

Instead I decided to hang on to the ropes and shout WHOA! WHOA! in my treble voice in an effort to slow the horses down. There were no reins to guide or restrain them—just the rope attached to each bit which normally was enough to control them. After what seemed like an hour the Shires slowed to a canter, then a trot, and finally their more familiar walk. I became less frightened so that when we reached the loading area I was pleased to hear one of the worker say "Well done, Mas' George, 'ee kept thoy head—but whoy did 'ee let they run away with 'ee at all!" I didn't mention my impersonation of Sir Galahad. I didn't think he knew enough about him.

By the time I was sixteen I was playing for the school team in hockey and the 2nd team in rugby football. I had also been made one of the five prefects in West House which made me proud but I was even prouder a year later when I was made a School Prefect, Captain of West House and also Captain of Hockey for the school. That was my last year at Cranleigh and I was fortunate to have a Mr. Bowyer as my House Master, a job that made him a surrogate father to us all. He was a large man with a walrus moustache, a warm heart and a twinkle in his blue eyes. I learned a great deal from him about a variety of things, one of which cause me some embarrassment. There was a certain amount of "boy-love" at the school just as I think there must be in any environment of that kind. It was not homosexual in the modern sense—there was no harmful destruction of a boy's mind or body as far as I knew. It was a case of temporary infatuation and a mild form of sexual play that was soon forgotten. On one occasion a young boy came to tell me that one of the junior prefects had made advances towards him. I was angry that a prefect would take advantage of his position, so went immediately to see Mr. Bowyer. I burst into his sitting room and said, "Sir, I am sorry to have to report a case of buggery." He looked at me quite pop-eyed for a full minute and then said, "Kitching, do you know what buggery means?" I was very embarrassed because I really did not know what it meant. I think we were all very naive in such matters. Mr. Bowyer gave me a two minute lecture on the body that frankly shocked me; he then had the prefect concerned attend his office where he admitted his guilt and was demoted. This was the only occasion of its kind in which I became involved—perhaps it would never have happened if we had been in a mixed school of girls and boys!

Having decided in 1927 that I wanted to go into the Army I took the examinations for the Royal Military College, Sandhurst in October 1928, just after my eighteenth birthday. An important exam was French Oral when I would have to spend perhaps twenty minutes discussing a wide variety of subjects in that language. My French teacher gave me a tip; choose a subject, learn all the special words and phrases used in that subject and then direct the discussion into that particular channel and keep it there. On his advice I selected travel by sea and the glories of such great French harbours as Brest, Le Havre and Marseilles. He said I must boost everything French because I would be examined by a young officer of the French Army. I studied all about ships, the oceans, and French ports. I went into the Oral Exam with confidence.

The examiner was in civilian clothes, very elegant, blond and good looking. He was obviously an officer from one of the crack French Cavalry Regiments. After the normal pleasantries and ''bonjours'' we got down to business. ''Why do you wish to go into the Army?'' was the first question. I was ready for it. One reason, I said, was that I loved travel—particularly by ship. I was about to launch into my long spiel about ships when he floored me by asking, ''How is your father?'' I replied that my father was well and that one reason he was so well was that he had travelled a great deal by ship, etc., etc., etc.!! I didn't get very far with that further attempt to display my knowledge of the seas because the next question was ''Which part of the Army is of the greatest interest to you—infantry, cavalry or tanks?''

It was clear that I was not going to get a chance to talk much about seas and ships and still less about Brest, Le Havre or Marseilles. Our conversation went on for about twenty-five minutes, at the end of which he told me I had done well and that he was awarding me 83%. I was so delighted and surprised that I confided in him that perhaps the reason why I had done so well was that he was a Frenchman which made him sympathetic to my efforts. I told him I could not have spoken as well if he had been a British officer. He immediately roared with laughter and as I said good-bye he told me, in English, that he was a Captain in the British Army!

Shortly after this interview I was informed that I had been accepted to enter Sandhurst in January 1929.

Schools like Cranleigh instilled discipline and a sense of responsibility in most of their boys. Whether these virtues remained in later years depended on the character of the individual.

I have always enjoyed some measure of discipline in my life and I think Cranleigh had a lot to do with it. Certainly the school gave me my first positions of responsibility and taught me that the higher you go in your job the more you should think about the increasing number of people who are working for you.

During these years at Cranleigh I began to feel uncomfortable in a crowd. Whenever a large number of us were turned loose to run or walk a few miles I would always try to get in front or to the flanks—I could not run with the herd and this feeling is still with me. I like to take the lead. In the same way, when I was given a task I liked to concentrate all my efforts on the job—I did not like to be distracted or have changes made unless they were important. I think I must have been learning to become impatient!

Perhaps the most important thing my brother Hugh and I learned during these years at school was to be self-reliant. With our parents away in China we spent our school holidays either at the Grange with our grandparents or elsewhere with aunts and uncles. Rather than burden them with our entertainment we always made a point of looking after ourselves either together or separately. The countryside was there for us to explore. This built up a feeling of independence in us and a degree of self-confidence that I would not have today if I had had to conform too much to other people's ideas and plans. I left Cranleigh in December with many regrets. I had been a school boy there for five and a half years and had many happy memories to carry with me into the future. Sandhurst was going to be quite a change.

My Father
George Charlesworth Kitching
1878 - 1963

My Mother
Florence Dagmar Kitching
1879 - 1956

above
The Island of Shameen, beyond is the
City of Canton in 1928

With my Mother and Brother Hugh
in England, May, 1926

above
My bungalow in Mhow, 1935
Chandu standing on the verandah

The Author, Madra, India, 1936
glosters full dress uniform

2

Sandhurst

In my day there were two military schools for the training of potential officers for the British Army; the Royal Military Academy (Known as the "Shop") at Woolwich in south east London for the training of Artillery and Engineer cadets, and the Royal Military College at Sandhurst which trained cadets for the Cavalry, Infantry and Tank Corps.

The course at both the "Shop" and at Sandhurst in the 1920's lasted approximately eighteen months—divided into three terms called Junior, Intermediate and Senior. R.M.C., Sandhurst is located in almost idyllic surroundings between the village of Sandhurst and the town of Camberley in Surrey. The entire area of the college comprises many thousands of acres which have been military training grounds for three hundred years. The college was founded in 1792 and moved to its present site in 1812. The original building, known as the Old Building, is of simple and classical design. Only two floors in height but four hundred yards in length, it is centred by a portico of Doric columns. It is one of the best proportioned buildings in Britain. As if to enhance this gem of architecture; eight cannon captured at Waterloo rest astride the central portico. The extensive lake lying in front of the building was excavated by French prisoners of war captured during the Napoleonic Wars. It is indeed an historic location.

About half a mile away is the "New" Building. It was built in 1912 and centred by a tall clock tower. Whilst the "Old" Building is of pale grey painted plaster, the "New" is of red brick and stone. In between the two buildings is the old chapel and the new and large gymnasium. In the rear of the Old Building is the new chapel to commemorate the thousands of ex-cadets who, as officers, were killed in the First World War. Behind this new chapel were many other training buildings including the extensive stables and riding schools of the Equitation Wing. Playing fields extended for about a mile in front of the "Old" and "New" Buildings, altogether a perfect setting.

The Commandant of Sandhurst when I was there was Major-General Eric Girdwood, an ex-cavalry man. He was of average height and powerful build, had a pleasant way of talking to cadets, and a good sense of humour.

The college was divided into four companies. Numbers 1 and 3 were in the New Building—Numbers 4 and 5 in the Old. there was no longer a No. 2. I was detailed to join No. 5—affectionately known by us as Lovely Five. Each company had about 180 Gentlemen Cadets divided equally into Seniors, Intermediates and Juniors. The Seniors provided the underofficers and N.C.O.'s in each company. The Intermediates and Juniors were formed into four platoons which were officered by the Seniors. Provided a G.C. (Gentleman Cadet) passed his exams he would move from Junior to Intermediate to Senior and only require three terms to Pass Out (graduate).

The Company Commander of Lovely Five was Major Cumberbatch of the Green Howards, a quiet gentleman who had been severely wounded in World War I. The Company Sergeant-Major was Neaverson of the Grenadier Guards and his assistant was Company Quartermaster-Sergeant Scotty Niven of the Royal Scots. These two men, whom we always had to refer to officially as "Staff," were really responsible for our efficiency at drill and for much of our discipline. They were complete opposites.

"Neavo," as we called Neaverson, was tall and ram-rod straight with ginger hair and ginger waxed moustache and his words of command were given in a high eunuch-like squeak. The tongue lashings we got from him as individuals and collectively were given with great emotion when his voice would go through several octaves in the same sentence. The names he called us would fill a dictionary. "Oh! you 'horrible shower of warts—that's what you are—little warts wot will never become soldiers.'' "Pig Eyes"—that's what you are—why don't you 'onk like pigs.'' "Cor and I'm supposed to make you into officers—that's h'impossible—you wouldn't even made good private soldiers.'' So it would go on day after day in the first three months of our Junior Term. But he was a superb Drill Instructor and became increasingly popular with us.

Scotty Niven was a quiet spoken Scot—not emotional in any way, at least he did not show his emotions. But his quiet words of command were effective and were so different from Neavo's that it was sometimes a relief when he took over. Both were first class soldiers. I do not know what happened to Scotty Niven after he left R.M.C. Neavo served with the Guards for another five years and then was persuaded to come to Canada. He was made drill-sergeant of the Canadian Grenadier Guards and got a fairly good job as Special Messenger for one of the big banks. I heard from him in 1973—he was living in Pierrefonds, north of Montreal.

The Regimental Sergeant-Major, (R.S.M.) the man who was far better known to us than the Commandant or the Adjutant, was Mr. Pearson. He had been an R.S.M. in the Guards and had a voice that could penetrate an artillery barrage. When he drilled the Battalion he would stand about a quarter of a mile away and give his words of command. He said he did this so that he could check on the movement of everyone. He certainly had an uncanny knack of finding fault and naming the unfortunate Cadet even at that distance. He knew which cadet was "idle"—in other words slow or sloppy in his movements—and he gave him hell unmercifully.

The first few months at Sandhurst were designed to be hell for the Junior Class and it was. The only time we had to ourselves was Saturday afternoon and evening when we were permitted to be away from the college until 10:00 p.m. We also had Sunday afternoons off but had to be back by 6:00 p.m.

During the Junior term the emphasis was on Drill, Equitation, Physical Training and outdoor Field work which consisted of digging extensive trench systems and filling them in again.

The purpose of this excessive physical exertion was either to build us up or break us. One or two would fail to make it and were removed but the great majority of us survived and were the better for it.

Each Cadet had his own small room furnished with a bed, dressing table, wash basin with hot and cold water, a work table and chair, and fairly good cupboards and shelves. Heating was by hot water radiators. To help us look after the rooms we had a "batman" or servant for each eight rooms. These men were all ex-Army and were a wonderful addition to the college—they kept us from going insane with their good humour and down-to-earth common sense. "Farmer" Giles looked after me and I was always grateful to him for his help. Many years later I was visiting the Staff College at Camberley and was able to contact Farmer Giles. He was not well but we had a few minutes together reminiscing about the Sandhurst days. He was a very heavy smoker and I'm sure his lungs had been affected.

Our uniforms, which were tailored for us, were Blue Patrol for evening wear and Khaki for everyday wear and ceremonial parades. Riding breeches, leggings and boots were also hand-tailored as were the Red and White striped Blazers and white flannels which were worn for Physical Training Parades. They all had to be kept immaculate and the accoutrements that went with them had to be shining like mirrors. Every piece of steel or metal was honed and buffed until it sparkled. Boots, belts, chin straps and bayonet frogs were polished until they, too, reflected like mirrors. In our Junior term this cleaning and polishing was done by cadets in the evening between dinner and lights out—and woe betide the individual who did not spend two hours each day on these cleaning and polishing chores. The punishment for having "idle" or unclean equipment was an hour of punishment drill in full battle equipment running up and down two adjoining flights of stairs without a break of any kind. It was not worth it.

What nearly broke our hearts was the continual changing from one type of uniform to another with only five or ten minutes allowed for the change. For instance, we would have as many as three changes in one morning for classes in equitation, physical training and Drill parade. In the fifteen minutes between sessions we had to run from the place of parade to our rooms, change into the uniform required for the next class and then run like hell to get there in time to "fall in" and still have everything faultlessly shining and correct. The fifth uniform issued to us was a denim jacket and trousers which were worn when we went into the training areas. This was always soiled so it was the one uniform that did not require a polish of some kind or other—a weekly wash in the college laundry brought it back to life.

This period of a new cadet's life lasted for about twelve exhausting weeks which culminated in the Drill Competition between the Junior Cadets of the four companies. It was an important event because it was one of the decisive stages in the overall competition for the title of "Champion Company" and the privilege of wearing the Red Lanyard, of leading the Parades at all times and escorting the Colours.

Neavo Neaverson coaxed and cajolled us, he sweated and swore at us and finally brought us to the standard he wanted. On the day of the great competition, which was judged by independent officers and warrant officers of the Guards, we excelled ourselves and won—it was a wonderful occasion and we were rightly proud of ourselves. Neavo was in tears—Scotty Niven was as calm as ever. This competition set the pattern for the rest of that first term and we came out as Champion Company.

The tough introduction of our first three months produced an esprit-de-corps at Sandhurst that would not have been possible without it. It was as if we had gone through the fire and had been cleansed by it. The spirit was truly "All for one and one for all." Because of this feeling of superiority through excellence, we tended to regard individuals who tried to get commissions in the Army by less energetic means as outcasts—as some of them were, particularly those who, having failed to get to Sandhurst in the normal way, would appear for a special four weeks' course prior to being given a commission in a Guards Regiment. The Duke of Norfolk did one of these short courses prior to getting a commission and I am quite sure that his stay at Sandhurst was the most exciting thing that ever happened to him. His room was invaded by cadets almost every day who would throw everything he owned out of the window. Had he been present he would have been thrown out, too. Mattress, pillows and sheets would be distributed all over the parade ground so that the Duke would have to spend half an hour collecting his goods and chattels to the accompaniment of cadet jeers and cheers. Fortunately for the Army, he only stayed for two or three years. He was the "Earl Marshal" of England by heredity and responsible for all national occasions such as Coronations and Royal

Funerals. Fortunately for England, he had an excellent staff who did all the work—without them Kings and Queens might never have been crowned.

Life at Sandhurst, however, was relieved by a great deal of good humour and understanding by both the Staff and students. On one occasion, the Commandant was returning in his car from London late one Saturday night. He was wearing civilian clothes and driving himself. He was stopped and asked for a lift by a cadet, also in civilian clothes, who was absent from the college without permission. The cadet chatted happily with the man who had picked him up, told him that he was absent without leave but would be okay because he knew of a special way to get to his room without being seen. The commandant dropped the cadet at the college gates and said, "Goodnight and good luck."

The next morning we paraded for Commandant Inspection prior to marching to church. The Commandant moved slowly down the ranks, examining each face. He stopped in front of the cadet whom he had helped the night before, looked him in the eye and said, "Did you get in all right?" "Yes, sir," stammered the astonished cadet. "Well done," said the Commandant, "but you must tell me sometime which special entrance you used—it didn't sound like the one we used in my day." Nothing further was said.

David Niven was at Sandhurst with me and put on several performances in plays and skits written for local consumption. He was the life and soul of any production and could always be counted on to bring the house down. He made a wonderful contribution one day to a large hall that, at one time, had been the college chapel. In it were still hanging from poles many colours and flags captured by British regiments when fighting against the French in the 18th and 19th centuries. Below each Colour was a small plaque which gave the details of the battle in which it was captured. "Taken in action, Blenheim, 1704" or "Taken in action, Waterloo, 1815." To these samples of valour Niven had hung, on one of the vacant poles, a pair of lady's silk stockings. On the plaque below was the inscription "Taken in action, David Niven, 1929."

The important subject of Tactics was taught us by a captain from the Gloucestershire Regiment, Maurice Gilmore. He was a down-to-earth instructor who was genuinely interested in both the cadets and the subject. It was not long before a great friend of mine, Kim Lacey, and I had decided that we would apply for a commission in Gilmore's Regiment. He was very helpful and encouraging but pointed out that we would have to pass out (graduate) fairly near the top of our term to be considered.

French was taught us by an officer of the French Army—my memories of him are not about the French language but about the need for the closest cooperation between France and Britain to deal with the German menace which, although then dormant, was bound to rise again. This was three years before the advent of Hitler.

Our officer instructors were generally very competent and professional. They knew how to instruct and, above all, they treated us as men. This was a noticeable change from our years at school where, no matter how old we were, we were treated as boys.

Field sketching was another important part of an officer's training in those years. The ability to draw a map showing the salient features, and to sketch a panorama which could be used to indicate enemy positions or possible targets, were vital in an age before aerial photographs and instant cameras became available. It is interesting to recall that many of the best drawings and water colours of early Canadian exploration were done by officers who had been trained in the art of field sketching.

P.T. or Physical Training was done mostly in the gymnasium except in good weather. Pull ups, press ups, rope climbing, parallel bars and the so-called "Horse" were all part of P.T. and without the benefit of sponge rubber to absorb the shock. In the final assessment of my work at Sandhurst I was given a "Distinguished" for P.T. which was some compensation for the grunts and groans of the previous eighteen months.

Amongst the cadets of my term at Sandhurst were a number who distinguished themselves. Many were killed or wounded in the early years of World War II as they were company and battalion commanders. Neil Blair of the Black Watch lost a leg in Sicily commanding his battalion. Dick Craddock went on to the rank of Lieutenant-General after losing a leg commanding his battalion—the Buffs. Hugh Bellamy went "Airborne" in the war and commanded a parachute brigade. Both Gerry Hopkinson and Harry Cumming-Bruce (Lord

Thurlow) commanded Divisions in Germany. They were athletes and played a full part in all sports and games. It was a joy to meet them again many years later.

A great friend was Doug Macdougald—a Canadian whose family lived in Montreal. Douggie was amost unusual type of man. He was very quiet and almost shy but a keen student of everything military. He was not only two years older than most of us but, having been brought up in Canada, he had a different view of life. To him, movie cameras were common-place—to us, they were almost unknown. To him a car was a necessity—to us, a luxury. On one of the first church parades Douggie took a smart pace forward, turned to the right, took out a pocket movie camera and shot a few feet of film of the Commandant advancing down the line on his Inspection. Neaverson was practically apopletic with rage and we could hear him muttering all kinds of dire threats about what he would do once he could lay his hands on Douggie.

Doug also bought a large Bentley which he drove, wearing a chauffeur's uniform as a disguise.

He requested permission to attend the Caledonian Ball in London. It was refused so he went and found himself sitting at the next table to the Commandant who pretended not to know him.

Doug made several short movies at Sandhurst which he still has in his collection. He went into the Cameron Highlanders, spent two years with them in India and then resigned his commission in order to return to Montreal. His father, who was a Senator, was in trouble through his association with the Beauharnois Dam project. Doug returned to help his father and once that was done, he joined the Princess Patricia's Canadian Light Infantry. His parents were very kind to me when I came to Canada in 1938.

My last term at Sandhurst was particularly enjoyable. On arriving back there in January 1930, I found I had been promoted to the rank of Under Officer to command No. 19 Platoon which I had joined as a recruit or Junior just a year before. Kim Lacey was also made an Under Officer so we were advancing together. Under Officers were accorded certain privileges because of their rank. There were only five of us in the total company of about 200. We were given a sitting room of our own, had no restrictions on our movements at weekends, wore swords on parade instead of carrying rifle and bayonet and wore blue blazers instead of the normal red and white stripes. It was quite a change.

During my time at Sandhurst we were inspected by a number of important people. One of them was General Sir Bindon Blood—a remarkable man of about 90 years of age and with almost as many medals. He had not taken part in the Indian Mutiny battles of 1857 but he seemed to have been involved in every one since that time. When we asked him how he looked so well at that age he told us that many years before he had been bequeathed a cellar of Port (and sufficient funds to keep it stocked) which allowed him one bottle a night up to the age of 100. He admitted that he did not drink all of it himself—''let me friends have a glass now and then, you know''—then added, with a twinkle in his eye, that he had no intention of living beyond his 100th birthday. He died at age 96. I was delighted to see him portrayed in the film ''Young Winston''—the story of Winston Churchill's youth. Apparently he had been a friend of Churchill's father.

Allenby, Plumer and other famous generals inspected us. So did the King of Afghanistan, who was assassinated shortly after his return home.

The King of Spain, Alfonso XIII, had been a cadet at Sandhurst. His visit was therefore particularly interesting. He had married one of Queen Victoria's daughters so that he had many relatives in Britain. I only met him for a brief moment but he seemed to have a pleasant and warm personality and I can understand the great loyalty that his staff, who remained in Madrid, had for him long after his death. We met one of them when we visited the Palace in 1961—he treated us with great respect when I told him that I had met and shaken hands with Alfonso some thirty years before.

We had a number of cadets from India many of whom distinguished themselves commanding companies and battalions. If they survived the war, they were immediately given great responsibilities when Partition came and Pakistan was created. When I first went to Sandhurst my section commander was Corporal Iftahar Khan. ''Ifty,'' as we called him, was every inch a soldier and I was saddened to read that he was killed in an aircraft accident shortly after Partition. At that time, he was a Lieutenant-General and Vice-Chief of the Pakistan Army.

We also had cadets from Iraq and Siam. Iraq maintained close relations with Britain in those years and there were a number of officer exchanges between the two Armies. Before the assassination of King Faisal and the whole Cabinet of Iraq in 1958 we used to say that their Cabinet functioned well because two-thirds of them had been to the Staff College at Camberley—including the Prime Minister!

The event that pleased me most when I was at Sandhurst happened at my final parade in July 1930; the celebrated Passing Out Parade when, after the normal inspection and March Pasts, the Senior Cadets march in slow time up the steps of the Old building led by the Adjutant. It was not the feeling of relief at graduating successfully from the College, it was the presence of my father and mother. I had not seen Dad since 1925 and Mother had been away for a year so it was a wonderful reunion. I was particularly glad for both their sakes that I was one of the Under Officer elite and had success both at at Cranleigh and Sandhurst. Quite apart from the strain of long absences, I knew that they had given up a great deal financially to send me to both. I was even more pleased whtn I received my graduating marks; I passed out 35th in my class of 175 with over 70% in all subjects. Shortly after, I received official word that I had been commissioned into the Glosters. Two others joined the Regiment, Kim Lacey and Digby Grist. Altogether this was a happy ending for me—gazetted a Second-Lieutenant at the age of nineteen years and eleven months. My Commission, signed by the King, arrived shortly after.

3

Gravesend, My First Commission

On Sunday, October 14, 1930, after two happy months with my parents and my brother, Hugh, I said my farewells and headed for Gravesend—a small town on the south bank of the Thames about thirty miles east of London. The 2nd Battalion of the Gloucestershire Regiment was stationed there. I was raring to go and felt I could take on the world.

My first impression of the town was that it had been suitably named. It was a drab conglomeration of Victorian villas strung together by streets like cheap beads on a string.

My impression of the barracks was even worse. Stucco and faded yellow brick predominated. The barrack rooms, officers' quarters, guard room and offices were all in rows of single-storey hutments. There were only two buildings that had any pretensions to architectural design in the whole barracks. One contained the men's dining room, canteen and some administrative offices—it was on two floors and had a clock mounted high above the portico. The other was the officers' mess which I am convinced was a copy of the many hundreds of brick buildings that had been built by the railways for housing their engines when in need of repair. It was an ugly building of dirty yellow brick with large high windows and high ceilings designed to ensure that what heat there was from the fireplaces stayed in the top ten feet of each of the large rooms. Certainly the temperature at floor level was anything but warm—the senior officers sat close to the fireplace—the subalterns gathered on the outer fringes.

But I was cheered on arrival to find Kim Lacey. He had just bought an old car and driven from his parents' home near Woolwich. He, Digby Grist and I were the newly commissioned Second-Lieutenants. Whilst Kim and I had not known Digby very well at Sandhurst, we soon found we all had much in common. Digby was always bubbling over with good humour and bright ideas, and in the interveening years he has not changed.

The following morning we were to meet the Commanding Officer and the Adjutant. The former was Colonel R.L. Beasley, D.S.O. I think his nickname was "Bolo"—not that I would ever have dreamed of addressing him in that way. He was a big man physically, kind and considerate but did not exude much in the way of personality. I am sure he was a capable soldier but he did nothing to improve my military education during the year I was under his command.

The adjutant was Captain L.C. (Elsie) Evans—a dapper fair-haired officer with a fair moustache which he was always brushing upward with the back of his hand. I learned a number of things from L.C. Evans of an administrative nature and always found him to be approachable.

He was certainly helpful and friendly when the three of us reported to him that Monday morning in October. We were each posted to a different company—I was to go to "B" Company then commanded by Captain Benjamin Vigrass. Ben Vigrass was a man of about forty-five years of age, medium height and one of the kindest men I have ever met. In many ways, I was very fortunate because the attitude of a person on first meeting stays with me for a long time. Ben Vigrass made me welcome, produced a mug of army tea and then spoke quietly and at length about the company.

He had been a Quarter Master Sergeant before World War I, and gained his commission during the war so that his knowledge of the administrative side of the regiment was second to none. He handled men rather like a good school teacher would handle his students. However, he could not enthuse anyone—he was just too quiet. Nor did he have much knowledge of tactics which suited me well. Whenever we had a chance to do any training of that kind he would let me take the company off into the countryside where we would practice elementary section and platoon tactics.

Ben Vigrass had one disconcerting habit. When discussing a point with me he would use my chest just like a blackboard. With his finger he would do arithmetic sums across my chest even writing down actual figures. I, of course, was at a disadvantage because not only where the figures invisible to me but they were upside down! He did this all the time even when discussing elementary tactics and on occasions I would want to turn my back to him in case he was running out of room on my chest!

The Gloucestershire Regiment was made up of two battalions: the 28th Foot and the 61st Foot.

Recruits, after sixteen weeks training at the Regimental Depot in Bristol, would join the 2nd Battalion or 61st Foot stationed at Gravesend. Following a further three or six months they would be sent overseas to join the 28th Foot. It was essential that the battalion serving abroad be kept up to full strength, about 900 men. The battalion at home, already reduced by financial restraint to about 400/500 men, was responsible for drafting enough men to keep the battalion filled abroad. Thus, the home battalion was more of a holding or transit unit than an organized and ready force and this was the condition of the 61st Foot or 2nd Glosters when I joined them.

Both battalions had long and outstanding records.

The 28th Regiment of Foot was raised in 1694 by William III to strengthen his army then engaged in the long struggle with France. After a few years on garrison duty in Ireland and the West Indies it joined Marlborough in his successful battles against Louis XIV of France—its first Battle Honour being Ramillies 1706. It took part with Wolfe in the capture of Louisburg, 1758 and the Battle and capture of Quebec in 1759. Wolfe was mortally wounded in that battle whilst leading the 28th Foot.

At the Battle of Alexandria in 1801 when fighting against Napoleon, the regiment was attacked in the rear by French cavalry. The rear rank of the regiment was ordered to turn about and fire on the advancing cavalry. So back to back the regiment fought. The front rank beat off the French infantry whilst the rear rank destroyed the cavalry. For this feat of arms, the regiment was granted the right to wear two badges on its helmets and caps. One at the front and one at the back—both badges are the Sphinx.

At Quatre-Bras, and at Waterloo the next day, the 28th won the distinction of being the only regiment named by the Duke of Wellington in his report on the battles.

Since then it has distinguished itself on many occasions culminating in its defence of Castle Hill in Korea against a full division of Chinese troops. For this action it was awarded the U.S. Presidential Streamer or Battle Honour. The only other non-U.S. regiments to be given this honour are Princess Patricia's Canadian Light Infantry which also held off the Chinese, and an Australian battalion.

The 61st Foot was raised in 1759 and distinguished itself during the Napoleonic War in Spain. It took part in every battle under the Duke of Wellington. In the Battle of Salamanca, it lost all except two of its twenty-four officers.

The 28th and 61st Foot were named the North and South Gloucestershire Regiments respecively in 1782. In about 1880 they were joined together as the Gloucestershire Regiment. In 1930 they had more Battle Honours than any other British regiment—a detail of which we were very proud.

The Glosters were a country regiment—with the majority of the officers from the County of Gloucester. Of the men I would think that about 55% were from the county and 25% from the adjoining Welsh county and the forest of Dean—the latter mostly from mining families who had been dependent on the coal mines for a century. We also had a fair sprinkling of Irish because of the trade contacts between Bristol and Dublin. For the most part the men were from small towns and rural areas and I am certain that this very solid base of countrymen—as opposed to city folk—has been the main reason why the regiment could take great punishment on many occasions and yet fight back with superb courage. Countrymen may lack imagination but they are a very stable element in adversity.

Life in the regiment in Gravesend from a military standpoint was dull and it was only on rare occasions that we did any field training at all. But I will always remember one occasion because it gave me a great "surge of power" and a great sense of well-being. I took the company off for two or three days of elementary training during which we spent a morning on the rifle range and then marched a few miles to a small training area to bivouac for the night. The weather was not good—we got wet and the amount of tentage available didn't give everyone a chance to dry out—after three days we marched about fifteen miles back to barracks. We arrived about 4:00 p.m., soaking wet, and I told the men to take off their uniforms and wait for "foot inspection." This was a normal inspection to ensure that no one had developed blisters or other ailments which might prevent him from marching the same distance the next day. It was a ritual that had started in the days of Marlborough in 1704—and we still did it!

After giving the men about fifteen minutes to strip off their soaking uniforms I went into the barrack room, had a look at their feet and said I wanted to talk to them. I was soaking wet as I had not had a chance to change and I must have looked like a very damp scarecrow.

I told the men how proud I was of their conduct, smartness and good spirits during the three rain-soaked days. I admitted we had not learned a great many military skills because the weather was against us but I went on to say that one thing I had learned was that they were the best group of men I ever hoped to command and thanked them for their support. I meant every word and did not put any emotion or rhetoric into my short speech. They were the first men that I had ever commanded and for whom I had full responsibility.

When I had finished I said, "Thank you once again," and turned towards the door. I was stopped by an almost naked corporal who then called for "three cheers for Mr. Kitching." After the cheers I was embarrassed to be surrounded by the soldiers who were clapping their hands as they came towards me. I did not know what to do—laugh or cry. I left the barrackroom, picked up my equipment and went to my quarters for a bath and change. When I returned to the company barracks in the morning, the Sergeant-Major said, "I don't know what you said to the men after they came in last evening—I heard about it in the Mess afterwards—But I want to thank you for what you said. It's what we need." At the time I felt almost embarrassed but after a few months with the regiment I realized that under the conditions that existed at that time the number of occasions when a company of soldiers got together for training as a company were very limited.

With the battalion at half strength because of financial restrictions and with the requirement to send reinforcement drafts to the 28th Foot then in Egypt, the important thing that held the regiment together was sport. Rugger, boxing and athletics were the cement of our existence and 80% of our energy went into training and practicing for those sports. In many ways this made sense because we had very little military equipment to make training interesting; furthermore, with companies reduced to half strength we did not have enough soldiers to make tactical exercises seem real.

Of the 400 or 450 in the battalion about 200 officers, NCO's and men became the nucleus of all our sports. the other 200 odd men were the ones who were standing by to go off as drafts to Egypt. This pattern was common throughout the battalions that were then stationed in England.

I think that the reason I received such an enthusiastic "thank you" from the men in "B" Company was that they were a part of the 200 who rarely got any of the limelight. They were not the elite 200 who formed the sports nucleus but the 200 draftees who were not as important and did not get the same amount of encouragement.

Leave for officers was two months each year—to be taken in the period September - December which, in the annual training cycle, was the period for the individual training of the soldier. So for my first three months we were running at about half strength in officers. Some were friendly and pleasant—others almost ignored the newcomers. Some were married and lived away from the barracks—we rarely saw them in the Mess.

But there were a surprising number of more senior officers who were not married. They were never in the Mess on weekends—always staying with friends or whooping it up in London which was only a half hour train ride from Gravesend. Bill Walton was our favourite unmarried captain—a large man with a happy face and great fun on a party. "Long-dog" Mirehouse was another—although he must have been married at some time because his son followed him into the regiment. The senior subaltern was Frank Priestley—somewhat dull and lacking in personality. He had been a lieutenant for about twelve years so perhaps he had reason to be dull. The majors that I remember were the

Hon. Nigel Somerset—a member of the Beaufort and Raglan families—and Arthur Capel. Both were somewhat dull from a subaltern's point of view. I suppose the difference in age had a lot to do with their aloofness and also the dullness of garrison life—with so little to do of a military nature. Several officers hunted with the local hounds for two or three days a week. It was considered good military training as it would develop an individual's "eye for the country". But generally life must have been boring particularly for those who had served in India and China with the 61st Foot before it returned to England in 1929 after spending twelve years abroad.

For us subalterns, life was made more interesting—we all took part in the sports programmes and kept fit playing rugger, hockey, cricket, boxing, etc. with the men. John Biddulph, a subaltern, encouraged us all to take an active part in athletics. He had been an army hurdler and was of Olympic standard. Captain Tom Barnard had also been a well-known athlete in his day—he was a great help in our training. Kim Lacey, Digby Grist and I entered fully into all the sports activities but we all agreed many years later that we didn't learn very much of a military nature in Gravesend. Fortunately for us all, Grist and I were destined for service in Singapore and India—and Kim Lacey became a pilot and joined the R.A.F.

Two events broke all the boredom of military life in Gravesend that year.

As "orderly officer" one day my duties included visits to the dining hall when meals were being served to the men. The purpose was to see that the food was palatable and to receive complaints from anyone who felt it was not. Generally I think the men were content with the quality but not the quantity. On that particular day I went to my quarters at about twelve o'clock noon, sat down, and waited for the clock over the dining hall to strike the one note for 12:30. Sure enough it struck a few minutes later, so putting on my Sam Browne belt and sword (the latter to indicate my official position) I headed for the men's dining hall.

Unfortunately the single chime I had heard from the clock was for 1:30—and not 12:30. I was late—so returned to the officers' Mess to have lunch myself. On entering the dining room I saw that the only officers still eating were Major Capel and the acting adjutant, Frank Priestley. Arthur Capel had been severely wounded during the war and had a glass eye. When I entered the room he turned and asked, "Why weren't you at the men's dining hall?" I told him that I must have fallen asleep—he was so astounded that his glass eye fell in his soup. Priestley stood up and told me somewhat pompously that I must report to the adjutant immediately. As he was the acting adjutant it seemed rather foolish to me—however off I went buckling on my belt again—to be followed a few paces behind by Priestley who was hurriedly buckling on his own Sam Browne. The farce continued. On arriving at the adjutant's office I held the door open for Priestley to go in. He told me to wait two minutes and then knock on the door.

I suppose the two minutes were needed for him to catch his breath and look composed. When I finally stood in font of him he looked at me fiercely and asked why I had made such a stupid excuse to Major Capel. I told him that it was the truth—I had fallen asleep. He looked almost as startled as Capel had been. "Damn silly excuse—I would have thought you could produce a better one that that—seven days extra Orderly Officer." Out I went for my long delayed lunch and in due course Regimental Orders showed that Second Lieutenant G. Kitching was Orderly Officer for the whole of the next week.

In June of each year the three services put on what was described as the "Military Tournament" at Olympia—a huge covered stadium in the west end of London. Early in 1931 the Glosters were selected to put on the Regimental Pageant. It was a great honour for us and preparations started immediately. Fortunately one of our best officers—Major R.M. Grazebrook—was put in charge of organizing the series of presentations which were climaxed by the marching on of a Guard of Honour and the Regimental Colours. The Guard was to be commanded by the Adjutant, Captain Evans, and three subalterns were to alternate in carrying the Colours. I was one of them.

After much practice we headed for London and were soon involved in the rehearsals necessary to coordinate the many battle scenes depicted, one of which was the spectacular Battle of Alexandria in 1801 when the regiment beat off attacks by French infantry in front and cavalry in rear.

The Navy and Air Force also put on first class displays and in due course His Majesty King George V and Queen Mary attended a special performance. About an hour before their arrival I was told to put together a small party of our spare men and form them up to line the carpet along which Their Majesties would walk on their way to the elevator which would then take them to the Royal Box. The party was also to line the same route after the performance when Their Majesties returned to their car. Furthermore I was to accompany Their Majesties to the Royal Box and remain there in case they had questions about the Regimental Pageant.

I got the men together, explained their duties and hurried off to change into my best uniform. All went well when the Royal Party arrived and in due course they moved into the Royal Box to receive the Royal Salute. This was the first occasion I had ever seen the King let alone being within a foot of him. I was very impressed. I remember feeling the surge of power and pride and I think I must have been very nervous because when the bands struck up the Anthem I saluted smartly only to realize too late that in the crowded area of the Royal Box I had, in bringing up my right arm to the salute, tipped the King's cap slightly forward over his eyes. I was horrified and could not think what to do. Out of the corner of my eye I could see that the King was slowly pushing his cap back with his hand as he remained at the salute during the playing of the Anthem. I wondered what would happen when the bands stopped playing; certainly three hundred years before I would probably have been executed. I waited for the end. When it came the King turned slowly and looked at me with a pair of the bluest eyes I have ever seen. Having reduced me to ashes by his look he turned back and waved to the crowds below before taking his seat. I quickly moved to the rear of the box!

After the performance I walked behind the King as he moved past our soldiers who were lined up on each side of the red carpet leading towards the car. When he got to the Royal Car he must have asked to meet the men responsible for the Tournament because he paused there for several minutes. As my small party were in fact blocking the public from crossing over the carpet to get to the exits I was asked to march them off. The men were facing each other across the carpet, had been placed there individually during the performance and were not organized as a front or rear rank. I felt the best way to march them off was to get them facing the lift (or elevator) and march off in that direction. Before giving the order "Outwards Turn" I explained to the men that on receiving that order they were to turn and face the lift. Unfortunately some thought I had said 'left' instead of 'lift' so the result was chaos with men facing in all directions. At that moment the King was saying his farewells to those around him and I saw him looking towards me. I knew from his look that he was thinking, "Thank God for the Royal Navy."

Shortly after this event the regiment received another officer, Second-Lieutenant James Heath. Heath was what was then known as a "university entry". If a student at Oxford or Cambridge wanted a Regular Commission in the army, he applied for it at university. He then had to spend three years with the officer training corps at university and after getting his degree would be given a commission. In order to compensate for his three years at university he was given a year's seniority on entering the army. This put Heath senior to Kitching, Lacey and Grist which annoyed us a great deal! Particularly as Heath did not appear to be endowed with many military virtues. I remember lecturing him very severely after a church parade of which his phoney seniority gave him command. I told him he was a disgrace, did not know how to march or salute, etc., etc. I gave him this lecture in his quarters after which I slammed the door and walked out.

During my months in Gravesend I had got to know "Henry" Heath well and greatly enjoyed his company. Although unpopular at first, his sense of humour and the fact that he was a "character" soon made him friends. Shortly after getting to Folkeston training area I went to call on friends of my parents who lived in the area—the Staple-Smith's. Their daughter, "Bonny", was most attractive so she became a part of our lives at the numerous parties which we had on arrival. One day she told me that a friend of hers was coming to stay with her—an Austrian blond aged about 19 and beautiful as well. Could I get one of my friends—preferably Henry Heath—to make up a foursome?" We would eat at the Staple-Smith's and then go to the fairgrounds in Folkestone for the roller coasters, etc.

All was arranged and in due course Henry and I arrived at the Staple-Smith house—a lovely place in the country. On the way out, Henry waxed ecstatic about Austrians—particularly blondes—and was obviously looking forward to the evening. As soon as we saw "Bonny" she took me aside and admitted that she had not seen her friend for about four years and that in the interim she had put on a certain amount of weight! She hoped Henry wouldn't mind. I knew that Henry did not like fat girls and it was obvious from the moment they met that things were going to be difficult. It became even worse as the evening wore on as "lilli" was obviously falling for Henry in a big way. The more he tried to avoid contact with her the more she closed in on him. She really was very plump and whatever beauty she might have had was hidden behind rolls of fat.

By taking refuge behind chairs and sofas Henry survived the early part of the evening including dinner when to his horror he found her sitting opposite him at the table. He immediately started an animated conversation with Mr. Staple-Smith, who sat at the head of the table on his left, on the glories of partridge and pheasant shooting. These were Mr. Staple-Smith's favourite sports but I knew that Henry hated shooting any bird and would normally have avoided discussion on the subject. But he was prepared to talk about anything in order to avoid having to look at Lilli across the table—she however was fascinated by his manner and ogled him throughout the meal.

After dinner we took off in the car—Henry insisting that he drive in order to avoid any possibility of her trying to embrace him in the back of the car.

At the fairground we played the usual games with hoops to win dolls—we threw balls at coconuts and then Lilli suddenly said she wanted to go on the roller coaster. Henry was reluctant—he didn't like them—but she pleaded and so the four of us climbed into the front car.

Off we went and it was obvious in no time at all that Lilli was scared stiff and was about to be ill. As soon as the cars stopped she leapt out and refused to consider another ride. This gave Henry his chance and he seized it. "I think I'll stay and have a few more rides. I get a great thrill out of these coasters." Henry remained in the coaster car for half an hour during which Bonny and I commiserated with Lilli. When he finally got off he was quite green in colour and staggered around holding his stomach. We piled into the car with Henry lying alone in the back seat threatening to be sick at any moment. This kept Lilli away.

So ended our party with Lilli but as Henry said as he was being physically sick on arrival back at camp. "It was worth it, old boy."

In late July I was warned that I was posted to the 28th who were then in Singapore, and would be sailing in October. I immediately took two months leave and headed for my parents new home near Cambridge.

October soon arrived and it was time to say goodbye to Mum and Dad. Looking back I realize now that I did not really appreciate the strong feelings of love and affection that my parents had for me and I for them. Although we had been parted from time to time between China and England, it was the fact that they were always there that counted. They were more than the backdrop to my school days, they were the pillars on which I leaned whenever I needed help or support. And they continued to be until the end of their days.

My mother had been a deeply religious girl in her teens and twenties as her diaries and writing show. She had been brought up in a simple Puritan household by parents who did not believe it was essential for a good Christian to be guided by a priest or attend communion. In fact, there were no priests, no altar, no silver or candles in the chapel she attended as a girl. When we were young in China we had all gone to church each Sunday but as my parents grew older they attended church less frequently. But they remained stout Christians and this gave them the strength to overcome whatever problems came their way.

My father was a very patriotic and proud Englishman. In writing that I do not mean he was a jingoistic "up the Empire and to hell with the rest of the world." He was proud of what England had accomplished He remembered his early years in China when an "Englishman's word was as good as his bond." He often recalled those years when a cheque on an English bank was regarded by the Chinese as the equivalent to gold and the cheques would frequently remain uncashed for many months because they counted as cash.

Having served in the Boxer Rebellion in 1900-1901, my father naturally volunteered to serve in the First World War. However, because of his position in Canton he had to be content with service as the commandant of the local Volunteer Forces on the Island of Shameen. In World War II he joined the Local Defence Volunteers in 1940 and was one of a happy band of L.D.V. in Barton-on-Sea who patrolled the cliffs each night armed with a variety of rifles and shotguns. The group had mostly been fairly senior in one or other of the Armed Forces but were happy to be privates or corporals. The lieutenant commanding the group had been a admiral four years before! They felt they had made a worthwhile contribution.

With many kisses and hand shakes I boarded a train at Cambridge and headed for the docks at Southhampton from which the troopship ''Neuralia'' was to sail with a full complement of about 60 officers and 1,000 other ranks. A number of families with children were also aboard.

The ''trooping'' season in those days was from October to May. During these months the troopships ''Neuralia'' and ''Nevasa'' plied between England and Hong Kong, stopping off at Gibraltar, Malta, Alexandria, Suez, Aden, Bombay, Colombo and Singapore to take out reinforcements for the various garrisons, exchange regiments between stations and bring back to the U.K. those who had served their quota of years abroad. They were not large ships—only about 12,000 tons and they generally averaged ten knots in good weather but only eight when the wind was against them. But they were moderately comfortable even though as junior officers we were crammed in four to a small cabin.

above
D Company of the Gloucestershire Regiment,
Singapore, 1932, winners: track and field
and tug of war

Beresford-Pierce, RAF, David Bayne,
RAF and The Author Port Said, 1935

4

Posting To Singapore

When we sailed on the Troopship "Neuralia" she was carrying drafts of reinforcements so we had none of the great ceremonies that accompany the embarkation of a complete regiment. We slipped quietly out of Southampton heading south-west to the Channel, passing the Needles—three huge isolated chalk cliffs at the western end of the Isle of Wight.

The two officers on board who were most helpful to me and took the greatest interest in educating me both became full Generals in the British Army and also good friends of mine many years later. One was Geoffrey Bourne who had lost an arm bobsledding in Switzerland in 1924 and later commanded an Airborne Division. On retirement he was given a peerage. The other was Hugh Stockwell who commanded the British forces in the Suez crisis in 1956 and later was Deputy Supreme Commander of Allied Forces in NATO Europe. He retired as a General and was knighted by the Queen.

After about seventeen days at sea we went through the Straits of Malacca between Sumatra and Malaya, I was struck by the incredible greenness of the many islands as we passed them—each seemed like a giant pin cushion with lush vegetation right to the water's edge. There was very little sign of life on them although we passed scores of fishing vessels—all sail powered and many of them of Chinese junk design—built high fore and aft to take big seas.

I was up early on the great day of our arrival, breakfasted by 7:00 a.m. and on deck as we entered Keppel Harbour with the beautiful islands of Blakang Mati and Pulau Brani on our right. Slowly we moved towards the main wharf on the south side of Empire Dock and after the usual pushing and pulling by tugs made ourselves fast alongside the dock. Although it was only 8:00 a.m., the sun was beginning to warm up considerably and the humidity rose with it. I could already feel the perspiration accumulating under my Wolseley helmet.

Suddenly I heard a cheerful voice behind me, "You must be Kitching—I'm Denis Biddle." I turned to find a very good looking subaltern, blue-eyed and fair moustached, smiling at me. Behind him was another officer of the regiment and to this day I can recall how impressed I was by their "turn out"—to use a military phrase. Leather was polished to a brilliant glow, brasses shining brightly and uniforms immaculately starched and pressed. Denis Biddle was wearing shorts and puttees but the other officer was in riding breeches and boots. He gave me a pleasant grin—"My name is Colin Campbell. I'm the Adjutant—welcome to the 28th."

I felt I was in a different world. It was not because Gravesend always seemed to be cloudy and grey whereas this morning in Singapore the sun shone brightly. It was partly the smart appearance of Biddle and Campbell, but it was obvious, after only a few minutes of collecting trunks and suitcases, that this half of the Gloucestershire Regiment had a sense of purpose and a military pride that I had not found in the 61st. Colin Campbell had a large convertible Buick which accommodated my trunks and boxes and still left room for the three of us in the front. We drove through the center of Singapore with Denis pointing out the important buildings—then up Orchard Road before swinging left for Tanglin and the area of the barracks.

The day of my arrival was a Sunday so the Officer's Mess was almost deserted. However Denis showed me my quarters, where I met the Chinese "boy" who was going to look after me. He was called Ah Too.

After lunch Denis took me up to the barracks in his old Morris Cowley car; it had no top so when it rained we used umbrellas. Colin Campbell told me that I had been posted to "D" Company and that the first parade in the morning would be the Commanding Officer's parade at 6:00 a.m. This meant my company would have to parade at 5:30 to reach the main parade ground in time. Dress would be jackets, shorts and puttees, Sam Browne and swords. I spent what was left of the afternoon unpacking and organizing my quarter. At dinner that night I met two or three other subalterns. One of them promised to guide me to the parade next morning, leaving the quarters at 5:00 a.m. Ah Too was a wonderfully tidy "boy"; he had everything arranged neatly in my room and guaranteed to have all my dirty laundry back by 4:30 a.m. when he was due to wake me! What service! I slipped through the mosquito net surrounding my bed, lay down and slept.

Sergeant-Major Oxenham was in the company office when I arrived there next morning soon after 5:00 a.m. He greeted me quietly and told me very quickly where to go and what to do when the company fell in for the parade. He was a good sergeant-major and I was glad that he stayed with "D" Company during the four years I was in it. He was commissioned during World War II and retired as a major. The Company Commander was Captain Bickley James.

In due course we marched off to join the remainder of the regiment on the parade ground. The regiment was made up of a Headquarter Wing comprising the band, the drums, signals, etc. and four companies, A, B, C and D.

Being in "D" Company we were on the left of the line as we formed up and being the only other officer, except for the Company Commander who stood on the right, I was on the extreme left of the line. There were about 900 men on parade drawn up in two ranks. In due course we "presented arms" to the commanding officer, Colonel Alfred Chapman, who then rode his horse along the parade as he inspected the regiment. Nothing seemed to escape his eagle eye as he passed slowly along followed closely by the adjutant. At last he reached the end of the line. "Captain James," he called out, "who is this officer and what is doing here?" I found myself looking up at a stern military face. Bickley James replied, "His name is Kitching, sir, he joined us yesterday." By this time I was beginning to feel a little unwanted in spite of my warm reception the day before. Colonel Chapman looked me over carefully and then said, "When I was young all newly joined subalterns had to carry a rifle and bayonet on their first parades—just to show the men that they were smarter than they were. Perhaps we should follow that example. I'll see you later.''

My interview with Colonel Chapman took place later that day. He was a tall powerfully built man—square faced and broadshouldered. His face when I stood in front of him did not show much expression.

I cannot remember his exact words although their intent stayed with me for many years. A young officer, he said, has got to show the men under his command that he can do anything that they can do—and do it much better. He must live with the men, get to know them and their problems, play every game with them: rugger, athletics, boxing, hockey, water-polo, soccer, swimming. He must make sure they feed well and are fit. He must train them as a military team so that in war the sections would function effectively. He must lead them at all times. He told me that this was the advice given to him when he had joined the 28th in the early years of the century. He would be watching to see that I was doing all the things I should!

Then he said, ''Do you have any money beyond your pay?'' I said I had a small allowance from my father. ''Do you drink?'' No, I replied, only on guest nights in the Mess.

''Do you smoke?'' ''Yes, I do.''

''Do you play polo?'' ''No, I can't afford it.''

''All right,'' he said, ''then stop smoking, I'll lend you a polo pony and you will play polo starting next week!!''

That was the end of the interview. I noted that the colonel lit another cigarette as I staggered out of the office. Colin Campbell was grinning from ear to ear. ''Now you know what we want from you.''

Quite obviously the authorities had no plans to defend Malaya from the north at that time. Everyone assumed the Royal Navy would keep an enemy from its shores.

Whilst the Navy had many plans for the development of Singapore as a major base, they had done very little by 1931. Some years before one half of a huge floating dock had been towed out to Singapore and moved into position at the dockyard on the north side of Singapore Island—however with the cuts in defence spending in '29/30, the ''other half'' was cancelled! It was some years before the halves were joined.

The Royal Air Force maintained an airfield close to the Royal Naval dockyard at Seletar, however, there was not much activity there except when flights of Wapitis came in from India. These ancient aircraft with pilot and Lewis gunner came down once or twice a year on training flights—they would remain in Singapore for a couple of weeks—scare us to death when we "volunteered" to go aloft with them—and then load up with duty free whisky and gin and fly back to India by easy stages. The pilots were great fun—some were Canadians on short service commissions.

There was only one battalion of British infantry in the whole of what was then Malaya—which included Singapore.

There was a battery of Coast Artillery—a part of the Hong Kong and Singapore Regiment which manned the coastal defence guns in those two important bases.

There was a volunteer force named the Singapore Volunteer Corps which included a complete company of Chinese. The standard of training was not particularly good but morale was high.

Regiments sent to Singapore were placed on "Colonial establishments." This meant an increase of about 150 over the establishment of regiments in India and Egypt. Presumably this was to enable us to carry out more effectively any duties in connection with "aid to the Civil Power" in case of riots between Malay, Chinese and Indian factions of the civilian population. Fortunately we were not called out to do this kind of distasteful duty—we remained on the best of terms with all elements and played many games and sports with them.

An activity that the Colonel introduced at short notice was an inter-platoon relay-race over a course of sixteen miles with each man running one mile. This meant each of the twenty platoons in the battalion had to produce sixteen runners—a total of 320 taking part altogether. This was the type of thing the Colonel liked—mass participation. It was the best way to get everyone involved and he did it frequently by ordering without notice a "dog and stick" walk for everyone, including senior officers, from the barracks to the top of some hill a few miles away. On the hill would be report centres to ensure that everyone except the guards and the sick had taken part.

In the inter-platoon sixteen-mile run my platoon came first. I had taken the whole platoon out the day before for a mile run so that we had some idea who to include in the team and it paid off. After the race

Colonel Chapman came to present us with the prize. I had a first-class miler in my platoon so I told him to go up and accept the prize. I remained in line with the other fourteen runners. After presenting the cup the Colonel came along our line and congratulated us on our victory. He then said he would like to speak to me alone. He asked me why I hadn't accepted the cup. I told him that the young soldier who had gone up was largely responsible for our win—he had gained a good 200 yards in his mile which made it easier for me when, as the final runner, I was able to keep the lead on our nearest competitor. The Colonel's face was expressionless. After a moment he said, ''Kitching, perhaps you were right on this occasion but I would never have done it that way. Well done—but next time you must accept the prize as you are their officer.''

That story shows what a first-class leader we had in the Colonel. He was not angry—he listened patiently and although he did not agree with my action he said, ''Well done.'' It was small thing really but over the two and a half years that I was under Colonel Chapman there were many other occasions when I benefitted from his advice and his instructions.

Although the countryside did not lend itself to large scale manouevres there were areas adjacent to the barracks where we could practice platoon deployments; however, the lack of suitable training areas was one of the weaknesses of serving in Singapore.

To compensate for this, Colonel Chapman would, on occasion, sound the alarm at about midnight with orders to parade immediately in full battle orders. Having assembled the battalion he would order us to wear gas-masks and then march twelve or fifteen miles through the city. Although the nights were fairly cool, the gas-masks were uncomfortable and we were always glad when after an hour or two the ''all clear'' was sounded and we could take them off. The men showed their complete disaproval by making rude noises through their respirators. It was almost impossible to tell where the noises came from so we marched merrily on our way and blamed the noises on the horses and mules.

When the Regiment had arrived in Singapore they found that ''the Army's name was mud''—to quote a local newspaper. This sad state of affairs had been brought about by the behaviour of the previous regiment during the last few months of their stay in the city. Something must have angered the soldiers a great deal to drive them into acts of vandalism and destruction which were almost unheard of in a disciplin-ed peace-time army. A strong commanding officer would never have permitted it in the first place. They obviously did not have one.

Colonel Chapman had to bend over backwards to restore public con-fidence in the army. He realized that if the soldiers of the Regiment were to get a fair deal from the merchants and others in the community their behaviour would have to be exemplary and, perhaps more im-portant, the merchants must have some way of identifying them. To force our men to wear uniform when walking out would have been un-fair—they wore it all day in barracks. On the few occasions when their finances would allow them to visit the dance halls and bars each month they deserved the anonymity of civilian clothes. What Colonel Chapman did was to ensure that the men were well dressed when in civilian clothes and that they wore the regimental tie. If a soldier could not afford to buy a suit, shirt and tie, Alfred Chapman bought him one and to make sure that it did not look like ''charity'' he would arrange for the soldier to pay him back ''sometime.'' But he was not concerned about being repaid—good behaviour and pride in the regiment were his return.

In many other ways Colonel Chapman set about restoring the faith of civilians in the army. The regiment threw itself into every sport with great enthusiasm—taking on Chinese and Malays at football and shooting, Europeans at rugger and cricket, Indians at hockey. The Colonel was not unduly concerned if we lost games—what he did insist on was good sportsmanship and fair play. Within six months of our ar-rival in Singapore, the name of the regiment stood very high. Our soldiers were treated with courtesy and became guests in many homes. The adjutant, Colin Campbell, always gave the credit for this change in public relations to the Colonel because of his insistence on high stan-dards and his interest in everything that was going on. However, I think that most of us gave a lot of the credit to Colin Campbell. Alfred Chapman was a hard taskmaster. He was very demanding and it was Colin Campbell's responsibility to ensure that the demands were met. This meant many long hours of work when the rest of the subalterns were relaxing. He had to maintain a strict routine to keep up with the commanding officer's energetic ways of exercising command. He did not have many opportunities to relax although he found time to put on a regimental concert in the large Victoria theatre in downtown Singapore. It was called "Tanglin Titbits" and whilst it started out as a rather humble concert it ended up as a well produced extravaganza which raised large sums of money for local charities.

From a subaltern's point of view, Singapore was almost ideal. Quite apart from the endless variety of games and sports we played with the men, we could play golf on a small course near the barracks and were always welcome at the Swimming Club halfway out to Changi. There were a number of attractive girls on the island, many of them visiting from Australia—they kept us busy! In addition, several large liners would go through Singapore each month. The U.S. President Line had a ship call each week. The P&O Line had one each week also. The Dutch ships including the "Marnix van Ste. Aldegonde" and the Polish ship "Batory" were frequent visitors. Both these great ships were a part of the Assault Convoy that later carried the 1st Canadian Division from Britain for the invasion of Sicily in 1943. For a change of scene, we would often visit these ships for dinner as they lay off the main harbour.

Our Warrant Officers were an exceptional group of men who were a tower of strength to the Regiment. Most had about fifteen years of Regular service and received well deserved promotion to Captain and Major in World War II. The senior sergeants had about the same span of service and I was fortunate in having as my platoon sergeant a great character known to everyone as "Battler" Bence. "Battler" was a man of about 32 when I first met him. He was about five feet eight inches tall, of stocky and strong build, dark brown eyes, black hair and large black moustache. He had not had much formal education but he had a good knowledge of men. In a way he was a Kipling soldier of the old school. Very straight and consistent for 90% of the time, but delightfully different for the other 10% when he had had a few drinks. Alcohol never made him belligerent—instead it made him generous and magnanimous—ready to give and forgive.

One day in March 1932, Battler Bence received the great news that an aunt had left him 5,000 pounds sterling. At that time that was a great deal of money and was equivalent of perhaps 75,000 pounds sterling in present values (approximately $150,000).

Battler was not married and didn't have a care in the world. He had always lived fairly carefully—husbanding his money so that when he did spend, he did so only on special occasions when, in the grand manner, he would indulge in expensive hotels, champagne and parties. On these occasions nothing was too good for him or his friends.

The 5,000 pounds was almost too much for him. He took three weeks leave and rented a bungalow out at Changi which was then an undeveloped rest camp. From this bungalow Battler sent out huge invitation lists to all his friends and acquaintances to attend a series of parties—and since Changi was about fifteen miles from the barracks, he arranged for a fleet of taxis to transport the revellers out to the parties and return them in due course back to the barracks.

All went well for a week or so and then unfortunately Battler had a bad fall that damaged a leg and put him into hospital. In those days we had to hold an Official Board of Inquiry into all accidents in case it might result in permanent injury which would entail a disability pension. Since I was Bence's platoon commander, I was ordered to conduct the Board of Inquiry—and since Bence was in hospital, we adjourned there for the proceedings. Fortunately, I went in to see him before the official party. He told me he could remember nothing about the incident. He had had a "small" party for some friends—he had said goodbye to them—then walked up the stairs to his rented bungalow and remembered nothing more until he was wakened by a native Malay gardener the next morning. He was found lying at the bottom of the stairs—that was all there was to it. I told him to stick to the story—and not enlarge on it.

Unfortunately once the Court was convened Battler started to enjoy the scene. He became the big actor and enlarged on the event to such an extent that I adjourned the Inquiry and on return to barracks arranged for another officer to head the Inquiry—and to start the proceedings all over again. I then returned to the hospital and had a few words with Battler. I told him that if he continuied to talk happily about the event in the way he had with the first Inquiry, he would probably end up with a Court Martial. Furthermore, I told him that I was so sure that it would end up in a Court Martial that I had persuaded the authorities to put someone else in to head the Inquiry so that I would be in a position to defend him at his Court Martial. This shook him up a bit and he agreed to be brief and repentant before the Inquiry. In due course the Board reported that the accident was unavoidable; that Bence was not primarily to blame, and recommended that the lighting at the top of the stairs be improved so that accidents would not happen again. Once his leg was well enough for him to walk with the aid of a stick, I made Bence go with me to Changi because I wanted to see exactly what had happened. We drove to the bungalow which like many houses of its kind in Singapore was built on concrete stilts as a protection against various ants. To enter the house one had to climb up twelve concrete steps. Like everyone else I assumed that Bence had fallen down the steps. However, when I questioned the Malay gardener, I got a quite different story.

Next to the bungalow rented by Bence were the beginnings of another bungalow which had never been completed. All that had been built was the fight of concrete steps—which led nowhere. On saying farewell to his guests, Battler had gone up the wrong steps and, of course, fell headlong in the dark from the top. He was lucky he wasn't killed—and he was lucky that the Board of Inquiry had accepted his statement that he had "fallen down the stairs". Had they gone out to the scene and questioned the gardener they would have been forced to report that Bence was entirely to blame "in that he had climbed twelve steps to enter a house that was not there". I am sure that the only reason Bence survived the fall was that he was drunk. I told him that the case was closed as far as I was concerned provided he came down to earth and stopped spending all his money. He did and was a model of propriety—for a while!

Singapore ws quite a good station for the British soldier. Although his pay was not very much, there were a number of places in the city where he could relax. One was the "New World"—a vast hall with dance orchestras playing for about twelve hours each day and hostesses available for "10 cents a dance." The girls were mostly of Chinese or Malay origin and the children of mixed marriages or liaisons. The girls, of part British -part Malay origin, were particularly good looking. There were also beer halls and other places of entertainment for the men and generally they seemed to enjoy Malaya.

I carried the Colours of the 28th, either the King's or Regimental, a total of nineteen times during my service with the battalion, either on battalion parades or as part of a Guard of Honour for a high-ranking visitor. One such visitor was His Highness, Ibrahim, the Sultan of Johore, a most interesting man. He was about fifty years of age at that time, had a powerful physique and was taller than most people of his race. But the stories about the wild parties he threw in his early years at his Palace in Singapore fascinated us. The Palace, named Tyersall, was only a few hundred yards from our barracks and, since the Sultan was not officially permitted to remain on the Island of Singapore because of his earlier misdemeanours, the Palace was empty except for a small caretaking staff. We often used to walk through its gardens and peek in the windows.

However, since the Governor of Malaya had his official residence in Singapore it was sometimes necessary for the Sultans of the various Malay States to pay official calls on him. It was on one such occasion that the regiment provided a Guard of Honour for the Sultan of Johore. All went well—the Guard of Honour was drawn up with the Colour Party in the centre, everything shone—buckles, bayonets and badges. When His Highness stepped onto the dais the command was given to present arms—I slowly lowered the Colour and with a turn of the pike on which it was carried I spread the Colour on the grass. Our Regimental Colour was one of the most beautiful I have ever seen. Its background was the primrose yellow adopted by the regiment when it was first raised in 1695. In the centre, surmounted by the Crown, was the Back Badge awarded to it at Alexandria in 1801 and surrounding this centre piece worked in delicate silks were emblazoned the battle honours of which the regiment is so proud. Much of the work of repair had been done by wives of members of the regiment over the years.

The Sultan was intrigued with the Colour and with the Guard of Honour and was most complimentary. He liked the primrose yellow—in fact he liked everything he had seen and invited me to visit him in Johore. I couldn't help but feel that the Guard Commander should have been the one to be congratulated—not me. A few days later the British Resident or Politcal Officer attached to the Sultan sent a car for me— I spent about an hour with him and the Sultan, consumed two or three large scotches, met the Sultanah who was a Scottish lady and then returned home. The Sultan certainly did not show many ill effects from the reputed debaucheries of his youth. He was intelligent and had all his wits about him.

The British Resident was a good looking man of about forty-five but his wife was one of the plainest women I had ever seen. He must have read my mind because when I met him a few weeks later he confided that his first wife had been a very beautiful girl and "some bounder" had stolen her from him. He said that he then made up his mind not to make the same mistake again!! He certainly hadn't.

Each year a Ball was given by the Governor to entertain local society and distinguished visitors. In 1932, Sir Cecil and Lady Clementi invited many distinguished people including Lieutenants Biddle, Heath and Kitching of the Glosters. We decided to go although we always felt that affairs of that kind were a little pompous. In order to make sure that it was not too pompous we also decided to have a few drinks before the party. In due course we arrived at Government House feeling in good form.

I do not recall Denis Biddle or Henry Heath doing much dancing. Instead we wandered from bar to bar, thoroughly enjoying ourselves mimicking some of the more distinguished guests. At about midnight Denis and I suddenly realized that Henry was nowhere to be found. We searched high and low and finally found him slepping happily on the official throne in the throne room. Fortunately huge curtains had been drawn around the throne which was on a low raised dais. Denis and I quickly seized Henry and, supporting him between us, moved towards an exit. All went well until we were just about to leave the building. There, standing very regally, was Lady Clementi. I should mention that at this point Henry was fine—he was suffering no pain at all and was no problem although he kept muttering about "having another drink, old boy."

"Oh, the poor young man," exclaimed Lady Clementi, "did he have an accident?"

"Oh, no, Lady Clementi," we said in chorus. "He has just fainted."

"Well, then, I will get him a brandy—that's what he needs," and she summoned a servant who returned shortly with a glass. Henry remained standing supported almost entirely by Denis and me Lady Clementi took the glass and, gently lifting his head, poured a little into his mouth. Henry took to it like a duck to water. He didn't just sip it—he gulped it down much to Lady Clementi's surprise.

"Oh, he needed that so badly," she said, "now take him home immediately and put him to bed."

Fortunately she then withdrew to join her guests. Had she remained she would have heard Henry mutter, "Thanks, old girl, but put a little soda in it next time."

In September 1932 we were told that the regiment would be moving in late November to India and that our next station would be Mhow. No one had been to Mhow—we knew very little about it but the news was greeted with groans and boos.

Singapore had taken the regiment to its heart and on the day that we sailed away the "Straits Times"—the largest English newspaper published in Singapore—came out with an editorial which eulogized the regiment for its contribution in so many different fields. Its final paragraph stated that there was no doubt in the minds of the people of Singapore that the 28th was the finest battalion that had ever served in Malaya. The two men who deserved most of the credit for our high standards and good morale were the Colonel and the Adjutant—Alfred Chapman and Colin Campbell. Of course, the men deserve the credit too—they were the ones who showed good sportsmanship and whose behaviour received so much praise but the man who set the example was the Colonel—and the Adjutant made sure we all followed it.

After many farewell parties we left Singapore late in November in the troopship "Neuralia" bound for Bombay which we reached five days later. From there we went by train to Mhow passing through an increasingly brown countryside in sharp contrast to the green of Malaya.

Colour Party, Mhow, India
Author holding King's Colour

British Infantry Barracks
Mhow, India

BRIT. INF.Y BARRACK
MHOW.

5

Mhow

In 1932, Mhow was a town of about 75,000 civilians with a military garrison of about 3,000. Whilst the economy of the town was in some measure dependent on the requirements of the military it was an important centre for the marketing and distribution of the extensive cotton and wheat crops grown in the surrounding area. It was a peaceful urban-cum-rural community situated in Central India just north of the Narbudda river and well served by rail to Rutlam in the north and Khandwa in the south where they connected with the transcontinental railway system.

The garrison consisted of an Area Headquarters, a British Artillery Regiment, A British Infantry Battalion and a battalion of the Indian Army. In addition, there was a large military hospital and the attendant supply services required of a garrison.

Mhow Military Area was a part of Bombay Military District. The District contained roughly a full division of soldiers made up of one-third British and two-thirds Indian Army. Mhow Area contained a full brigade because in addition to the garrison in Mhow itself there was an additional battalion in Jubbelpore, three hundred miles to the east. The Area Commander was a Brigadier Conry of the Indian Army—a pompous little man who, like many senior officers of that Army, had a strange attitude towards the British Army. Perhaps this was due to the different outlook within battalions of the two Armies. In the Indian Army, the Colonel of a regiment was looked on as a "father" figure by his Indian soldiers—they had a fierce price in him—they were a family in spite of the different "races" which might make up the regiment. He could do no wrong The Colonel Sahib was omnipotent. The men had a childlike faith in him. This was not the attitude in the British Army.

Although Alfred Chapman was an excellent commanding officer we never looked on him as a "father" figure. The British solider is too independently minded for that form of hero worship. In war, a British regiment can be inspired by their commanding officer to follow him to Kingdom Come but in peace time the men like to take a longer look.

In addition there were many more officers in a British regiment than there were in the Indian. All our platoons were commanded by British officers whereas in the Indian Army platoons were commanded generally by Viceroy commissioned officers who were Indians. There was nothing wrong with their system because they had to find some way of training Indians to climb the ladder of promotion. But it did mean that there might be as few as ten or twelve British officers in an Indian regiment whereas we would have more like twenty-eight. And with only twelve officers, the colonel would naturally stand out more clearly and appear more important. With us the men looked more towards their platoon commanders as their leaders and they were encouraged to do this as we needed them to get our initial training in leadership. There were many differences between the two armies but the main one was that many senior officers of the Indian Army did not understand the British soldier and his motives. Brigadier Conry was one of them.

When we arrived I was approached by an Indian who told me that he had been selected to be my Bearer; he didn't tell me who had selected him. His name, he said, was Chandu. He was a good looking man of about 45 and of a fairly high caste in the Hindu hierarchy. I like him at the outset and he stayed with me during my years in India. He had a nice family with two of the most attractive young children—a boy and a girl. He was completely honest, had a good sense of humour and didn't hestitate to tell me if, in his opinion, I had done something wrong. He was one of the best things that happened to me in India.

The British Infantry Barracks were located well clear of the town and comprised six huge stone barrack blocks, one for Administration and the other five for the Companies. In addition there were the usual Messes and canteens scattered through the barracks and beyond that again lay the rifle ranges. In the distance were the hills of the Narbudda—an area we were to get to know intimately in the years ahead.

We were a subdued group of officers during our first month—we took quite a while to adjust to the change. There had always been so much to do in Singapore—never a dull moment. We quickly realized that we would have to change our habits. The Officers' Mess we took over was quite inadequate—it was an old house and a disappointment after the luxury of the Mess in Singapore. We spent Christmas in it three weeks after our arrival and the only thing we could think of for entertainment was to hire a magician and a couple of snake charmers. Cobras were swaying lazily in their baskets to the reedy music of a local flute—the magician made trees grow before our eyes. It was colourful but hardly Christmas.

This was monsoon country in which everything was based on a period of about two months of rain commencing in the third week of June. The monsoon was generally on time.

A week or so before the rains the farmers would be out ploughing their fields laboriously with all movement based on the speed of the water-buffalo. Small catchment areas were repaired so that they could be temporary reservoirs and channels were cut in the fields in order to direct the rain along the courses required. Seed was sown and then came the rains. Within two weeks the new wheat appeared, the cotton shrubs turned green—in fact everything turned green. In mid-August the rain would cease and the sun regain its warmth. In October the crops were gathered and thereafter the fields and countryside turned brown. Around the villages and farms small areas stayed green planted with vegetables and watered by wells and irrigation ditches. From a military point of view it was a paradise with endless training areas and a wide variety of landscapes. From November to June there were very few crops to damage—we could move across country almost anywhere in an area of over 400 square miles! It would have been difficult for an infantry battalion in those years to do much damage to crops anyway—we had no vehicles of any kind! It may be hard for a young officer of a modern army today to imagine a regiment without wheeled or tracked transport. The only wheeled "vehicle" available were two-wheeled carts pulled by two bullocks or, on occasion, by the ubiquitous water buffaloes.

In 1935 a small R.A.F. flight, flying ancient Wapiti aircraft, visited Mhow. It was an early beginning to the Army Cooperation Squadrons of later years. On this occasion I volunteered to be the first "brown-job" to go up and report by radio on the movement of some of our troops who were deploying about three miles away. It seems incredible that as late as 1934 we had no means available on our large scale exercises of looking "over the hil" at an enemy.

Communication on operations or exercises was either by heliograph, lamp, signal flags, field telephone for short distances, or by runner. There were no radios. Communication between 99% of all the inhabitants of Mhow—Indian and British—was by a runner carrying a written message. Telephones were only available on a very limited official basis.

The absence of radios, vehicles and the myriad of sophisticated equipment which are now a part of an infantry battalion gave us one big advantage. We, as young officers, were always within sight and sound of our men. We marched with them, played with them, we were always a part of them and they of us.

The mention of communications and the use of runners reminds me of an incident on one of our exercises. In this case the battalion was being "tested", by a visiting general, in offensive operations. This particular general had his own son as his A.D.C.

At one point the general required quick action from the regiment—he sent his son to deliver a verbal message to our colonel.

"Sir," said the A.D.C., "my father wants you to capture One Tree hill immediately."

"And what does your mother want me to do?" was the reply.

Shortly after we arrived at Mhow our company commander, Bickley James, was posted to the U.K. He was replaced by Captain Willoughby Chapman, no relation of Colonel Chapman. "Willow," as he was called, had had a distinguished career during World War I rising from lieutenant to acting brigadier in command of a brigade. He was twice decorated with the Military Cross. After the war he had dropped back to the rank of captain! "Willow" was about 6'3" in height, handsome and well built—he was to many of us the perfect "Bulldog Drummond" of the Ian Hay stories. He was the only company commander under whom I served at that time in the Glosters who took seriously his responsibility for the training and development of the officers in his company.

One of the first things Willow did on taking over the company was to get the officers and senior NCO's together and ask each one of us in turn "What ideas do you have and what plans have you made to keep your men happy in this environment?" Most of us were a little nonplussed. We hadn't had such a direct question thrown at us in this way. Willow went on to explain his philosophy—if it was obvious that there would be problems of man management ahead then he wanted action taken well in advance that would minimize the problem—he wanted to avoid the rocks and not have to be rescued from them. He would be getting us together each week—at these meetings he wanted each one of us to report on our activities during the past week and our plans for the weeks ahead.

What Willow did was give each one of us a much greater sense of purpose than we had had before and when we did things that led to greater efficiency he would be full of praise; when we failed he would be quick to point out our mistakes but then always come up with suggestions to improve that particular situation.

When the company went off on field training, Willow would conduct the exercises himself and each evening discuss with us the rights and wrongs of the actions that we had taken. He was an excellent teacher. He was an inspiration to us all and I will always be grateful to him—he taught me much of what I know about infantry tactics and man-management.

John Vicary still commanded the Machine-Gun Company. I never served under him but from what I heard at the time he was a good commander. He was a good teacher but he didn't have the patience of Willow and he was sometimes too scathing in his comments. Bobby Seldon commanded his company well. He was human and people enjoyed being under his command but he did not have the dedication of Willow. Captain Douglas—suitably nicknamed "Porridge" commanded a company. He was an import from one of the disbanded Irish regiments. I can understand why the Irish were unhappy when they had people like him around. He was fat, wore a monocle and oozed phony "bonhomie". He wasn't popular and didn't stay with us very long.

Colin Campbell was still Adjutant. He had a delightful bungalow and cultivated an attractive garden—Henry Heath and I were fortunate to move into it when Colin left for the U.K. In our early months in Mhow I can remember Colin remarking on a problem that might arise with the band and drums. In Singapore they had reached a pitch of excellence both in their playing and in their drills. But there they had always had an audience for their performances. Wherever they played or marched a crowd would gather. They were appreciated.

But here in Mhow there was no crowd—we were a mile and a half from the native town. The only times they were seen or heard was when we marched that mile and a half each Sunday on Church Parade or when they muffled their drums and draped them in black for a soldier's funeral at the same church. Colin Campbell was determined to keep them up to a high standard and was already thinking of ways of doing it.

On the subject of Church Parades it is interesting to recall that in India all British troops went to church with rifles, bayonets and twenty rounds of live ammunition which they kept in the pews beside them. It was a reminder of that occasion at the start of the Great Mutiny in 1857 when Indian soldiers waited until the then unarmed British soldiers were in their various garrison churches before raising the flag of rebellion and massacring both soldiers and families, without mercy, as they left the churches.

In the same way, since artillery guns in the hands of the mutineers had played an important part in their early successes, all artillery regiments in India in 1932 were British—there were no Indian gunners at that time. Nor could any of the Indian Princes who were permitted to maintain small armies of their own, have any artillery or heavy machine-guns in their forces. For saluting purposes they were allowed bronze muzzle-loading cannon of ancient vintage. Their forces comprised only cavalry and infantry armed with lance and rifle respectively.

I got permission from Willow Chapman to take my platoon, and any other men of our company who might want to come along, on a camping trip. Altogether about 60 of us went on this first expedition which was really designed to give the men a holiday, a break from the routine of barrack life. I hired ten bullock carts and on them we loaded tentage, food, medial supplies and beer. The beer was in huge barrels and I allowed eight pints per man per day—I should have allowed much more.

We took along six rifles and a small amount of ammunition as I wanted to ensure that we had an armed guard on our store of food in case some light-fingered native might think we would be easy pickings.

We wore shorts, shirts and sandals. There was no formality. Once we had pitched the camp, arranged cooking and eating facilities and made out a roster of Guards, I told the men they were on their own. Beer was available from 10:00 a.m. to midnight. Some kind of food was always available. Native villages and homes were out of bounds.

It was a wonderful setting with the roar of a nearby waterfall as a backdrop to the songs and merriment. We swam in the small lake at the foot of the falls, played hockey and football, climbed surrounding hills, sang and drank beer, ate and then drank more beer. The small guard on duty each day remained sober. On this occasion I had a lot of fun with "Battler" Bence. He became convinced that he had heard a panther growling further down the valley and was most anxious to go and shoot it. The more beer he consumed the louder were the growls. Finally he asked if he and Corporal Webster could go and search for it and would I please lend him my shotgun. Looking very warlike with his long black moustache curling towards his ears he took off followed by Corporal Webster who carried my revolver in case of emergencies!

About three hours later "Battler" returned and after a couple of beers regaled us with the dramatic story of the shooting of his panther. Everyone in the camp gathered around to hear the details. "Battler" was in his element, he had an audience and they were in a receptive mood. Still grasping my shotgun he gave a lifelike imitation of his quiet approach to the unsuspecting animal. Then in hushed tones he demonstrated how he had parted the undergrowth to get a better view—levelled the shotgun and fired. "Got him right between the eyes," he shouted. "But where's the panther?" we asked. "Oh, he was much to heavy for me and Webster to Lift—we left it right where I shot it." With that, and a thank you for the loan of the gun and revolver, Bence and Webster retired to quench their thirst.

About half an hour later I could hear the sounds of weeping and wailing and gnashing of teeth coming from the valley below—and, furthermore, it was approaching our camp.

I called for Chandu and together we went to meet the long line of villagers who were straggled along the path leading from the village. I was glad to have Chandu with me because the Headman, who was in the lead, spoke no English. After the usual salaams and greetings the Headman, who was about 60 years of age, spoke with some emotion for about ten minutes, his voice rising and falling to emphasize his gestures. It was obvious that he was talking about Battler Bence because he went through the motions of raising an imaginary rifle. Finally he stopped and Chandu turned to me and told me quietly that Battler had not shot a panther—he had shot one of their domestic cows!!!

Cows are holy to the Hindu and may not be killed—in fact, they may not be hurt or injured in any way. If one is sitting in the middle of the highway—you go around it—you may not disturb it. This was a serious matter and I asked Chandu's advice. He spoke at some length with the Headman who agreed that the cow had wandered some distance from the village and was grazing on the edge of the jungle. By this time most of the villagers were crowding around us—they were a friendly crowd and didn't seem very upset. I asked Chandu to find out how much I should pay the Headman by way of compensation. This led to another ten minutes of heated discussion during which Chandu was beginning to laugh. Finally he turned to me and said, "Master, the Headman does not want money. He knows that we have many empty tins from the food the soldiers eat. He will settle for 100 empty tins." We gave them about 200 and they went away very happy. Tins were not a normal container in Indian villages in those days—they used pottery and occasionally glass which were often broken. Two hundred tins would set them up for life. Battler Bence never lived that incident down and many months later the troops on seeing cows in a field or a street would call them "Bence's Panthers."

One night my friend Henry Heath and I decided to dine at a club in the neighbouring city of Indore. We knew we would have to leave there early as the regiment was marching at 6:00 a.m. to take part in a five day manoeuvre. After a good dinner we were about to leave when the Club Secretary told us that a Colonel Bence was dining alone in a private room—would we care to meet him.

As soon as he mentioned the name I had a horrible feeling that his guest was none other than my platoon sergeant—Battler Bence. Henry and I moved towards the private dining room and, as we went, agreed that we would not expose him. We would play along.

When we entered the room, poor Bence nearly dropped his glass. For five seconds or so he remained staring glassily at us as if hypnotized. He was being waited on by two of the club's Indian staff and it was quickly obvious that he had had quite a few drinks.

"Good evening, Colonel Bence," I greeted him. "What a pleasure to see you again." Henry was equally effusive. For a moment Bence was obviously off his guard but as soon as he realized that we were not going to expose him he started to put on the act again. He summoned the waiters to bring us drinks—everything was done in the grand manner. He was thoroughly enjoying himself and with each drink he became more insistent that we have another. Each time we protested he reminded us that he was a colonel and that we were only lieutenants.

Unfortunately, the Indian servants remained in the room otherwise we would have quickly dealt with Battler. So I wrote a short note and passed it to him.

From the inner pocket of his immaculate dinner jacket he drew a monocle, stuck it in his eye and tried to read my message which said, "We are leaving in five minutes and you are coming with us."

With some difficulty Battler focussed on the writing and, without a minute's hesitation, called for the secretary and announced to him that he wouldn't be able to finish his dinner because he had just had a message that a great friend was dying in Mhow and he had to go there immediately. He produced two one hundred rupee notes (in Canadian each about $40) and said he was sure they would cover his bill. In fact, that was enough to pay for twenty dinners—so with a bow and a hiccup, Colonel Bence left the club and stepped into our car where he quickly became Sergeant Bence again! The effect of the alcohol on him had been in abeyance when he was acting the part of the Colonel—I supposed he kept his wits about him and wouldn't allow it to have too much effect on him. But once in the car he went out like a light. By this time it was well after one o'clock and it was exactly 2:00 a.m. when we delivered him to his bachelor room in the barracks. Reveille was to be at 4:00 a.m., breakfast at 4:45 and company parade at 5:30! God knows how he did it but at 5:30 Battler was straight as a ramrod—paraded smartly and swung away with the rest of us when we marched out of barracks shortly after six o'clock. Each hour we halted for ten minutes rest and still Battler appeared fit and well. I noticed that he was drinking rather more water than usual from his water bottle but knowing that too much alcohol dehydrates an individual I thought nothing of it.

We completed our march at about 5:00 p.m. I called Sergeant Bence over and congratulated him on his stamina—I told him that I knew he had been out on a party the night before and that he must have felt terrible during the march. He grinned happily and then admitted that he had filled his water bottle with gin—and then astonished me by looking me straight in the eye and saying, "How did you know I had had a party last night." We never discussed the subject again.

One Christmas I joined a group of officers who were going shooting in the jungles south of Jhansi. The idea was to get a panther and if one of those wasn't around we might get a samba or deer. Samba skin made excellent suede for shoes. I won't write about our shooting forays, and only mention the expedition because in the middle of it I developed a terrible toothache. To return to Mhow or Jhansi would take too long—I was in some pain. I asked Chandu to find out from the shikar (chief hunting guide) if there was a town in the vicinity. Yes, there is a small town with a dentist—it is only five miles away. Grabbing my rifle (and a bottle of gin for comfort) I took off up the track accompanied by Chandu and one of the guides. We reached the small town about two hours later and there on the dusty street was a big sign in both Urdu and English

"V. Naidu—Dentist"

and underneath in equally large letters was the somewhat doubtful message:

"Failed in Dentistry—University of Wisconsin"

Mr. Naidu's establishment was old-fashioned by North American standards—the chair had obviously once graced a barber-shop and the implements were laid out on a nearby table reminiscent of the implements of torture on display in the Tower of London. There were no windows in front, in fact, there was no door. Everything opened up to face the street although the chair was in the rear of the room and faced towards a rear window. Mr. Naidu had an assistant—a teenage and cheerful boy who smiled with the whitest teeth imagineable. A good advertisement.

Having been seated in the chair, Mr. Naidu examined my bad tooth. I told him not to keep looking at it—just pull it out. I had taken one look at the foot-operated machine for drilling teeth and decided against it—the cheerful young assistant was obviously the operator.

The dentist explained that he had no gas to put me to sleep nor did he have any pain killer. I took another long pull at the gin bottle, which Chandu was holding as if it was blood plasma, and bravely told Mr. Naidu to take it out anyway.

He clipped a leather band across my forehead and one on each wrist and went to work. The tooth was obviously so far gone that he had little trouble removing it. With a sign of relief I asked the reason for the leather bands. ''That is to make sure that you cannot strangle me as some of my customers try to do when I hurt them—I strap down both their heads and their hands!''

Whilst I gargled with some quite pleasant disinfectant I asked Mr. Naidu about his days in the U.S. He said he had found it difficult to understand the instruction he had received in dentistry—the technical words were quite different and, he said, ''They don't speak proper English.''

The fact that he had even studied in the U.S. was a point in his favour and he had the fact printed on his cards. I was grateful to him for his help and by the time we had walked back to our camp I was feeling no pain. The gin bottle was empty.

One of the ways that Colin Campbell devised to keep the band and drums busy and in the public eye was to resurrect the very successful show ''Tanglin Titbits'' that we had put on in Singapore. We made many changes and introduced more topical items of interest. The first shows were staged in the dining hall of the barracks and of course we were applauded loudly and boisterously by an audience of our soldiers who were heavily biased in our favour. From this early start, Colin got the idea that we would put the show on the road. He wrote to friends and brother adjutants in Jhansi and Cawnpore and having received favourable replies, we designed new dresses for the chorus (Designer: G. Kitching), practiced new dance routines, packed up all the scenery, stage props and electrical system and away we went.

The whole party was about fifty strong and we went by train. Colin paid all the bills for travel and food, and all the theatrical props, and just prayed that our audiences would be large enough to reimburse him. The distance to Jhansi by rail was about 400 miles with Cawnpore another 150 beyond that. In Jhansi we put on the same show for two nights and had a full house on each occasion. Greatly encouraged we headed for Cawnpore, but the theatre facilities we had found in Jhansi did not exist there. Instead of a good theatre located conveniently in the barracks we found that the theatre we had booked was right in the centre of the native city of Cawnpore and was not too well supplied with stage lighting or the normal scene changing pulleys. Colin and his carpenter crew went to work for about 18 hours. He reorganized the whole lighting system to conform to our requirements. We were able to put in a rehearsal on the newly transformed stage a couple of hours before the public were to be admitted. All went well, we relaxed and ate sandwiches before putting on our make-up and costumes. With half an hour to go before the curtain the doors were opened to the public. At twenty cents a seat they would be getting good value for money. With only ten minutes to go Colin came back and told us that no one had paid admission to come in! The audience at that moment were the Indian Manager and his wife!

We held a quick war council. What should we do? What had gone wrong? Was it bad advertising?

We decided we would go ahead with the complete show even though it was to be an empty house. Colin got the entire cast together, explained the problem and told them to go ahead as if the King himself were in the audience. The men were terrific and responded like veteran troupers; and Colin, unbeknown to us, had sent for a case of champagne and ice to cool it! After the show he thanked us for our efforts and we all sat around until the champagne was gone.

Some days later we found out what had happened. Ghandi had recently visited Cawnpore and had preached his theory of non-violence. The population were advised to avoid any contact with the British. In turn, all British soldiers were ordered by their authorities to keep away from the native city in order to avoid provoking an incident. We were the only people who hadn't been told anything! The Manager was too frightened to tell us for fear that he would forfeit our rent for the theatre.

Fortunately the Cawnpore Club saved our bacon. Instead of only playing for one night they invited us to stay on for a second one. They also advertised our presence well. We had a most successful stay there which, with the higher price for seats, raised enough money for Colin to take his account out of the red.

Shortly after our return to Mhow, Digby Grist arrived. He had been posted from the 61st in England and was a most welcome addition to the 28th. He was not only a good athlete but he entered into the spirit of "Tanglin Titbits" in a way that raised our morale even further. We produced new skits and songs in which Bill Percy-Hardman, Henry Heath and Digby and I played our full parts. I'm sure these shows all helped in the somewhat monotonous life of our soldiers. We made them laugh.

In 1934 I was made Weapon Training Officer for the regiment. Apart from the bullets of our rifles, Lewis guns and Vickers machine-guns the only offensive weapon available to an infantry battalion was the World War I Mills hand grenade. These small but deadly grenades had been designed for trench warfare and the normal method of using them was to throw them by hand into the enemy trench. Towards the end of the war someone had found a means of lobbing these grenades a distance of about 200 yards from a cup discharger which was fixed to the rifle.

On examining our supplies of explosives and ammunition I found we had quite a large number of the Mills grenades. Hardly anyone had ever thrown a live one although we had all had instruction on dummies. Live grenades could only be thrown from an official grenade range—and there wasn't one in Mhow! We decided to build one.

Fortunately I had an excellent sergeant to help me in Weapon Train-ing. His name was Wallis. He was young and energetic and in no time at all we had the plans for a range and permission to build it. Since con-crete was not available we had to build it of tubular steel and corrugated metal sheeting with several tons of stones and sand as a filler. It worked well and very shortly we had a fair number of soldiers who were trained in their use.

The next item on our agenda was to build a field firing range where the soldier would have to engage targets that looked and behaved like an enemy. The only targets that most soldiers shot at were the four foot and six foot square targets which were raised and lowered in the butts on every range in the British Army. In the centre of each target was a half circle in black—that was the aiming mark. It looked as much like a potential enemy as a street car. The idea that an enemy might be moving or that, if still, his head might be difficult to identify amongst leaves and undergrowth did not appear to be important. What was important was that every soldier fired a total of 120 bullets each year at the square targets in order that he could qualify for extra pay as a first, second or third class shot. Shooting was not related to the battlefield in spite of the fact that it was the only weapon in the infantry.

Sergeant Wallis and I decided to change the pattern of a soldier's shooting so that once he knew that his rifle was shooting straight he could start to take on a moving enemy and targets of opportunity. With Colin Campbell's approval and the help of a dozen soldiers we planned and built a field firing range through which we could put every section in the regiment. We dug trenches and deep dug-outs from which we manipulated, by ropes and other devices, small parties of cardboard "enemy." Each enemy party would appear in turn—some running in groups, some running as individuals, some standing, some kneeling. It was up to the section commander to give the orders to his men to engage the enemy as they appeared and at the end it was possible to tally up the number of hits so that the men in the section would have a good idea if their shooting had been effective or not. After most of the sections had gone through the system we changed the pattern, dug new trenches, and made it appear as if the enemy was advancing instead of retiring.

The sections liked what they were going through—it was different and appeared worthwhile. In these and other ways, Sergeant Wallis and I tried to make rifle shooting an everyday part of a soldier's life instead of the existing four day period each year when he fired his rifle on the ranges to qualify for pay.

In 1933, Colonel Alfred Chapman gave up command of the regiment and retired from the Army. He had had his four years of command but had developed phlebitis. He was succeeded by Lt. Col. Vinen.

Colonel Vinen took over command of the 28th at a time when the regiment had reached a peak of efficiency in many fields. Our drill as a battalion was excellent. The men were meticulous in their dress—everything was clean and bright. We were proud of our band and drums who always led us on parades. The discipline was good and the morale of the soldiers was high. We were winning most competitions that we entered. The monentum of this high standard carried us for the next eighteen months because without it and without the firm hand of Colin Campbell as Adjutant, the regiment could have falled on bad times.

Colonel Pewsey Vinen was not a good commanding officer. I understand that in private life, after he retired, he was a kindly man who took an interest in the countryside around him. I was glad to hear this and I am glad to acknowledge it because as a commanding officer he was a poor choice. Looking back, after fifty years, I suppose the people who selected Vinen to command were as much to blame as he was.

He was fifty-three years old and a bachelor. He had served in the Boer War. In World War I he had risen to command a company and was awarded the D.S.O. I don't know what he did between 1918 and 1933 but by the time he got command he was physically and mentally an old man. He hated Indians and India—he would never speak with an Indian and refused to have any Indian servants in his house—he employed our soldiers in these tasks. He refused to be served by an Indian servant in the Mess—he had to be served by one of our soldiers. He would not read any newspaper printed in India—he read each morning at breakfast the London ''Times'' which came by sea and took three weeks to reach us.

He had a ''charger'' named ''Sherry.'' This was the quietest horse that could be found because Pewsey didn't like horses. He was not happy on a horse. Sometimes, on our regimental and brigade Parades, Sherry would fall asleep and we often wondered if Pewsey had dropped off, too! On one parade he actually fell off the horse when it was standing still!

During one parade he suddenly gave the order to "Form Square". The British Square was a military formation devised by Wellington during his wars against Napoleon. It was used primarily as a defence against cavalry when the infantry would form up in a square with all ranks facing outwards and capable of firing on the horsemen as they swirled around the square. It had also been used against the Zulus and "Fuzzy-Wuzzys" in the 1890's but had never been used since. It was as out of date as armoured knights and the long bow. But not with Pewsey—oh no! We solemnly formed a square and faced outwards with front rank kneeling and rear rank standing. He rode into the centre of the square in accordance with the Victorian drill books where I am sure both he and Sherry had a quiet nap. It was difficult to explain the purpose of this manoeuvre to the men.

On one occasion, Pewsey was returning to his bungalow after a battalion parade. He was riding Sherry and was on a public street when an Indian walked past him on the other side of the road. The Indian had an umbrella which he had raised to keep the sun off his head. Pewsey was enraged and, drawing his sword, crossed the road, hit the umbrella with his sword and shouted, "Don't you dare to go past me without lowering your umbrella." I understand that the incident was reported and that Vinen had to make an apology. Apparently in Victorian India a native always lowered his umbrella as a sign of respect when passing a British officer. With people like Pewsey Vinen around, it is not too difficult to imagine why they soon lost that respect.

Pewsey always breakfasted alone on the verandah of the Mess, waited on by one of our soldiers, and reading his out-of-date copy of the London "Times".

One morning we heard a shout from the direction of his veranda and then a roar, "Good God, they shot him." The Mess Sergeant, Berry, rushed out of the dining room where we were all enjoying our breakfast, to go the aid of the Colonel. He returned in a short while and standing to attention but with eyes lifted heavenwards, he announced, "The Colonel has asked me to let you know that the King of Yugoslavia was assassinated in Marseilles yesterday." His assassination had been reported accurately in the Indian Press three weeks before!

Who or what committee would select such a man to command a

battalion in India? They have a lot to answer for, particularly when we had a number of very able majors like Nap Grazebrooke and Charles Bagot waiting in the wings.

One one occasion Mahatma Gandhi visited Mhow. His arrival was, of course, well planned and large numbers of country-folk came to the city for the occasion. To me, the greatness of Gandhi stemmed from his preaching of non-violence. Had he been a fire-eating advocate of revolution, he could have caused many problems for us. Instead, he always spoke against violence with the result that visits such as the one to Mhow were happy events for the people and they came in the thousands to hear him.

In 1935 I decided to take six months leave in England; whilst there I saw a movie with actual battle scenes from the First World War. It was not an anti-war movie per se but I was shocked at the continuing slaughter shown on the screen. One series after another showed men "going over the top" and being decimated before getting to the wire ahead of them. I began to wonder at the mentality of generals who would continue to throw in regiment after regiment across the same ground without thinking up some other means of getting at the enemy. That film stayed in my mind until 1939 and 1940 when the German Blitzkrieg tactics changed the whole pattern of war and swept away the cobwebs and the older generals whose minds could not keep pace.

What a highly disciplined but poorly equipped force the British Regular Army was in the early 1930's!

I had not seen a tank with a gun in it until I was shown one on a visit during my leave to the Tank School at Bovington. On my return to India in October the military news was about the increased activity of the Fakir of Ipi on the North West Frontier and of the action being taken by two brigades commanded by two recently promoted brigadiers—Alexander and Auchinleck. Tanks were not mentioned.

Early in 1936, the King died from pneumonia after a length illness from which it was understood he was recovering. Only six months before we had celebrated the 25th Anniversary of his reign. Both he and Queen Mary were popular with all classes in Britain. Their example of rationed simplicity in World War I and their decision not to serve or consume any alcohol until Germany was defeated put them on a level with the millions who had to live on a similar scale of rations.

In India we knew nothing of Edward VIII and his infatuation for Wallis Simpson. He was solemnly declared King and Emperor of India. At dinner, in India, we toasted him, just as we had his father, as the King-Emperor.

In January we were warned that our next station would be Madras and that we would be leaving in March.

Before we left Mhow, Henry Heath and I decided to visit for the last time—Mandu. Mandu was located in the State of Dhar, only about eighty miles from Mhow, and was originally a fortress designed and built by the Moghul Kings and Emperors in the 14th century. These great warriors, direct descendants of Genghis Khan and Tamurlaine, swept through the northern passes of the Khyber region with their hordes of horsemen and soon established themselves in Delhi. From there they rode south and eventually came to the rock face that encircled a plateau about three miles by two miles. The rock face was a cliff about 100/150 feet in height and surrounding it in the valleys was the Narbudda River and one of its tributaries. They were quick to realize the military significance of this geological mass. Elephants and slaves were used in great numbers to build a road up the rock face and a strong defensive gateway to protect it. Over the years a number of palaces and outer forts were built, crops were sown and gathered. Water was in abundance from natural wells and many of the wells were converted to luxurious bathing pavilions. At one time at the height of Moghul power an army of 10,000 soldiers was maintained within the fortress. However the warrior soon preferred the silken couch to the saddle and for one glorious era, Mandu was ruled by a Moghul who employed only women in his army. The only male allowed in the fortress was the King himself—he was surrounded and protected by thousands of women trained and drilled as soldiers. I think it was for that reason that Henry and I always enjoyed tramping through the ruined and deserted palaces. How lucky can a King get! The era ended when, for unrequited love, the Princess Rupmati flung herself from the battlements of her palace onto the rock of the Narbudda below. We drank a pink gin to her memory on this last visit and threw the glasses down the cliff after her. This was a foolish thing to do because when we got back to our rented car we found there weren't any others!

And so to Madras.

The Author, England 1941

lower right
General Simonds, the Author and
Admiral Vian en route to Sicily 1, July, 1943

below
Brigadier Penhale and the Author,
Sicily, September, 1943

General Leese, Admiral Montbatten, General Montgomery, Sicily, July 10, 1943

below - Scout Officer, Brigadier Cris Vokes, the Author, July 26, 1943

6

Back to England

In both Singapore and Mhow the regiment had always been together except for short periods when companies were training on their own. This was a source of strength and we got to know each other well. In Madras we were going to be divided. The Headquarters and one-half battalion would be in the superb Fort George in Madras itself. The other half would be twenty-five miles away at St. thomas Mount. But without any motor transport in the regiment, twenty-five miles was a long way. We were not looking forward to the split.

The City of Madras in 1936 was the capital of what was then known as the Madras Presidency. The Presidency was one of the political divisions and extended for nearly 1,500 miles along the south and south-west coast of India. Although the official head of the Presidency was the Governor, representing the King-Emperor and the Viceroy, the people enjoyed a fair degree of autonomy in local affairs and were able to elect their representatives to the Parliament that met in Madras. The population was in the area of one hundred million—one of the most densely populated areas of India. It had a buoyant economy based on a wide variety of agricultural and mineral products—tea, coffee, tobacco, rice and jute; coal was mined in the north; gold was mined in the Nilgiri Hills and pearls were found in the south.

On arrival in Madras I was posted to St. Thomas Mount with the two companies that were to be quartered there and warned that I would soon be sent to the Machine Gun School at Ahmednagar on a course.

The flat plain west of the City of Madras was marred at intervals by "mounts" of about 400 feet which from the distance looked like the pyramids.

St. Thomas Mount was in fact two of these low hills, on top of one of which was buried Saint Thomas, an early Christian missionary of the 4th Century. Our barracks lay at the foot of the hills—they were comfortable and well planned with large trees to give as much shade as possible.

A short distance away from us were the barracks of a regiment of the Indian Army, the 10th Baluchis. These men—the Baluchis—are Muslim and were recruited from the fiercely independent tribes of Baluchistan, the most-westerly province bordering on both Afghanistan and Iran.

An interesting painting hung in their Officers Mess. It showed a commanding officer of the late 1800's mounted on his horse with a well-dressed soldier standing to attention beside him. Beyond them were the companies of the regiment drawn up on parade. Apart from its vast size there was nothing remarkable about the painting until the presence of the lone soldier was explained. The Colonel apparently had a weak bladder—in fact it was so weak that he could not go for more than half an hour before having to relieve himself. To overcome the problem he had a device made that fitted over his private parts and by a series of tubes descended into his knee length riding boots and then to what appeared to be a spur. But it was not a real spur—it was a tap that looked like one! The job of the lone soldier was to turn on the tap when ordered!

In preparation for my course at Ahmednagar, I was put through my paces in elementary gun drill and range finding by Sergeant Taft, a very able and tough sergeant. Every morning at 6:00 a.m. he would drill me for an hour "on this spot—Mount Gun"—the spot would be marked each time by the heel of his boot. Stop watch in hand he would urge me to greater efforts. By seven o'clock I would be sweating like a pig and hs cheerful grin would be wider. But he was a good instructor and I had no difficulty in passing the entry exams on reaching the Machine Gun School. Ahmednagar was a delightful army station about

100 miles east of Bombay. Situated in the foothills, the climate was quite agreeable—not unlike Mhow. It was in this part of India that Wellington had won his great victory at Assaye when, with only 5,000 men and 17 guns, he had defeated a Mahratta Army of 60,000 and 100 guns. Wellington's force had also captured a number of forts including the one in Ahmednagar. After the fall of the fort there the Mahratta leader was reported as saying:

"These Englishmen are strange people and their General is a wonderful man. They came here in the morning, looked at the wall, walked over it, killed all the Garrison and then returned for breakfast."

During the course I had the opportunity of travelling for half an hour in a light tank which was a part of the Royal Tank Corps unit nearby. The tank was only armed with a Vickers Machine-Gun which I was allowed to fire as we advanced up the ranges. Since the gun was fixed to a steel mount which, in turn, was fixed to the tank it was almost impossible to maintain accuracy—each minor lurch of the tank was imparted to the gun. It was a most inaccurate weapon when in motion. I remember discussing with the young officer in command the possibility of mounting the gun in such a way that it was stabilized or at least did not react so violently at each minor jerk of the tank. He said he thought someone was trying to design such a mount but that by the time it was invented that particular tank would be out of date. I felt that it already was.

The course was an interesting one and well planned. I didn't do quite as well as I should have, however, because I whooped it up with a couple of other subalterns the evening before the final exam. We were told that we had been singing the Imperial Russian Anthem outside the Commandant's house at 3:00 a.m. Perhaps we had!

On my return to the Regiment I found that it had been further split up as one of the companies would now be in the Nilgiri Hills, at Wellington some 300 miles southwest of Madras. Although I enjoyed my four weeks in the hills away from the steamy heat of Madras I found the camaraderie of our lives in Singapore and Mhow was missing. Split up as we were in three different stations we began to come apart and when we did meet it became an occasion instead of an everyday occurrence.

There was very little that could be done beyond platoon training except in the Red Hills. We continued to play every kind of sport with added enthusiasm.

In September 1936 I was warned that I was to return to the U.K. for posting to the 61st early in 1937. Denis Biddle got the same warning. We both paraded to ask if the order could be changed since we both preferred to serve abroad.

Unfortunately for us a new ruling had been made by the War Office which no longer allowed officers who were posted back to the U.K. to trade postings with some other officer who wanted to return to or remain in the U.K. In the past this had always been possible—in fact it was often a source of funds for the ones who wanted to remain abroad—paid by the ones who for family reasons preferred to serve in the U.K.

I was sorry to leave the 28th; it had been my home for over five years and I knew so many of the officers and men. Also, I was not looking forward to the somewhat inconsequential life in a half strength battalion in England. Following a great send off from Madras I boarded a troopship in Bombay and after five weeks leave joined the 61st in Plymouth.

Crownhill Barracks, on the edge of that city, was fairly modern by the standards of that day. Our commanding officer was Lt. Colonel Cox—known as "Bouncer" Cox. He was a large cheerful man and a good mixer but like some others of his vintage in the British Army he did not appear to be interested in the military education of his officers.

I was posted to Maurice Bryant's Company—we were the Machine-Gun Company of the Battalion and although we were supposed to have sixteen machine-guns and a complement of 128 all ranks we had, in fact, only 47. I was second-in-command of this company but to have that position when I had commanded a company of 120 for a year in India did not look to me as an exciting prospect.

Since the regiment was earmarked to receive the new equipments planned for infantry battalions I was sent on a whole series of courses to learn about these new weapons. The courses were well organized and I noted that there were a small number of officers from the Canadian Army attending one or two of them.

One of the officers was Bobby Clark of the Royal Canadian

Regiment. The RCR was allied to the Gloucesters so I made certain that he visited us later in Plymouth. I had already met another officer from the RCR, Captain Gil Foster. Gil was a quite brilliant officer who graduated at the top of his class when he attended the Staff College at Quetta in India. Both Clark and Foster intrigued me because the difference in the pay of a Canadian subaltern and his British Army equivalent was about 2 to 1.

On a series of visits to London during the summer of 1937 I applied at the War Office for a number of jobs overseas, including two connected with the League of Nations. I also asked about exchanges of officers between the U.K. and Canada.

I was introduced to Lt.-Col. Georges Vanier who then had a job at Canada House known as the "Secretary." In reality, he was the Deputy High Commissioner. He told me that if I decided to visit Canada at any time, he would be pleased to send letters of introduction to his friends. I was very struck by his firm but gentle manner.

I was also interviewed at that time by a man who could have come out of any modern spy story. I had thought that I might continue my Russian lessons with the idea of going into Intelligence. I was told to report at ten o'clock one morning for an interview with Major Loden-Hena-Lewinsky (that is not his proper name but it was very similar). Overnight I tried to conjure up to myself the image of this man with the long impossible name. I finally decided that he would be tall, immaculate in a dark suit and wearing a monocle. He would obviously have an office which would be covered with photographs of his family connections in Europe—he would be smoking a long Russian cigarette from an even longer holder.

At 10:00 a.m. I knocked on the door of room 315A. Nothing happened. I knocked again. This time there was a sound as if someone was covering up a number of papers and then finally a voice said, "Come in." I paused a little to allow him to hide the important documents that he obviously did not want me to see, then I took a deep breath and stepped in. I was glad I had taken a deep breath when I saw my friend with the long impossible name because if I hadn't I think I would have choked.

There, behind a very ordinary issue desk, was a small fat man sitting in what was obviously a very ordinary issue chair. He had very little hair on top of his head but compensated for it with a large walrus moustache. On a wooden stand behind him was a bowler hat and umbrella and also a grey suit jacket. I assumed that the grey jacket went with his trousers and that he had removed it in order to be more comfortable in the blue blazer that he was wearing. It was the best-fed blazer I had ever seen with the remains of many meals spread across its ample girth. Eggs, porridge, gravy, rice pudding—it was almost possible to diagnose which cookery book his wife used.

"Kitching," he said and then, as if to keep reminding himself of such a repugnant name, he kept repeating Kitching, Kitching, Kitching. As he repeated it he fumbled in one of the drawers. Finally, through the walrous moustache, I recognized that he was saying that he didn't have a file on me.

I told him that was understandable because I was only there to ask him about going into Intelligence.

"Good heavens, man," he said, "you wouldn't be any good in that sort of work—you look much too English!"

I don't recall whatever conversation we had after that but after taking my leave I couldn't help but feel that if I had to look and behave like Loden-Hena-Lewinski, I wouldn't be much good in whatever field he was in.

My the end of March 1938 I was becoming restless; I had an interview with the Colonel, Bouncer Cox, who accepted my resignation of my commission, effective 1st May. I was to remain as apart of the regiment on its reserve of officers. Two days after seeing Bouncer I was in London being interviewed again by Colonel Vanier in Canada House. He very kindly wrote letters to old friends of his in the Canadian Army, Brigadier R. O. Alexander and Colonel Logie-Armstrong.

Whilst in London I had also asked about exchanges of officers between Canada and the U.K. In this I had a great deal of help and advice from a Colonel Shaw who lived near my father in New Milton. He was so enthusiastic about Canada and its opportunities that he and his wife had decided to retire there but unfortunately an illness had prevented it. He advised me to "go over and have a look at it—you won't come back!!!" He also recommended that I go back and see Colonel Vanier in Canada House.

I had already written to my friend of Sandhurst days, Doug Mac-dougald, who kindly asked his parents to meet me in Montreal when I arrived there. Doug was then stationed in the West with the PPCLI.

I booked a passage on board the old Canadian Pacific "Montcalm" sailing from Liverpool. My father thought I was crazy to cut loose at the age of 27, but, he gave me a handsome cheque to help me on my way. In later years he agreed with me that it was the best thing I could have done.

I bade a sad farewell to Colin Campbell, Denis Biddle and my other friends in the regiment, then spent a couple of days at home with my parents—my mother packing more things into my trunks than I could ever do. Finally the time came to leave for Liverpool and Canada.

General Montgomery, Prime Minister MacKenzie King,
General Crerar, England May 1944

The attack on Agira by the
Edmonton Regiment, July 28, 1943

The Canadian Cemetery, Agira, Sicily

7

Canada and Mobilization

On the "Montcalm" I shared a cabin with a strong and buoyant young Canadian named "Scotty" Brown. He was from Edmonton.

As soon as we docked in Halifax all passengers were herded into a large shed for customs clearance. My two trunks eventually appeared. I claimed them and unlocked them preparatory to taking out some of the heavier articles of clothing so that the customs man could examine the contents more easily. This was what most passengers were doing although I noticed that some had been ordered to remove all the contents which would mean a laborious problem of repacking.

My friend, Scotty Brown, was beside me and assured me that I would have no problem. He would have a word with the customs officer. In due course the officer came along and Scotty started his routine:

"Officer, this gentleman is Mr. Kitching. He is an officer in the British Army and he is going to be staying with Senator Macdougald in Montreal. I'm sure you don't want him to unpack all his trunks, do you?"

The customs man looked at me, then looked Scotty straight in the eye, and said, "No, I don't want Mr. Kitching to unpack anything but you will empty your trunks and I want to see everything—and I mean everything!" Poor Scotty, they kept him on tenderhooks for about an hour and finally cleared him in order that he could catch the train.

We arrived in Montreal during a minor snow storm—somehow I hadn't expected snow after being regaled by some of the passengers on the ship with stories of the glorious spring awaiting me. However, there on the platform to meet me were Doug's father, Dr. Wilfred Laurier Macdougald, and his younger brother, John. I could not have wished for a warmer or kinder reception.

I had met Dr. Macdougald on his visit to Sandhurst in 1930 when he was at the top of the financial and political ladder. Since then he had been the butt of an official inquiry into the sale and distribution of the shares of a company that had been established to finance the building of the Beauharnois dam and hydro project on the St. Lawrence a few miles west of Montreal.

Dr. Macdougald was a tall, distinguished looking man with a strong squarish face. He had a good mop of hair which was turning grey. He and Mrs. Macdougald continued to be most kind to me as they introduced me to family friends. Dr. Macdougald sponsored me for my "landed immigrant" status which was granted without delay. He also showed me a number of papers and letters in connection with the Beauharnois Enquiry. It was obvious that Dr. Macdougald did not feel that he had done anything unethical and from the documents he let me read, it did appear that a number of individuals high in the Liberal Party, including Mr. King, could have given evidence that would have been of help to him. However, they had not done so. I asked him why he hadn't brought these letters and documents forward in his defence. His reply was simple and straightforward—"George, it would have wrecked the Liberal Party and that I would never do." I admired him even more from that day on.

My letters of introduction to Brigadier Alexander and Col. Logie-Armstrong were helpful as I had the opportunity of meeting them. They were not optimistic about my being able to join the RCR which, at that time, had its full slate. However, they gave me a letter of introduction to Major Archie Campbell who was commanding the company of the RCR stationed in the barracks at St. Jean about twenty miles south-east of Montreal.

On arrival in the Mess there, I was greeted by Dan Spry—a subaltern in the regiment who became a very firm friend. Dan commanded the regiment in Italy, then got command of 12th Brigade prior to coming to Normandy to command 3rd Canadian Division.

I met other RCR officers in the course of my many visits to their Mess including Eric Snow, Neil Hodson and his father, "Uncle Bill" Hodson, who commanded the regiment when we went over to Britain in December 1939. Neil Hodson was a very quiet individual—almost anti-social in some ways—but having heard him lecture to militia officers in Montreal and join in discussions on many military subjects with them, I realized that he had a degree of professionalism that was surprising when you consider the scarcity of weapons and modern equipment that were available. It could not have been easy to keep the interest of militia officers under those conditions. Perhaps it was because the very small "Permanent Force," as it was called then, knew it was heavily dependent on the militia in the event of an emergency that made it take such an interest in the training of its officers.

I was impressed by the quality of the men in the St. Jean Company. Many were well educated and had joined during the depression—there was, in fact, a waiting list of recruits in almost all areas. I think the strength in St. Jean was about 60 and of those more than 50% were commissioned early in the war.

In the spring of 1939, I went to see Davidson Dunton, then the young editor of the Montreal Standard. After some discussion he agreed I should write a series of articles on the training of the militia with particular emphasis on their work at the Summer Camps at Mount Bruno.

The Bruno Camp had a good rifle range and a small training area and, being only about thirty miles from Montreal, was used frequently by militia units and also by the RCR Company at St. Jean. At the annual summer camps the general administation was handled by the RCR and they also produced a demonstration platoon when required. In 1939 they gave a first class demonstration of how to "wire in" a platoon defensive position. At the end of the demonstration the militiamen expressed their appreciation with a considerable amount of applause.

In my daily report to the Standard, I mentioned this demonstration amongst the many other activities and gave the RCR a special pat on the back. In the newspaper next morning they had left out all reference to the RCR. They just mentioned that a "demonstration of wiring" had been given. When I checked with the editor, I was told that the RCR weren't important. They didn't sell copy!

Before leaving England, my father had said that I would find people in Canada quite different in their outlook to those I knew in Britain and had met in Singapore and India. My father had been in the U.S.—he had a number of Canadian and American friends. He appreciated that the North American background was dissimilar to that in Europe; and that geography and the different social systems were producing a people whose patterns of thought were distinctive and sometimes at variance with those of the British people. How right he was. It took me about six months to appreciate the fact.

There is no doubt that the visit of the King and Queen in 1939 played an important part in setting the stage for the quick response of Canadians to the invasion of Poland by Germany three months later. The good looks and friendliness of both the King and Queen had a profound effect even in Montreal where the crowds were as warm and enthusiastic as elsewhere. I saw them also in St. Jean on their return journey by train. It was only a whistle stop for perhaps 45 minutes, but a large crowd was there to welcome them from an area that was predominantly French-speaking. When mobilization came early in September and I joined the many thousands of men who besieged the recruiting offices in Montreal, I could tell from the talking and conversatons around me that the Royal visit had had an impact, if only to remind us of our link with the Crown.

Amongst the more senior members of the militia whom I met were Col. Phelan of the Canadian Grenadier Guards whose son won a Military Cross when commanding his troop in a spirited action in Normandy.

Another was Colonel Basil Price who was then the Honorary Colonel of the Royal Montreal Regiment. He had won a Distinguished Conduct Medal for bravery and leadership when serving in the ranks during the First War. In 1939 he was running a very large dairy, the Elmhurst Dairy which delivered milk and other farm products to a great many homes in Montreal. Whilst speaking with him one evening in the Officers Mess of his Regiment I asked him why his dairy did not sell orange-juice at the same time that it delivered milk. Those were the days before "frozen" juices were available. At his request I went along to see him in his office at the Elmhurst plant. He said he wanted his manager and his chief chemist to hear my suggestion and they were then summoned. I went through my proposal in some detail—why couldn't a large squeezer be installed in each milk cart which would be operated by the wheels of the cart transmitted through a series of "worm-wheels," gears and differentials? All the delivery man had to do was feed oranges into the machine when it needed reloading and turn on a tap to fill a bottle whenever a customer requested it. Basil Price seemed quite enthusiastic but his ardour was dampened by the chemist who kept harping on the good hygenic record of the dairy and the difficulty of maintaining the standard when squeezing oranges in horse drawn vehicles!!!

"Well, then," I asked, "why not squeeze them in the dairy and have the juice delivered with the milk in that way?"

The Chemist still had an objection—if the oranges were squeezed before the carts left the dairy in the morning the pulp and the liquid of the juice would separate—and the customer wouldn't like the appearance of it!

"Then put it in an orange coloured bottle and shake it up on delivering it," I almost shouted at him! But he wouldn't budge so after he and the manager had gone, Basil Price told me he had to be guided by the opinions of his chemist and so would have to turn down my suggestion. Basil was a very kind man and I know that in his heart he felt my suggestion had merit—but he didn't want to upset the operation of the dairy at that time. I reminded him of my efforts some years later when he was commanding 3rd Canadian Division—he told me then that he wished he had gone ahead with my suggestion.

In July 1939, I received my first unofficial notification from the Gloucesters in England that they were starting to recall officers who were on their Reserve Lists. At that time it was more of a warning, checking on possible changes of address. In August I received official notificaiton as the authorities felt more and more that Hitler would ignore his promises to Chamberlain of the previous September. He appeared determined to bring the whole of eastern Europe into the German orbit even if it meant war.

I was in a quandary. I owed a great deal to the Gloucesters—that regiment had been my home for eight years and I had many friends in it even though some of them were now dispersed to other jobs. Would Canada go to war if Britain did? Would it mobilize divisions for overseas service as it had in the First War? If it did, would there be a long delay before any action was taken?

Archie Campbell and Dan Spry knew that, if possible, I would like to join the RCR. Archie's advice was to be patient—he felt that if there was to be any expansion of the RCR I would be amongst the first to be taken in. Eric Snow had just been appointed to a job at National Defence Headquarters in Ottawa—he promised to put my name forward as soon as the order came to mobilize the RCR. In order to short-circuit the possible delays in procedure, I sent him my official application.

In early September, the mobilizing of the 1st Canadian Division was ordered. Archie Campbell advised me to go through the recruiting centres in Montreal where medical inspections and other formalities were completed. At the same time, Eric Snow went to work on my behalf in Ottawa. I was interested to read my file in 1946 when, after the War, I was posted to Ottawa. In my application I had listed all the courses I had attended over the years with the Gloucesters and all the positions I had held. When the Adjutant-General of the Canadian Army had approved my commission in September 1939 he had written "Approved—but how can the British Army do without him!"

Dan Spry very kindly gave me set of RCR buttons, "beavers" and a cap badge which I was proud to pin and sew on one of my uniforms that I had formerly worn in the Glosters. The first weeks of mobilization at St. Jean were hectic as new stores and equipment started to arrive. Early in November the Regiment was ordered to concentrate at Valcartier near Quebec City.

Dan Spry was appointed Adjutant and did a superb job of organizing a thoroughly unorganized battalion. Lt.-Col. Beak Holloway commanded the regiment at that time although he was shortly to hand over command to "Uncle Bill" Hodson whom I had met in St. Jean. On the 20th of November I was warned that I would be leaving on the 27th November as head of the Advance Party of the RCR with the task of taking over the accommodation allotted to us in Aldershot, England. The Advance Party included a number of Warrant Officers and NCOs who had experience in the handling of barracks stores and accommodation. I was particularly grateful for this expertise because, in addition, I found myself being the ''advance party'' for the 1st brigade Headquarters and one or two units whose officers were quite unfamiliar with the problems.

The ship containing the Advance Parties finally sailed towards the end of November in a Canadian Pacific liner which, because of its speed, travelled alone and without escorting destroyers. Most merchant ships in this category had had a gun of some kind mounted on their aft deck so that they would have some means of engaging an enemy when challenged. Our ship had a 6'' gun of indeterminate vintage.

All went sell for the first 48 hours. The senior officer aboard was Major R. Brownfield of the Artillery. ''Browny,'' as he was known, had a distinguished career and retired as a Major-General in the late fifties. As we crossed the Atlantic he was full of fun, always cheerful and rarely downhearted. When we were south of Iceland we suddenly had a warning. The German battleship, ''Deutschland,'' was believed to be about 100 miles north of us. The captain of the ship called Major Brownfield to the bridge and asked him to take command of the 6'' gun and also select eight officers from amongst the Advance Parties who would help in operating it.

Fortunately, ''Browny'' knew all there was to know about bringing this gun into action. The crew he chose from amongst us included Captain Jim Lister and Orme Barrett, both of the Royal Canadian Army Service Corps; George Renison of the 48th Highlanders and myself. ''Browny'' explained the mechanism and the actions we were to take, including the hoisting of the heavy ammunition from the nearby lockers to the gun breach. As it was now dark and our ship was running without lights, it was not possible to fire a sample round to get the feel of the gun. ''Browny'' explained that the captain had altered course slightly to the south and with luck we would be well clear of the enemy by dawn. He asked us to remain on deck through the night ''just in case.'' It was a chilly vigil relieved shortly before dawn by a kindly steward who brought us each a tot of rum courtesy of the captain who thanked us for volunteering and told us that we could stand down. The ''Deutschland'' was gone. ''Browny'' said later that he was glad we hadn't had to fire the gun because he wasn't too sure just what would have happened! He didn't think the rivets holding the gun to the stanchion looked too strong!

We arrived without further incident in Liverpool from where we went by train to Aldershot.

The Author, Colonel Bill Matthews and The Queens Own Rifles on their return from Korea, 1955

8

Preparations For Action

In 1939, Aldershot was the biggest military centre in the United Kingdom. The sandy soil in the surrounding countryside made it an ideal manoeuvre area. The barracks allocated to the First Canadian Brigade, of which the Royal Canadian Regiment was a part, were the original ones built after the Crimean War. They were of red brick and each barrack block had two floors with a central staircase dividing the building into four barrack rooms: two up and two down. Each room was designed to hold about 30 men—a total of 120. To accommodate this number there were four latrines and four urinals. The washing facilities were equally inadequate. In each barrack room there was a small fireplace which was the only device for heating the room; and there were four large windows, single-glazed and so positioned that they successfully prevented the fire in the fireplace from heating the room at all. The Barrack Stores personnel of the British Army from whom we took over the barracks told us that the allowance of coal for each room per day was one bucket-full. They said it would be adequate because no one was permitted to light the fires until 6:00 p.m.

Another system that intrigued our advance party as much as the heating was the careful way all plumbing outlets were taken outside the buildings before entering the sewers. This ensured that in very cold weather most of the exterior outlets were frozen, thus putting them "out of order."

The barracks allocated to the Regiment were named "Barrosa" after the victory in the Peninsular War. We were told that they had previously been occupied by a Guards Regiment. The Officers Mess was heated primarily by fireplaces which in mild weather might have been adequate but on a cold winter evening were not very effective.

The Royal Canadian Regiment had no difficulty settling in to the barracks. We had a fair sprinkling of experienced officers and N.C.O's who made light of some of the problems that were to cause difficulties in other units.

"Uncle Bill" Hodson commanded the Regiment and Major Milton Gregg, V.C. had been appointed Second-in-Command. Milton had won his V.C. with the Regiment in World War I but had spent many of the intervening years in various appointments in Ottawa.

Dan Spry was Adjutant and brought a lot of military expertise and good humour to the job. The Quartermaster was Jack Adams, The Regimental Sergeant Major was Frank Darton. Altogether a strong team.

I was posted to 'D' Company which was commanded by John Macdonald, a shrewd and discerning subaltern who was not taken in by some of the stories and excuses which started to plague us on Monday mornings as the men tried to explain their "absence without leave" over the weekends.

One of our most interesting "problem" absentees was a Private Picard. This soldier was an excellent cook and the company appreciated him. Unfortunately he was also fairly attractive to the ladies with whom he dallied too often and too late. His first two absences were excused; however, on the third and fourth occasions he was punished with short periods of "confinement to barracks." All went well for a couple of weekends and then he was absent again. On his return he knew he would be for the high jump and prepared himself. He was marched in to the Company office by Company Sergeant-Major MacKenzie. There, facing him, was the company commander who, after the evidence was read, asked him if he had any excuse. Picard tried the same kind of sob story that he had pitched on other occasions. 'He was helping an old lady to cross the street when he was hit by a bicycle—the injury wasn't bad but in getting it fixed he had just missed the train.' etc., etc. John Macdonald listened patiently but told Picard that he could not let him get away with it again. He was going to punish him severely. On hearing this, Picard held up his hand and said, "Stop, sir, please. I have something for you," and to our astonishment he extracted a magnificent open-faced jam pie from his battle dress blouse, whipped off the protecting paper laid the pie reverently on the desk. "For you, sir, I made this special pie." By this time C.S.M. Mackenzie was nearly apoplectic with rage and astonishment but John Macdonald took it calmly. "Pte. Picard," he said, "I have never had to deal with anyone like you before and I hope I never have to again. Next time you appear before me I will throw the book at you—and your pie as well! March out!"

We didn't have a problem with Pte. Picard again.

The 1st Canadian Division had a real problem during its first three or four months in Aldershot and surrounding camps. We were a division of civilians with very little discipline. I do not think half of our fifteen thousand men had ever worn uniform before or had been subject to any form of discipline. Some of the senior militia officers were not really fit to command. They had been all right at home in their armouries because discipline did not have to be too strict; and in an effort to keep the men in the regiment they were too often forgiven instead of being punished.

We arrived in Aldershot in time to suffer from the coldest winter in England for over a century and the very new Canadian soldiers did not like the conditions under which they had to live. The damp cold was the biggest factor in any breakdown of discipline and gradually it grew worse. The authorities in the town complained that seats in the parks and at bus stops were disappearing. Wooden fences, even bannisters on stairways, were spirited away at night. Coal yards suddenly found that their levels were falling. Since the pubs were warm they attracted those that needed the extra warmth. Invariably the men stayed until the pubs closed at 10:00 p.m. and frequently consumed more than they were used to. They sang their way back to barracks with a bawdy song or two, interspersed with a little profanity.

We were not very popular in Aldershot during those first few months, and I think that the authorities were glad to see us leave that summer. The Canadian divisions and other units that followed us into the area had time to instil some discipline into their men and, besides, there were not any more benches, bannisters and fences to burn.

In the Regiment morale was boosted when a group of drummers and other musicians formed a band. That small group marched us on and off hundreds of parades, and for many miles along narrow English roads. They were a tonic.

On one occasion we marched a distance of about five miles to the ranges and ''Rolled out the Barrel'' hundreds of times as we sang our way through the countryside. For some reason John Macdonald was not with us that day. Once there we had started in zeroing our rifles when General McNaughton, who commanded the 1st Division, arrived in his big Buick. The men were glad to see him—it was the first time they had had a chance to talk with him. When he asked if there were any complaints that he could look into the only one who stepped forward was Sergeant-Major McKenzie. His complaint, he told the General, was that the boots that were being issued at that time were not leather—the sole was some soft composition which was not wearing well.

''Take your boot off, Sergeant-Major, and let me have a look.''

The Sergeant-Major took off his boot and handed it to the General who took a large penknife out of his pocket. He scraped around for a while, then digging the blade into the sole he cut out a piece about as big as a silver dollar. He examined the piece, handed back the boot and thanked McKenzie for his interest. ''You are quite right, Sergeant-Major, it isn't leather. I'll have this piece examined and promise you it will be corrected.'' With that, and a cheery wave to us all, he stepped into the Buick and drove away.

I shall always remember the expression on McKenzie's face as he stood clutching his boot with the large hole in the sole and wondering how he was going to march the five miles back to Barracks. He made it with the aid of a strip of canvas torn from an ammunition box!

In early January we had a visit from a group of officers from the Glosters and I was delighted to welcome amongst them Colin Campbell, John Biddulph, Bill Percy-Hardman and Denis Biddle. It was like old-home week to see them all again and it gave a change for people like Dan Spry and Eric Snow to meet my old friends about whom they had heard many stories from me. Alas! not many weeks later Colin and

Bill and many others were taken prisoners by the Germans during the withdrawal to Dunkirk and spent the rest of the war in prisoner of war camps.

In March 1940 we had a visit from the King. Each regiment was drawn up on one of the roads in its Barrack Area and His Majesty walked slowly down the center of the road. He appeared very interested in seeing the men as he looked from one side of the road to the other. At the end he congratulated Colonel Bill Hodson on the smart bearing of the Regiment.

In April the Regiment went to Salisbury Plain where we took part in the preparation of a trench system of the type built during the First War. Trench warfare was still considered to be the probable pattern of our war. In fact the Chief of the Imperial General Staff of the British Army, Sir Edmund Ironside, had told us in a lecture to all officers of 1st Canadian Division in March, that trench warfare would be the pattern and that he knew we would win the war because our generals had so much more experience that their opposite number in the German Army. He had a lot of humble pie to eat when the German Army started its blitzkrieg.

By May, the Royal Canadian Regiment were in good shape although we had been handicapped in our training by lack of equipment and vehicles. All the talk by senior officers about "trench warfare" had slowed down our thinking but the German onslaught which started on 10th May soon corrected this. On 23rd May, we were warned to put ourselves on a war-footing and to take train immediately to Dover. I was still second-in-command of 'D' Company under John Macdonald. It was a period of great excitement and we travelled through the night, arriving on the docks at Dover at 6:00 a.m. We understood that we were to board a ship that would take us to Calais. Once there, we would take part in its defence. There was no question of a "Dunkirk" at that time. We were going to France and would be there until the war was won.

"Canterbury" was our ship—a cross channel ferry boat. As we waited for it and were given a stand-up breakfast of tea, bread and "bangers," a ship came in through the entrance to Dover Harbour and, without delay, tied up to the dock on which we were breakfasting. The gangway was lowered immediately and down it came an endless procession of badly wounded men lying on stretchers. Blood seemed to be everywhere. Breakfast, which had been unappetizing before, suddenly became impossible.

Since "Canterbury" did not have much stowage space it was decided to load the most important stores first. Our anti-tank 2-pounder guns, mortars and ammunition had priority. Then, company stores with enough extra uniforms, books, socks, first field dressings to take care of 20% casualties. They were followed by the less essential items including rations for a week and finally, if there was room, a number of items for the Officers Mess. There was room.

Just as we had completed loading a message was delivered at about 9:30 a.m. indicating that we would probably be opposed by the enemy as we went into Calais since they were in possession of a part of the city. Now the important priority before landing was to have the anti-tank guns on deck, ready to shoot if necessary. All stores were unloaded and went back in reverse order. The 2-pounder anti-tank guns were strapped to the bows of two of the ship's life boats—they were our only offensive weapons. The picture had changed rapidly. Instead of a nice dock on which to unload our stores we would have to fight our way into the port. By 11:0 a.m. we were reorganized and restowed—ready to go. Shortly after we received a further message to remain aboard but not to sail until further orders. We began to wonder what might have gone wrong—surely we could not have given up Calais already? After all, we were only an hour's sailing time away from it.

At 5:00 p.m. we were told to disembark, unload stores and return to Aldershot by train. We arrived back in our barracks at about 1:00 a.m.—it had been a hectic and tiring 24 hours.

At about 9:00 a.m. the next morning I was walking from the Officers Mess down to our company lines to see that all was well after the "Dover Dash" as we had christened it. We really had very little news about the change of plans.

Brigadier Armand Smith was walking along the road and hailed me. I went over and walked beside him as he went towards our Battalion Headquarters. He stopped and facing me said very quietly, "Kitching, it's a good thing for your regiment that you didn't sail yesterday—if you had there wouldn't be many of you alive today." He was our Brigade Commander.

He did not enlarge on his remark at the time as he apparently wanted to go to our Headquarters to see "Uncle Bill" Hodson. But later that day we heard that General McNaughton had personally visited the French Coast in a British destroyer and had seen at first hand what was happening. His information had been passed to the War Office with the firm recommendation that our attack be cancelled.

Naturally we were very relieved but I think it is fair to say that we were disappointed. As we were going to bed that night we were again ordered to reload and head for Dover. I remember thinking at the time that I wished Armand Smith hadn't made his remark to me in the morning.

We reloaded all our equipment on the train and stood by for immediate take off. The next day we were ordered to "stand down" but to leave the trains loaded. After another alarm to be ready to move we were advised that the whole operation was cancelled.

Shortly after this I was moved from 'D' Company and became second-in-command of 'B' Company which was commanded by Willis Moogk. Willis had developed a disorder in his digestive system which, it was first suspected, came from milk that had not been pasteurized. Whilst he was out of action the 1st Canadian Division was suddenly ordered to move to the area of Northampton, about 90 miles north of London, to be in a better position to counter German forces should they attempt a quick invasion of England by landing on its east coast. To enable us to move effectively we were issued with about 70% of our vehicle requirements. Many were new three-quarter ton trucks built in Canada. We were told that when the move came it would be done at night. Battalion H.Q. was to be in Rushden twelve miles east of Northampton, and 'B' Company which I was commanding was to be billeted on the good people of Higham Ferrers, a village nearby.

Unfortunately, that week, the Home Guard, or Local Defence Volunteers as they were called at that time, were ordered to remove all signposts from all roads in Britain. Milestones which had stood for centuries indicating distances between ancient villages and towns were taken up or buried on their sites. At the same time the Home Guard of civilian volunteers were warned that they must not give anyone information about the names of villages in their area or directions to any town or city. If the Germans came they would be preceded by parachutists—possibly in British battledress—whose role would be to cause chaos in the rear area and seize vital installations. Every stranger must therefore be treated with suspicion. Apparently, no one had bothered to tell Headquarters of the Canadian Division about these instructions to the Home Guard. Headquarters just issued orders that we would proceed by certain roads which would be well sign-posted and numbered; to proceed via Reading, subsequently north west towards Oxford, then avoiding that city turn northeast and go for Northampton. Very simple. Since we had only just been issued with our vehicles very few of the drivers had had an opportunity to get the feel of the roads. They would now be driving Canadian vehicles with left-hand drive on the British road systems where they were to keep on the left of the road. Everything was set for a night move of sixteen thousand Canadians in a thousand vehicles which resulted in a dispersion the like of which had only once happened in history when the twelve tribes of Israel finally left Egypt.

I was used to English roads and the excellent maps with which we were provided. In fact, I knew many of the roads along which we would be travelling, but 99% of Canadian officers and drivers had no knowledge of the roads or maps. Add to this the inconvenience of a "blacked out" Britain with no lights showing anywhere and the additional problem of driving without lights.

Come the dawn, my driver, Pte. "Rocky" Anderson, and I were in Higham Ferrers accompanied by one of the three trucks which had been in my small convoy. The other two arrived shortly after. The Royal Canadian Regiment had little trouble and we were complete by noon. However, the Headquarters of the Division was besieged with calls from lost individuals and units from as far as North Wales and Lancaster. In the Regiment, the funniest incident occurred not too far from Oxford. Fred McRobie was commanding the carrier platoon at that time. The "carriers" were light, armoured and tracked vehicles designed as a regimental work horse on the battlefield. Fred was heading his line of carriers when they came to a sharp turn in the road. Unfortunately, he had not seen the turn ahead so the carrier continued straight on until it hit and went through the bay window of the local pub—its front end in the public bar, its rear in the garden. The pub was fairly full of local people at the time but fortunately no one was hurt.

The "locals" showed their astonishment at this intrusion by putting down their beer mugs and glaring at Fred and his driver. Fred stood up immediately. "I'm so sorry to disturb you like this but can you tell me if I'm on the right road to Oxford?"

When they finally extricated the carrier, and were bidding farewell to the owner, one of the locals stuck his head out of the broken windows and said, "Next toime 'ee come, come in thrue the roight door."

The people of Higham Ferrers were extremely good to the men of my company. They made them welcome in their homes, gave them the best bedrooms in the house or cottage, fed them as if they were their own family. If this was war we were prepared to rough it forever!

When I went to 'B' Company, I took on as my batman, Pte. Vanneuvenhof and as my bodyguard, Pte. Silas. They were two of the most interesting men whom I met in the war. Vanneuvenhof was of Belgian origin; his family home in Belgium had been destroyed and pillaged by Germans in the First War and he was anxious to pay them back with interest.

Silas was one of the strongest men I have ever met. He wasn't a muscle man who had built up the body beautiful, he was just built like an outhouse. Every part of his body exuded power. He would remove the cap of a beer bottle with his thumb nail or, when it became sore, with his front teeth. The people in Higham Ferrers would stand in awe of him as he crushed, with one hand, a half pint beer mug.

My driver, Rocky Anderson, was of medium build but was a well-known and aggressive welter weight boxer. I felt that between Silas, Van and Rocky, I would be in good hands in an emergency.

Our stay in Higham Ferrers was unfortunately cut short after only a week when we were ordered at short notice to return to Aldershot. This time we went in daylight and all was well, although we moved into a tented area instead of our old barracks. The day after we arrived we were inspected by the King and Queen; it was a beautiful warm June day and it was noticeable that the Queen went out of her way to talk to as many soldiers as possible. That night our advance party was ordered to drive to Plymouth and we realized that this time it meant action.

The Battle of France had reached a critical phase. Belgium had surrendered. The British Army and a number of French Divisions were

isolated in front of Dunkirk. French Armies, confused and demoraliz-
ed, were being overrun by the lightning thrusts of the German Panzer
Divisions. The French people, without any accurate information or
guidance, were in panic and fleeing from the advancing enemy. In
Rouen the civilian population were not even told that the enemy were
ten miles from the town and they went on shopping and walking in the
streets. They were an easy target for the Stuka dive bombers which, as
usual, 'softened up'' the opposition before the entry of the Panzers.

The French Government was disintegrating in spite of Winston
Churchill's visits and exhortations but there appeared to be one hope.
General Weygand was ordered to hold on the line of the Seine. As that
line crumbled a decision was taken to hold the Brittany peninsula. The
1st Canadian Division was to be one of the divisions to do so under the
overall command of Lt.-Gen. Sir Alan Brooke. Our vehicles went
across to Brest just before us and arrived in the evening of the 12th
June. We went through Plymouth arriving in Brest early on the 14th.
Whilst we were waiting for our train to take us inland Bobby Clark and
I went in search of a few rolls of good French bread. ''Uncle Bill''
Hodson had decided that all Company Commanders would travel with
him in his carriage so that if there was any emergency he could issue
orders quickly in transit. It was to feed this small group that we under-
took our search which was to include also a little wine! We were
shocked at the expressions on the faces of the French men and women
in the pastry shop and the small bistro. We were certainly not made to
feel welcome. The owner of the bistro refused to sell us any wine at all
although we were able to buy a few loaves of bread in the pastry shop.
The radio in the bistro was turned on full blast so that people in the
street might listen. To us, it was a sad commentary on the impact of
radio on this group of good solid French people. Almost every
sentence told of the advance of the German Army, nothing was said
about the French Army or, of course, the British. The Germans were
here, the Germans were there, the Germans were almost everywhere.
''Sauve qui peut''—''run—keep running—save yourselves and to hell
with your neighbours.'' The Germans entered Paris as we were buying
bread.

Gus Taschereau, who was commanding one of our companies, had
been able to lay his hands on a few bottles of wine. Gus was a rugged

Quebecois, excellent in both English and French and very proud of his French heritage. I remember he was carrying four mills grenades in his battledress pockets and had two pistols!

The train started about 10:00 a.m. with our soldiers hanging out of every window waving to the people. In the city they got little response but once out in the countryside the peasants in the fields and farms waved enthusiastically. Whenever the train halted for some reason they would crowd around anxious for us to taste their wines and cheeses. Our spirits rose; these people were worth defending.

As we moved east the stops became more frequent—no doubt the engine men were phoning ahead to find out if all was clear. I do not think "Uncle Bill" Hodson really knew where we were supposed to go—there had already been a mix-up in Brest. General McNaughton understood that the division would concentrate just to the west of Rennes; that was the arrangement he had made with General Brooke. However, the authorities responsible for our movement assumed we were to go to Le Mans, only fifty miles from the advancing enemy. We were beginning to see panic-stricken civilians in the stations and on the roads. They were pushing carts and prams full of household furniture and cooking utensils, their children running beside them. In the station many of the women were crying unashamedly and some of our men would run over to try and comfort them, almost missing the train as it moved away without notice. Everyone seemed numbed by the shattering course of events.

At some time late in the afternoon, the train came to a halt in a fairly large station. I do not recall its name but we felt it would be near Laval as we had already passed through Rennes. The station was filled with refugees, old people, young mothers and their children, all frightened and asking when the next train was leaving for the west or the south. After about fifteen minutes "Uncle Bill" Hodson told Gus Taschereau and me to go forward, look for the stationmaster and find out what was happening and why the delay.

We eventually found him talking to the engin drivers at the front of the train, telling them that the train was not to go any further until he had more information. He told us that he had received orders that we were to wait in the train.

It was obvious that the stationmaster was a frightened man and he was starting to infect the two engine drivers with his fears. Gus Tachereau was getting more and more angry and asked me to go and get Col. Hodson. "I'll stay and look after these bastards and if anyone so much as moves I'll shoot him—dead." And to emphasize his intentions he pulled a revolver from its holster and a grenade from his pocket!

As "Uncle Bill" Hodson moved up the station I told him the news we had received from the stationmaster. Gus had checked with the two drivers. They were both from Brest area and quite prepared to drive the train back there if the orders came through to that effect. It was equally obvious that they would hesitate to go any further to the east unless coerced into doing so!

At this time Dan Spry, Tommy Powers and others were phoning Movement Control to find out just what was happening. Gus Taschereau and I washed our hands of the stationmaster although Gus felt he must have been a fifth columnist and should be taken out and shot. Two NCOs with Tommy guns stayed with the engine drivers just to make sure they didn't play any tricks.

It was becoming increasingly difficult to handle some of our own soldiers at this time and I think the NCOs and young officers who were riding herd on them were getting a little concerned. After all, they had been on the train for about eight hours, the available food was limited and we were not able to tell them just what was going to happen. In addition, a few of them had obviously had too much to drink. At this difficult period the decision was made to return to Brest. Apparently the French Government and Army had both given up. General Alan Brooke gave orders for us to re-embark in Brest and return to England.

In the morning as we neared Brest we saw many hundreds of French soldiers standing in the fields close to the railway. They had been ordered to go there, unarmed, to surrender to the Germans. Gus Taschereau was absolutely mad with rage and if he had had a machine-gun I think he would have turned it loose on them. I can remember his anger. He was descended from these people and had been proud of it, but from now on he swore he would never speak to a French bastard again!

On returning to the docks we found our old friend of the Dover Dash days waiting for us, the "Canterbury." I do not know how many passengers the ship was supposed to carry in peacetime, perhaps 700. In no time at all we had our own 800 men aboard and an equivalent number from British units, which had been ordered to withdraw. All our transport which had been issued for our Higham Ferrers move was ordered into a field nearby—about 300 vehicles. There they were set alight to ensure they were not available to the Germans.

During our day of waiting aboard ship in Brest several enemy aircraft flew over the harbour area. Many of them dropped mines in the narrow channels through which we would have to pass and one dropped a bomb in a neighbouring dock area. The French Navy did not fire a single shot at the German aircraft although in the harbour there must have been at least fifteen ships of all sizes from a battleship to destroyers. Our men, however, let go with everything they had—rifles, tommy guns, Bren guns and pistols. We did not hit any aircraft but we made about 500 holes in our ships' two lifeboats and cut every steel hawser holding up our masts. At a neighbouring dock was a British destroyer which was no more anxious to sail up the mined channel than we were. It radioed for a minesweeper and, by the Grace of God, one came over from Plymouth, reached Brest in the early dawn and cleared the channel. We steamed through the cleared channel before breakfast and as we passed the French Navy's docks we emptied about 400 barrels of lovely red wine by riddling them with bullets of all descriptions. We hoped they would go thirsty for weeks.

After we climbed aboard ''Canterbury'' my two musketeers, Vanneuvenhof and Silas, sought me out to say that they were so mad at the way everyone was leaving that they had decided to desert, and were going to report to the office of the French Foreign Legion in Brest and join that great regiment. It was certain to go on fighting the Germans even if no one else would! I tried to dissuade them, told them of the penalty for desertion, but they were determined. They handed over their rifles, saluted and, with muttered apologies, climbed down the gangplank and started up the hill towards the town. Having found the Headquarters of the Foreign Legion they marched smartly up to the sergeant in the recruiting office and said they would join his great Legion.

He drew their attention to a large sign on a wall. It said that recruiting had been stopped temporarily but that it would be resumed in a month's time.

"Would you care to wait a month?" asked the Sergeant.

Van and Silas returned to our boat, picked up their rifles and soldiered on.

We returned to Aldershot but this time we were in other barracks on a temporary basis. It was there in early June that I got my promotion to Captain.

Group-Captain MacNab and
Admiral Pullen learn about an Army
Scout Car from the Author, 1955

9

Meeting With
General George Pearkes V.C.

During the first few months of the war there had been little promotion amongst the officers serving with the Royal Canadian Regiment. Of course, many members of the regiment were promoted at the outset to take on responsible jobs elsewhere either in command or on the staff.

Generally, however, our companies were commanded by lieutenants for a large part of the time. I think the reason for this was that the Ottawa authorities felt that, being a regular regiment, we would be expected to put in more time in each rank than the regiments from the Militia which promoted their members to fill vacancies as they occurred. All their companies were commanded by majors or captains, many of whom were nothing like as well qualified as our subalterns. When I mentioned the disparity to our brigadier, Armand Smith, he grinned and said, "Don't forget your promotions are made in Ottawa—the 48th Highlanders make their promotions here and tell Ottawa later."

In June, among the officers promoted to captain was Len Lavoie, an Albertan French-Canadian, who had been with us in Brest and who, like Gus Tascherean, said he would never speak to a Frenchman again. He had been deeply hurt by the actions of France and Frenchmen. The bright image of the land of his ancestors had turned into an indistinct mirage. After a few days of reorganization the regiment moved to one of the most lovely areas of countryside in southern England—Charlwood, six miles south of Reigate.

To those who know that part of England now, and who may read this chronicle, I must add these words. In 1940 there was no Gatwick Airport, There was no "new town" of Crawley, there was no M23 motorway. In 1940, "Gatwick" was a race course, in the centre of which was a grass strip on which light aircraft might land.

Crawley was a small country town with the villages of Three Bridges, Pound Hill and Ifield comfortably and happily separated from it.

Motorways had not been heard of. When we had to drive from Reigate to Brighton we drove along narrow roads and lanes passing through small towns and villages, each one of which was different.

The decision had been taken that the 1st Canadian Division should form part of a Corps which would be responsible for the security of the counties of Surrey and Sussex. The Corps was an Anglo-Canadian one commanded by General McNaughton; in addition to our own division the Corps would also comprise the 1st British Armoured Division and a large part of the 2nd New Zealand Division. Major-General George Pearkes, VC, DSO, MC took over command of our 1st Division in place of McNaughton.

Overhead the Battle of Britain was beginning. As company commanders we were told to carry out a number of reconnaissances in the coastal areas so that we would get to know the salient features, the best ways of defending them and of retaking them should the enemy be there first. There was real purpose in what we were doing. On our reconnaissances in July and early August the enemy bombing was directed to the coastal airfields and the fledgling radar system. From our vehicles we watched as shipping and coastal installations were bombed without too much interference. We did not realize at the time that the fighter squadrons of the RAF were being kept for the titanic struggle which must develop as enemy attacks moved inland against more vital targets.

In the latter part of August the real struggle began. We watched from our fields and woods as hundreds of enemy bombers and fighters spread across the sky, their targets the fighter bases of southern

England. The summer of 1940 was one of the warmest and driest recorded. Each day, in an almost cloudless sky, two hundred, three hundred, perhaps four hundred bombers would come in from the south while above them, with their wings and fusillages twinkling in the sun, were the German fighters waiting to pounce on anything that might interfere with the orderly procession of bombers. We noticed for the first time the intermittent sounds of the reciprocating engines of the bombers with which we were to become familiar each night that winter.

Suddenly the whole sky would erupt with additional sound as fighter squadrons of the RAF roared in amongst the bombers, guns blazing. The bomber groups would be broken up and their orderly pattern would disintegrate. Perhaps two or three will have been hit and their crews, if alive, would be parachuting slowly to earth. A great cheer would go up from our men as we watched and then, if there was any chance that one of the parachuting crew might land nearby, our stand-by truck would roar off, the soldiers standing with Tommy-guns ready in the hope that if the unfortunate airman landed in our area he would at least pull out his pistol and try to run away. Instead they always surrendered peacefully and were given cigarettes and a drink.

Once the bomber formations had been broken up the RAF fighters had to deal with their opposite numbers in the German Air Force whose job it had been to protect their bombers. The sky would truly become a maelstrom of sound as ace fought against ace. Squadrons broke down to individual pilots. We could see the flame of the machine-guns and cannon before we could hear their roar, just as we could see the orange explosion of a dying aircraft before we heard the detonation of its end.

We, on the ground, could do nothing but cheer and admire.

In September the pattern of the bombing changed. After a daylight raid on London when large areas of docks and waterside industry were set on fire, the German Air Force returned that night with devastating effect. We, in Charlwood, watched as only 25 miles away the whole of London seemed to be in flames. The sky for almost 90°, was so bright with the red, orange, and yellow fires that we could read a book quite easily by its glare. And always, overhead, we could hear the intermittent drone of new bombers moving in to add to the confusion and flames below.

A few weeks later we were moved from our tented homes into the towns of Reigate and Redhill. A number of large houses and buildings had been taken over from their willing occupants and became a part of our regimental life for the next four months. Many kind and generous civilian families in the area, including Arthur Rank, the film producer and owner of Odeon Theatres, opened their doors to us. Many of them set aside a room or two where our men could relax in the nearest thing to home.

Around Christmas I was sent up to brigade as a temporary staff officer and the link with the regiment which was to move to the Brighton area to take over the beach defences for a period of a month. At this time, Lt.-Col. Murray Green took command of the regiment. It had apparently been decided that "Uncle Bill" Hodson should return to Canada to get a well-deserved promotion to brigadier. Col. Green had commanded the regiment in peace time; he must have been about 50 years of age and his appointment was a surprise.

General George Pearkes* was at this time very busy putting the units of his 1st Canadian Division through a series of battalion exercises so that he could judge their overall efficiency. These exercises were taking place in an area known as South Park Farm, south of Oxted. Since I was not doing anything important at Brigade Headquarters, I was detailed to be an "umpire" and told to report to South Park Farm. The exercises were quite simple ones designed to test the deployments drills of each battalion in the attack. A small "enemy" force was positioned to take the toll of any unwise movements made by the attacking battalion. I was the umpire with the enemy force.

General Pearkes was a great trainer in addition to his other qualities. He loved to stride about the training areas during exercises spurring platoons on or correcting some mistake or other. He was more active than most of the soldiers under him.

On this particular occasion the Princess Patricia's Canadian Light Infantry were the battalion being tested, and as a spectator, General Pearkes had with him Major-General Lee of the U.S. Army, then

* Major-General George Randolph Pearkes V.C.; the Canadian Army's most decorated soldier. Minister of National Defence 1957-60. Lieutenant-Goverfnor of British Columbia 1960-68. Died 1984, aged 96.

visiting the U.K.

All went well for a while but I soon noticed that three carriers of the PPCLI were about to try and move across an open field only about 300 yards from two anti-tank guns of my "enemy" force. When they reached the centre of the field I put each one of the carriers "out of action" and told the sergeant with them just why I had done it. They put up a blue flag indicating they had been knocked out.

About five minutes later I saw three figures moving towards me. In front was General Pearkes whom I had never met before. He was striding purposefully in my direction, followed immediately by his ADC and well to the rear, puffing mightily, was General Lee.

"Why did you put those carriers out of action?" asked General Pearkes. I explained what had happened, pointing out the two well-camouflaged anti-tank guns that had done the 'damage.' "Well, put them back into action," said General Pearkes and, turning to General Lee who had arrived on the scene, said, "This young man has put three of the Patricia's carriers out of action, no German is ever going to be able to do that, are they, General Lee?" General Lee clearly had no option, he had to agree. However, I obviously could not put the carriers back into action, too much had happened since. And anyway, they had deserved to be 'killed.' I explained this as best as I could. General Pearkes looked me up and down and strode away. He did not appear very happy.

Shortly afterwards his ADC came back, introduced himself as Dick Danby of the Seaforth Highlanders and, taking out his notebook, asked my name. The General wanted to know my name and what job I was doing. I couldn't help but feel at this point that I would not be doing my present job much longer. After the exercise we all congregated to hear General Pearkes sum up the lessons learned and the mistakes made. He was cheerful and in good form—he made no reference to the idiot who had dared to put three of the Patricia's carriers out of action. I breathed again.

Some weeks later I received an order to report to Divisional Headquarters at Nutfield Ridge. I was to contact Dick Danby on arrival.

Nutfield was a small village about two miles east of Redhill. The Divisional Headquarters was in a large red brick mansion of doubtful architecture. As I walked up the drive I could not help but wonder whether I would be dead or alive after the visit. I reported to Dick Danby who told me to wait a couple of minutes.

He soon reappeared, knocked on the General's door and announced "Captain Kitching, Sir." I went in and saluted. George Pearkes was sitting at a desk which was uncluttered by 'in' and 'out' baskets. He obviously did not like paper. "Come in, Ketchin" his voice was kindly. "I want to talk to you." It took George Pearkes some time to get my name right. He had a great friend in Winnipeg, who was also a soldier, named Ketchin. The General got to the point very quickly. "Do you know anything about chemical warfare?"

"No, sir."

"Good, that's very good. Now, I want you to know that I took your name off the list of officers who are now taking Staff College training under Col. Simonds. You can go on the next course. But now, I want you to take a short course in chemical war so that you will be qualified; then, you will officially be my GSO III (General Staff Officer) Chemical Warfare. But you can forget about gas and all the chemical gadgets because I don't think that Hitler will use them. What I want you to do is be a training staff officer. You have more experience in that field than most, so that's how I shall employ you. When I send you to observe the training of a unit I want an honest report from you. Understand? Good."

I was glad that Pearkes did not really want me to be his chemical warfare expert. I had no real interest or knowledge of the subject; and I was sure I could not learn enough on a seven-day course at the Chemical Warfare School at Porton to pass even an elementary exam.

A few days later I left my phoney job at brigade, said a quick farewell to the regiment which happened to be near Brighton at the time and headed for Divisional Headquarters. I was to live in 'C' Mess in an old rectory on the hill below the church.

We generally slept two or three to a room in which there would be no furniture except our own camp-beds. The dining room only had standard issue tables and chairs. The 'sitting room' had a few beaten up old leather sofas and chairs. Heating was obtained from the fireplaces. Hot water was obtained by lighting a very dangerous looking gas-operated water heater which was located at one end of the bath. To light the flame you would turn on the gas then light a match and apply it to the hole indicated by an arrrow. There would immediately be an explosion that would rock the machine and send everyone for cover. However, as we were only allowed four inches of water in the bath the machine was never overworked.

I went on my chemical warfare course to Porton and was delighted to find the Chief Instructor was none other than Fred Ollis, one of the majors in the Gloucesters whom I had known in Mhow. Fred Ollis remembered me because I had been a too frequent visitor to his house when he had a most attractive niece staying with him.

On the course we were told of plans being made by the German Army to use nerve gas in a very big way; just before their troops hit the beaches special landing craft without crews would run up onto the beaches and paralyze the defenders the new nerve gas. To the sceptics this was rather like saying that we would soon land on the moon!

Once back at Divisional H.Q. I began settling into their routine. The G.S.O.I.—or Chief operations officer—was Lt.-Col. Rodney Keller. Rod was a regular Army officer, having served with the Patricias. He had at one time been the undoubted head of Physical Training in the Army and had almost driven some people to suicide with his toughness. He had red hair and a red moustache. He was a very efficient officer from whom we all learned a lot.

The AA & QMG or Chief Administration Officer was Lt.-Col. Chris Vokes. He and Rod Keller had many similar traits and characteristics: they were physically strong, first class officers, good teachers, rough and yet soft hearted. Both had red hair, were obstinate, and commanded Divisions in action. They were a wonderful pair to work for and they ran a happy Headquarters.

George Pearkes, of course, set the tone of the whole division. He commanded it for over two years and during that time he never relaxed. He was constantly on the go. He laid on exercise after exercise, each one designed to rehearse accepted theories or try out new ones. One or two ended in complete confusion, particularly at the beginning when our new equipments had just been issued and commanders and drivers had not got used to deploying and handling them. Whilst General Pearkes was an inspiration to us at his Headquarters and to the troops in his division he was, I think, a very difficult subordinate. He did not think highly of General McNaughton as a soldier although he always gave great credit to him as a scientist and an organizer. There is no doubt that without McNaughton's ability to influence Mr. King and the Cabinet the Canadian Army overseas might have been much smaller and might well have been so dispersed that its Corps and Divisions would have become parts of British formations. But as a tactician and leader of infantry he felt that McNaughton would have been a failure. We noticed that whenever a staff officer from Canadian Corps Headquarters was brash enough to attend General Pearkes' conference at 8:00 a.m., the General would look around the room, fix his eyes on the unfortunate officer and say, "Who are you and what are you doing in this room?"

The wretched officer would say, "Sir, my name is Smith. I have been sent from Corps Headquarters."

"Who sent you?"

"Colonel Jones sent me, sir."

"Well, then, get out of this headquarters and go and tell Col. Jones to ask permission before he sends anyone down here to find out what I'm dong."

This may sound like a harsh way to handle a subordinate but it did have its effect. When people later came from Corps Headquarters they came with a purpose and we used to insist that they send us copies of any reports they made.

To his own staff, General Pearkes was always considerate. One evening early in April 1941, I was Orderly Officer. This meant that I manned the Operations Room during the night and received and reported any undue occurrences. This particular evening was a Saturday and as that was the only night when we could go out and have fun the Headquarters was empty. As far as I knew the Sergeant on duty with me was the only person in the building except for myself. At that time the German Air Force was returning in strength to bomb Britain prior to turning its full fury on the Soviet Union and on that night there were a number of bombs dropped in the Divisional area. At about 9:00 p.m., the General walked into my office, looked at the bomb reports and invited me to go with him to his small 'A' Mess to have a drink. Leaving the sergeant to 'hold the fort,'' I followed General Pearkes to his Mess. He ordered drinks and asked me how everything was going in the R.C.R. He knew that I had been to see the Regiment the week before. I told him that I felt that things were going downhill and there was not the same spirit in the battalion. He naturally wanted my opinion on the reasons for this. I told him that I felt I should pass on to him the remarks made to me by a major in the regiment, Neil Hodson. I reminded him that Neil had no axe to grind, he was not looking for promotion but was deeply affected by the present state of the regiment because his father had been the commanding officer from November 1939 to December 1940 and had brought the regiment to a high state of efficiency. Now, after only two months of being commanded by Murray Green, it had slipped badly and discipline was suffering. Green did not appear to be interested in the welfare of the men. I told the General that, according to reports from the Regiment, Murray Green went up to London almost every night, leaving his driver outside in the army station wagon during the air raids, and did not leave London until about 2:00 a.m.

General Pearkes said very little as I spoke—he was obviously upset. I finally excused myself but before going I told him that I was sorry that, as a captain, I should have to report on a commanding officer whom I did not know. I was only thinking of the regiment. Finally he said, ''Then who would you put in to command?'' I said, ''Eric Snow.'' He looked at me in astonishment and said ''But Eric Snow's much too young, he's only 35.'' He bade me goodnight and I thought no more about our conversation.

About three weeks later General Pearkes sent for me. He asked me if I remembered our conversation about the R.C.R. and what I had said about Col. Murray Green. I told him I remembered it well. 'Good,'' said the General, ''now I want you to write a letter for me to sign to the Corps Commander (General McNaughton) informing him that I am dissatisfied with Col. Green as a commanding officer and that I would like him replaced immediately. You are to put in the letter all you said to me that night including the fact that he spends several nights each week in London.''

I went away and wrote and rewrote several drafts all in longhand as I hesitated to have even the confidential clerks see what I had written. Eventually I felt I had the best draft possible so went to give it to the General. He read it and said it was all right, he might change it a little but he thanked me for doing it. I then said that the evidence about Col.

Green going up to London should be checked because I had only the word of Major Neil Hodson on it, and I hadn't seen what was happening myself. He smiled and told me that he had had the Provost Marshal check that point and that what I had told him was correct. Murray Green gave up command shortly after and Eric Snow was promoted to take over from him.

Two events of great importance raised our morale and also our Mess bills. The sinking of the Bismarck after an exciting four or five days chase all over the North Atlantic was a tonic at a time when we needed one badly. I happened to be on my way to divisional hedquarters from a visit to Brigadier Potts' 2nd Canadian Brigade Headquarters when I noticed a commotion in front of a pub in one of the neighbouring villages. Everyone had a beer mug or a drink of some kind and they were cheering and shouting. We pulled in just in time to hear someone shouting ''Three cheers for the Navy'' and this was followed by another shout of ''three cheers for Winston.'' They had just heard the midday news which had reported Mr. Churchill's speech to Parliament in which he had announced that the ''Bismarck'' had been sunk.

The other event which preceded the sinking of the Bismarck was the landing in Scotland of Rudolf Hess, the Deputy Fuehrer, and Hitler's righthand man, and leader of the Nazi Party. The news reached us on a Monday morning and was another cause for celebration. The details of this incredible happening, and just how much Hess knew about the German plans for the future and how much he talked about them, were not announced for some time. Certainly it must have worried Hitler.

I normally avoided London unless it was to attend a meeting called by Canadian Military Headquarters. But for some reason I was there close to noon on a Sunday in April or May 1941. I was walking along Jermyn Street wondering when the pubs would open and which one I would visit when I saw across the street a young officer of the Royal Canadian Engineers, Captain Malcolm Sutherland-Brown. We chatted for a few moments and decided we would find someone who would sell us a drink.

A little further along the street was the Cavendish Hotel, a rather genteel looking establishment with only a narrow frontage. Full of hope we entered. The foyer was not large and slightly right of centre was a grouping of five or six elegant but comfortable chairs and a "carrying chair" of Georgian days. The shafts had been taken from the carrying chair and only the box remained.

Seated in one of the comfortable chairs was a lady of perhaps 55 or 60, possibly more. In the carrying chair was a man of 60 or 70; he was small but made himself conspicuous by wearing a check suit and yellow waistcoat.

Perhaps Malcolm and I looked a little sheepish. I had not been in the hotel before and somehow or other we had not expected to see two elderly people sitting in such surroundings. We stood still, smiling happily.

"What can I do to help you two young gentlemen?" the lady inquired. She had a nice voice which put us at our ease and unashamedly we said, almost together, that we had hoped we would be able to buy a drink in the hotel. Could we do so?

With that she turned to the man in the check suit and asked him to fetch a bottle of champagne and four glasses. She then invited us to sit down. We introduced ourselves and she asked a few questions about Canada and about one or two Canadians whose names I have forgotten. 'Check-suit' returned with the glasses and a bottle of champagne wrapped in a white napkin. He filled the glasses. We thanked him and toasted her. He filled the glasses again. So it went on for a while until she told us that a bomb had hit the top floor of the hotel and had wrecked the suite of which she was obviously very proud. Would we like to see it? She took us up to what I suppose was the 4th floor. The windows in the hall had been boarded up and we went into the suite. There the windows were badly damaged and one wall was a mixture of plaster, brick and wallpaper, the ceiling had a large tarpaulin stretched across one part of it.

We surveyed the scene for a moment. Then, with a triumphant "But they didn't get him" she pulled aside a curtain which hung above the end of the large bed. There was a life size oil painting of King Edward VII wearing the full dress uniform of a Field Marshal!

We descended to the foyer where she ordered another bottle. 'Check-suit' soon returned and in due course the second bottle was emptied. She wouldn't let us pay for anything and she talked excitedly about the 'old days.' I think she enjoyed talking to Malcolm and me just as much as we enjoyed her stories. 'Check-suit' rarely spoke.

We eventually excused ourselves and said good-bye with many words of thanks for her kindness.

She was Mrs. Rosa Lewis, the famous lady who, from being a superb cook, became a mistress of King Edward the Seventh and the owner of the hotel. 'Check-suit' was the doorman, concierge and friend who had been with her for over 30 years. Rosa Lewis was the 'Duchess of Duke Street' and 'check-suit' was Harry, the doorman.

In July Dick Danby and I were warned that we would be attending the next course at the Staff College at Camberley.

I used to accompany General Pearkes on a fair number of his visits to units. On one occasion he decided to go to the Rifle Ranges at Bisley and to go there via the Hogs Back—a road running west from Guildford. He loved the views from the Hogs Back which apparently had many memories for him of his earlier days at the Staff College. We drove along happily in his official Buick—finally came to the Hogs Back and were driving slowly along it when, at a small intersection ahead, a solitary figure in riding breeches and uniform stepped onto the road. It was Major-General Victor Odlum who commanded the 2nd Canadian Divisionl General Pearkes stopped the car, lowered the window and said, 'Are you looking for a horse, Victor?' I don't think Odlum was very amused by the remark. I had never met him before and didn't see him again. When I mentioned to Col. Keller on my return to Headquarters that we had seen Victor Odlum he grinned and said, 'You know his decorations are CB, CMG, DSO: and some people say they stand for: 'Come Boys, Call Me God, Don't Say Odlum'.

On the ranges with General Pearkes that day I was delighted to meet Col. Alec Vicary, formerly of the Gloucesters, and now Commandant of the Small Arms School. I had not met him before although I knew his brother, John, from Singapore and Mhow days. He and General Pearkes had met some years before.

As a result of the visit to the Ranges, I was given permission to organize a competitive shooting day on the Ranges for any volunteers within the Division. I was determined to get away from the "Bull's Eye" targets at which most of our soldiers had been shooting since joining the Army—and to produce imaginative targets that made the firer think.

On the great day we had about 300 of the best shots in the division

Attending. All our shooting was done at 300 yards range and I had two
ordinary targets available with an armourer who could adjust rifles if
they required zeroing. The remaining targets varied greatly. On one I
had 20 coloured balloons filled with gas to keep them floating. Two of
the balloons were white—the remainder were mixed colours. The problem was to hit the white ones which of course were intermingled with
the others and turning with the wind. The firer had to put the equivalent
of 10 cents down for each bullet fired—if he hit the white he got a
dollar—if he hit a blue balloon by mistake he forfeited another 10
cents—and so on.

Another "target" was a highly painted surface 4 feet square with as
many as 15 different coloured squares, circles, triangles, hexagonals,
etc. Camouflaged in this mix of shapes and colours was the aiming
mark, a small square 3 inches by 3 inches. It was painted black. The
firer had an exact miniature replica of the target on a card in front of
him which allowed him to assess the juxtaposition of the aiming mark
to the variety of forms and colours surrounding it. He paid 10 cents for
each bullet but this time he got $2 for a correct hit.

Another was a circular target with 12 windows radiating from the
centre, each window was a different colour—black was the aiming
mark. The target turned full circle at varying speeds. Ten cents a
bullet—$1 for a hit. There were other types of "targets".

General Pearkes and Colonel Keller came out for the day to watch—Rod Keller, who was a good shot, tried each one in turn. He didn't
hit a jackpot and his language got worse and worse—however he seemed to enjoy himself. At the end we had a shoot off—firing at normal
targets. The quality of marksmanship was superb—the winner getting
18 Bulls in a row. He was an armourer from RCEME named English
or England (I forget which). He certainly deserved his gold medal. It
was a very informal occasion and I think that General Pearkes enjoyed
it particularly because he was able to talk to so many men in such informal surroundings.

Dick Danby and I became great friends during our time together at
the Headquarters. After doing a year as the ADC to the General, he
moved over the operations side as one of the GSO III's with me. Later
that year he and I went to the Staff College together at Camberley—but
more about that later. The spring and summer of 1941 seemed to race

by—there were always a number of exercises to prepare or to observe.

In September the division took part in the biggest military exercise ever staged in Britain. It was named "Bumper". Four Corps Headquarters and twelve divisions were involved. As a staff exercise I'm sure that Bumper was of great value. It lasted about ten days which allowed us time to establish a routine at the Headquarters. On short exercises everyone thinks he has to take part if only to learn what's going on—but it teaches bad lessons because in war staffs must be spelled off in order that everyone gets the necessary sleep, rest and meals. We learned that lesson very quickly in Sicily.

General Montgomery was the senior umpire on Bumper—this was the first time I saw him. He had some strong comments about the way in which someone had tried to cross over the main axes of two Corps one of which contained two Armoured Divisions. I can't remember the details of his criticism but I can remember afterwards hearing General Pearkes remark that in his opinion England in wartime was not the place to train an armoured division. There were too many restrictions on cross country movement that made it almost impossible to be realistic. He thought that the north of Scotland was the place to manoeuvre—not the vital food producing fields of England.

During my nine months at Divisional Headquarters I had learned a great deal from George Pearkes, Rod Keller and Chris Vokes. Prior to being there all my service had been in an infantry battalion and from that vantage point at the sharp end I had seen Staff officers come and go but had not quite understood their functions or their relationship with commanders. I knew that in the First War the British had closed their Staff College, relying on staff officers to learn their jobs by in-job training in action. One result was that the staff officer became the butt of all the jokes. If there was a failure, blame it on the staff.

We, in the Canadian Army in 1939, did not have anything like the number of officers trained to staff and maintain the Corps Headquarters and two Divisions that were raised in that first year. In an effort to help us the British gave us extra vacancies at their Staff College in Camberley. Unfortunately our selection of students was poor and instead of sending regular officers we sent some Militia officers who simply did not have the background to grasp the instruction. The result was that about 50% of those who went on the course were failed. It was a waste of vital positions which we could ill afford. In 1940 the decision was taken to open a Staff College of our own. Eventually it was to move to RMC Kingston but the first course was to be in England to take advantage of support offered by the British Staff College. Lt.-Col. Guy Simonds of the Royal Canadian Artillery was Commandant. There were about 50 students on the course and this infusion of qualified, although inexperienced, staff officers was essential to the efficient functioning of the formations of the new Canadian Army. The British still continued to give Canada vacancies at their Staff College and it was to fill two of those vacancies that Dick Danby and I were selected.

The Author, April, 1944

10

Beginnings With Crerar And Simonds

The Staff College at Camberley was situated at one end of the extensive land and training areas on which the Royal Military College, Sandhurst is located. I knew the region well from my earlier Sandhurst days.

Whilst the peacetime courses at Camberley were as long as two years, the wartime ones were reduced to six hectic months. One hundred and twenty students lived in the Staff College itself and another 60 were in Minley Manor, a country house nearby.

Dick Danby and I were in the Minley Manor group along with Major Lewis Clarke of the Royal Canadian Artillery. We were the Canadian component. On arrival we celebrated my promotion to Major.

Amongst the directing staff at Minley Manor were Neil Blair and Dick Craddock, two friends from my Sandhurst days who had been Under officers in their companies at the same time that I had hit that dizzy rank. The commandant was Maj.-Gen. Stopford who later distinguished himself as a Corps Commander with General Slim in Burma.

During the six months we were at the Staff College we worked six days a week from 8:15 a.m. to 5:00 p.m. After dinner, except Saturdays and Sundays, we would spend two hours writing essays or military appreciations which would have to be handed in next morning. Our only break was at Christmas when we had four days off. I have never worked harder in my life nor learned so much in such a short period.

One of the highlights of our course was a two hour talk given by General Sir Alan Brooke who had taken over the job of C.I.G.S. (Chief of the Imperial General Staff) only a few days before. We had all been shattered by the news of Pearl Harbour, but the fact that the U.S. was now completely involved in the war was very comforting. In his two hour talk General Brooke summed up just where we stood on that February day and what we could do to improve our position in the months ahead. Not only had the whole of the Far East been over-run by the Japanese but the German onslaught had already reached Stalingrad and the oil rich Caucasus.

I can still see General Alan Brooke standing alone on the stage, speaking quietly, listing one terrible defeat after another. But at no time did he indicate that conditions were hopeless or that we might ultimately be defeated. In fact, I do not think there was anyone in the room who thought that that might happen. We were strangely buoyant considering the state of the world. After speaking about the few actions that could be taken to counter the Japanese, Germans and Italians, General Brooke spoke about the plans that were in the making for the Allied Invasion of France! He did not indicate the year or the place but he told us of the Staffs that had been working in great secrecy on the problems that must be overcome and the means to overcome them. He lifed our eyes from the gloom of the present to the sunshine of the future. His manner gave us all renewed confidence even though at the last moment, just before stepping down from the stage, he said, "Before coming here this morning I received news that our 18th Division, originally scheduled to help in the defence of Burma but redirected to strengthen our forces in Malaya, is surrendering to the Japanese as it leaves its troopships in Singapore! He was almost crying as he spoke.

The two most important legacies that the Canadian Army has acquired from its long association with its British opposite number are the Staff system and the Regimental system.

The commander of any force needs a staff, not only to help him make a plan but also to ensure that the means to make that plan successful is at the right place at the right time.

The British Staff College starts its students a the lowest levels and then brings them through various stages to the top.In this way the student becomes familiar with all the details and problems at each level and is required to exercise his mind in solving those problems. The 'broad brush' is not permitted. The study of detail is encouraged.

Perhaps the Dardanelles Campaign is the best example of poor staff work. If the commanders had had good staffs who were doing their jobs correctly, they never would have made the decisions they did. The best example of excellent staff work must be the incredibly detailed work that went into Operation ''Overlord,'' the cross-Channel invasion of 1944, planning for which started in 1940.

The British system, in my opinion, is the most suitable for the Canadian Army because it teaches the most economical use of human and material resources knowing quite well that, certainly at the outset of any war, they will be short of both. Great Powers, with almost unlimited resources, do not have to give the same attention to detail in the use of those resources that we do. They can use the 'broad brush' treatment. We can't.

I was shocked six years ago to be told that one or two ignorant generals in our presently Unified Forces had recommended doing away with the Army Staff College. It would be better to do away with the generals!

The course finished in late March when I was delighted to be shown the report that had been prepared on my work. It was complimentary and recommended me to command a battalion. I knew that I was to be GSO II Training at 1st Canadian Corps Headquarters. In April 1942 the Corps was commanded by General Harry Crerar. The head of the General Staff was Brigadier. Guy Simonds to whom I would be reporting directly. The Headquarters was located in a large stone house known as Wakehurst Place in Sussex.

General Crerar had his small ''A'' Mess there. ''B'' Mess, in which I was to live, was located in a superb old Elizabethan Manor known as ''Gravetye'', a mile or so south-west of East Grinstead.

This was the first time that I had met General Crerar. He was quiet spoken and spoke slowly—rather as if he was teaching a rather dull class. He struck me as being very kind; he was certainly kind to me at that time and continued to be until he died. He was rather too particular and formal to be called a ''warm personality.'' I had no way then of judging his military ability as a commander.

He sent for me on my first morning at his Headquarters and asked me to 'cull' through the operations logs of three divisions that had recently taken part in a large scale exercise and come up with the 'lessons learned.'

As I had not even been on the exercise I was a bit shaken by his request and I was even more shaken when I got hold of the Operations Logs. There must have been about 150 typed pages giving in great detail the moves and countermoves, the orders and the counterorders of each formation. They included masses of figures showing where everyone was at certain times but no word of why they were there.

General Crerar had asked me for my report ''in a couple of days.'' I went to see him once I had the Operations Logs to explain the problem. He was not in and would not be back until evening.

So I went to see Brigadier Simonds. This was the first time I had spoken with Guy Simonds as he had been away when I reported the day before.

We are told now that when Guy Simonds was a cadet at RMC, Kingston he was known as the 'Count' because of his elegance and the way he wore a uniform. I can well understand the nickname. In 1941, Guy Simonds was a man of about 38. He was handsome with even features, dark hair, dark moustache. The most noticeable feature about him were his eyes—blue, penetrating and observant. He was of average height.

I told him my problem and showed him the Operation Logs. He glanced at them for a minute or two and looked up, ''they are not much help, are they?'' He went on to say that he was sorry that General Crerar had given me such a strange assignment, particularly as I had not even been on the exercise. He was preparing a report to Crerar on the 'lessons learned' and would be presenting the report at the conference the next morning. He would tell Crerar at that time that I had helped him prepare the report. If I agreed to this I was to sit down with him there and then and call out the location of certain formations at certain times by using my Logs. I could not have been more relieved and all went well the next morning. Needless to say I became a Simonds' man from then on.

Unfortunately Brigadier Simonds left the Corps H.Q.'s in June to go on a special assignment. I was sorry. He was so easy to work for and knew what he wanted. At that time we used to get reports each week from divisions outlining their training plans for the following week. I would go through them and mark the ones that I felt were important enough to warrant a visit. He would return the reports to me with notes of what to look for. After each visit I would report to him and it was a simple but effective arrangement. I did not see much of him socially as he lived in "A" Mess with General Crerar but he came down and had a drink with us in "B" Mess occasionally.

His place was taken by Brigadier Churchill Mann, a Regular Army officer from the Royal Canadian Dragoons.

Church Mann worked quite differently from Guy Simonds. He was an ideas man and every day I would receive as many as four or five little slips of paper, signed by him, asking what I thought of such-and-such a suggestion; or would I go and meet the Chief Engineer and see if it wasn't possible to make bigger fascines to carry on our tanks so that the tanks could cross deeper ditches! For the first two or three days I tried to keep up with his little notes but after a while I tore up most of them and just dealt with the few that I felt were my responsibility. He didn't seem to mind.

We had a good group of officers at my level at the Headquarters including Malin Harding of the Artillery and Bob Hilborn of the Toronto Scottish. Another member of the staff who lived in our mess was the GSO II Chemical Warfare, Major Eric Smith. He had been at the Headquarters for about a year and I remembered him well from my days as a phoney Chemical Warfare officer. In my day, gas was a possibility and a certain amount of attention was given to it but now, a year later, it had no priority at all. This used to make Eric Smith very angry. He was a man with a great deal of ability and here he was wasting his time and no one would listen to him.

One night he was feeling very sorry for himself so he decided to get drunk. It took a lot of doing but he finally succeeded and staggered up the stairs to his room. About ten minutes later he lurched down again saying he needed a final drink. This time he was wearing his belt from which hung his revolver in its holster. He had a double Scotch, bade us farewell again and headed for the stairs. Suddenly we heard a shout followed by a shot, then another shot and a shout, "I got you that time, you little bastard." We went to see what was happening. Eric was shooting his way upstairs just like a Western movie only, of course, there weren't any 'bad guys.' Whatever it was that he thought he could see received a total of six lead bullets of .38 calibre. We all assumed, including Eric, that it must be dead. He was happy and went to bed to sleep soundly.

The panelling around the stairs was the original wood of 1588. He had made four holes in it; the other two bullets hit the ceiling. The repairs made by our Engineers were so good that the damage cannot be seen, but to this day, high in the corner of the ceiling, there is still one original hole.

General Montgomery was at that time the General Officer Commanding, South East Command. His area of command comprised the counties of Surrey, Sussex and Kent. Amongst the forces under his overall command were the 1st Canadian Corps and the 12th British Corps.

It was interesting to see the way that General Montgomery impressed his personality on his command. When he felt that he had a number of points which should be stressed in our training he would order all the officers of a division to attend a briefing or lecture in a certain theatre at a certain time. If the theatre was big enough he would have the officers from two divisions—a total of over 1,000.

Before entry into the theatre all cigarettes would be extinguished—there would be no smoking. Everyone would be seated five minutes before the time of the briefing. At exactly the hour appointed General Montgomery, wearing battle dress, would walk onto the stage from one of the wings. Everyonewould come to attention and remain standing. After a moment the General would say, "Thank you, please be seated." He would remain standing with his hands behind his back whilst everyone sat down; invariably in an audience of that size a few officers would cough or clear their throats. When all was silent, Montgomery would say, "Good, Now that you are seated I want you to know that there will be no more coughing—no more coughing. People who cough make it difficult for others to hear what I am saying—and that's no good. No good at all. I will be speaking for

30 minutes, after which there will be a break for 10 minutes. You may cough then if you have to, but not before. Now, I have got you in here today to point out three weaknesses that I have found in your training.'' He would only speak about those three weaknesses and would tell the audience how to overcome them. He never allowed himself to get off the subject and he used very simple language, emphasizing some points by numbering them on his fingers or by repeating himself twice or sometimes three times.

He used to throw in a few laughs occasionally. One of his favourites was to say that he sometimes repeated himself twice for ''audiences who are a bit slow—a bit stupid. And that when he repeated himself three times it was because he could see one or two people in the audience falling asleep.'' He would then repeat the words ''falling asleep'' three times! The effect was, of course, electric and those of us who might be dozing would get the message very quickly.

But the most extraordinary thing about these talks was that no one coughed and everyone remembered the two or three salient points of his message.

There is no doubt that he was a first class instructor. I have read articles and books by some of his detractors and by some people who never met him who said he had no ''presence.'' I must agree that Monty was not a large, dominating man, in fact, he was quite small and slight and I suppose that if he were walking along a street in a crowd, he would be no different from anyone else. But if everyone in the crowd was asked to stop and give you a chance to look into their eyes for a moment, you wouldn't hesitate to pick his eyes as being the dominant ones and the ones of a leader. They alone gave him a 'presence.'

He was also a bit of an actor but which great general in history hasn't been? If, in times of crisis and difficulty, a commander puts on a confident expression to raise the morale of those around him he is an actor. When Monty put on an Australian hat in the desert and wore two badges he was putting on an act which pleased the troops and raised morale. Certainly our troops got to know Monty because he made a point, in that spring and summer of 1942, of visiting each one of our regiments. First he would speak with the commanding officer and the senior officers in private, then he would go to where the men were paraded, stand on his jeep and ask them to gather around him.

Although he did not know Canada at that time he knew enough about the rivalries between cities and provinces to be able to joke about them and get the men in a good mood and listening to him. In every sentence, he showed himself to be a leader, utterly sure of himself. I think the men appreciated his simplicity.

General Montgomery's theory of the training cycle for this period was adopted by us in the Canadian Army. Normally this training cycle would be for a twelve month period, starting with individual training of the soldier—then section and platoon training—then company and battalion training—then exercises on a brigade level and so on up through each level of command.

What General Montgomery suggested was that the twelve month period should be telescoped to three months. This meant, of course, a hectic programme but the constant change of pattern kept us on our toes.

He also laid down that every man would march ten miles in 135 minutes with a twenty minute break after five miles. We all had to wear full equipment and carry 70 rounds of ammunition. The weight of our equipment, rifles and ammunition would be about 50 pounds. We all did it.

I mentioned on the last page that I felt that Montgomery's eyes alone gave him a presence. I must enlarge on this.

When speaking to an individual his eyes remained on the individual. He looked directly into the eyes of the man or woman he was addressing. I believe someone is said to have written that "the eyes are the mirror of the soul"—perhaps they are, but I have never met anyone whose eyes mirrored his feelings more than Montgomery's. His eyes were blue and showed clear against the "whites" surrounding them. You could see them sparkle with interest or dull over according to his feeling for the subject matter or his interest in an individual. They would have given him away in a game of poker.

In May 1942, 1st Canadian Corps took part in Exercise Tiger—the last large-scale exercise run by General Montgomery in South Eastern Command.

It lasted for twelve days during which some of the regiments marched and countermarched as many as 250 miles. It was a great test of endurance for the regiments and a great test of our organization at Corps

Headquarters. General Crerar had only taken over at Corps in January 1942. He had never commanded a brigade or division because of a number of shuffles of senior officers which always seemed to land him in Staff jobs. However, the Exercise went off well and the Headquarters functioned effectively. General McNaughton was impressed by the standard of fitness and training. General Montgomery was well satisfied. This was the first occasion when he was able to observe at first hand the organizing ability of Brigadier Simonds. He must also have seen that many of the successful tactical decisions made by General Crerar had stemmed from Simonds' brain.

Unfortunately, at some period towards the end of the exercise, a large staff car containing one or two very senior officers of the British Army and General McNaughton went past a line of marching infantry at such a speed that it sent up a cloud of dust and gravel into the faces of the troops. Some of the men showed their anger by "booing" the car. I am sure they also used other ways but the "boos" apparently upset General McNaughton most. He could see from the 'flashes' on their shoulders that the men were from the Edmonton Regiment; shortly after the exercise ended he started an inquiry into the incident. It was found that the 'bad guys' were from 'B' Company of the Edmonton Regiment; somewhat naturally the company was immediately christened "Boo" Company and has stayed that way ever since.

Towards the end of July I was sent for by General Crerar who told me that I had been selected to command the Edmonton Regiment in place of Lt.-Col. Wilson who had been moved to 1st Divisional Headquarters. He told me the story of the "booing" incident and said that the regiment needed a real shakeup. He went on to say that General Montgomery had not been very impressed with some of the senior officers in the regiment. They were too old, too slow in their thinking. I was to have a good look at them and get rid of those that were not carrying their weight. Finally, he said that he thought my English accent might upset some of the troops—maybe I should Canadianize it! He would be down to see the regiment in about a month. I was to take over on the 1st of August.

General Crerar had spoken in a very kindly way to me, almost fatherly in his advice. He told me that at one time in the First War, a Major McLeod of the Edmontons had commanded the Royal Canadian

Regiment and my going to the Edmontons was just a return of the compliment.

All my uniforms naturally were RCR, and badges, buttons, flashes and everything had to be changed. I had two days to do it. I must be wearing the correct regalia or it would be like a red flag to a bull to appear in RCR uniform.

I immediately got a military car, filled it with my uniforms and headed for London. The only place that could handle this kind of emergency was Hobson's, a tailoring and military supply company on Lexington Street. I had a letter of introduction to Miss Miller who, I was told, could perform miracles.

Miss Miller was well known to Canadians and many knew her personally. I went into Hobson's and climbed the stairs to her departent. There were a number of officers there, many of them American, examining the mass of material in the glass show cases. A nearby office door was half open; I knocked and went in. A lady of about 45, smallish and very wide awake looked up from her desk. I gave her the letter of introduction which she read. " So Colonel Kitching is it?" She accented the colonel as she could see I was still a major.

"Now, dear, what will you want?"

I showed her my pile of jackets that needed alterations.

"Edmontons, oh, yes, I like the boys that have been here from that regiment. Now just wait a moment and I'll see what I've got and how soon things can be made that I haven't got"! She went off leaving me to read the interesting testimonials and letters that were framed on the walls. Letters from Kings, Princes, Generals—all most grateful to Miss Miller for her help.

She returned after about five minutes. She had enough to outfit one of my service dress jackets and one battle dress and she would do this now as I waited. The other uniforms would be ready the next morning; she had ordered the bits and pieces from Birmingham and they would be on the train that afternoon and she should have everything ready for me the next day for sure.

She pressed a bell, a girl came in and removed my pile of clothing and when she had gone Miss Miller opened a small cupboard and took out a decanter of sherry and two glasses. "Now, have a glass of sherry and tell me about yourself." We sat and talked for a short while, then came a knock at the door. "Excuse me, Miss Miller," said a girl trembling with excitement, "But Clark Gable would like to see you."

"All right, dear, don't get excited, just ask him to wait a moment. I'm talking with Colonel Kitching."

What a remarkable lady Miss Miller was and evermore will be for me and many thousands of other Canadians.

She introduced me to Clark Gable who was looking for some U.S. Air Force insignia. In the thirty seconds of our meeting he seemed like a very normal person and was fascinated at the wide variety of militaria in Miss Miller's establishment. "I've got all countries on our side, dear, but no German or Japanese, of course, though I'm keeping some Italian because they'll be on our side soon!"

Miss Miller lived up to her word and my uniforms were all complete on the following day. I was now one of the "49th Battalion" then known as "The Edmonton Regiment."

Canadian National Exposition   Toronto, 1963

11

My First Command

On my way down to the regiment which was stationed in Shoreham, Sussex, I called in to see General Pearkes who had some good advice for me about the regiment. He was very familiar with its record in the First War and had maintained close touch with it in the 1930's. In fact, I think it was his recommendations of 1938 and 1939 that persuaded National Defence Headquarters to choose the Edmontons for inclusion in the mobilization plans for the division.

From 1st Division HQ, I drove to the headquarters of 2nd Infantry Brigade, the brigade in which the Edmonton's were grouped. There I saw Brig. Chris Vokes who had been with George Pearkes at 1st Division Headquarters when I had first reported there early in 1941. He wished me luck and introduced me to Major Jim Jefferson, the second-in-command of the Edmontons, who had come to brigade to escort me to the Regiment in Shoreham.

I was particularly interested to meet Jefferson because he had been one of the officers who Montgomery felt was "too slow." We had a pleasant drive to Shoreham where I met the Adjutant, Captain Fred Reesor and the Regimental Sergeant-Major, Alan Sachse.

When Harry Crerar told me that I was going to command the Edmontons I immediately tried to recall the do's and don'ts of my early years in the Glosters when the qualities, or lack of them, of the commanding officers under whom I served had had such varying impacts on the regiment. Based on my experience I wrote down a number of things that I must do. The salient points were:

1. I had the responsibility for training all officers just as they had the responsibility for training their men.
2. All officers should be trained to take on the responsibilities of two levels above them, i.e., a platoon commander should be able to be second-in-command of a company and also command it. Company commanders should be able to be second-in-command of a battalion and also command it.
3. We must expect heavy casualties among our officers and NCOs once we are in action, therefore we must train replacements now; ensure a steady flow of young officers by encouraging the men to go to officer training units.
4. Once satisifed that an officer knows his job—decentralize and give him has head—it's his best way of learning.
5. Check all faults as they occur—don't let anyone think they can get away with anything.

Shortly after arriving in Shoreham we were told that we would be moving to Eastbourne, a city about 26 miles to the east and also on the coast. We were to march so I decided we would do it in two days, covering 20 miles on the first—with only six miles for the second day which would allow the men almost a full day to settle into their new billets.

We started at about 6 o'clock one morning in order to avoid upsetting traffic in Brighton through which we passed at about 8:00 a.m. I marched an hour with each company in turn which gave me a chance to get the feelings of some of the officers and senior NCOs.

We soon settled down in Eastbourne and I think that the men enjoyed their stay there as much as any of their previous billets. Houses had been taken over for the duration of the war, some took 15 men, others took 30. A small park with a football field became our parade ground and a nearby school playing area was our rendezvous for early morning Physical Training. All ranks attended.

We maintained patrols on the beaches supporting the Home Guard. We mounted anti-aircraft sentries armed with Bren guns to counter the terror tactics of German fighters and light bombers which would sweep in from the sea at low altitude, drop their bombs or spray the streets with machine-gun fire before heading out to sea again. We had several such raids, one only two nights after arriving in the city. The regiment was up all night dealing with the fires and clearing the streets. We received some very nice letters from the Mayor and people of the town; there was no doubt that the Canadian soldier was greatly appreciated for his initiative and ability to work far harder than most.

On 16th September there was a night attack which caused heavy damage and casualties. Our men were again thanked for their excellent work, particularly the stretcher-bearers and medical officer. The day after that raid I had a message that General Crerar would be visiting us on the following day. I remembered his admonition to change my English accent "because no one will understand you." I decided to play a joke on him.

My Regimental Sergeant-Major, Alan Sachse, had been born in China like me; he had also been to school in England and in fact had an accent that was as bad as mine. I told him about Crerar's advice to me and asked him to play ball by being very very English when introduced to Crerar. The General arrived the next morning and I went to meet him accompanied by Reesor and Sachse. Crerar was in a very jovial mood and asked if my accent was any better. I said I thought so but I wanted him to meet our R.S.M.

Alan Sachse advanced, gave a salute that would have done credit to the Guards, held out his hand and said in the heaviest English accent he could muster, "How do you do, Sir." Crerar looked at him pop-eyed and blurted out, "Good God, Sergeant Major, you've caught Kitching's disease!"

I showed Harry Crerar round the town and the damage that had been done by successive raiders. He met the Mayor who also thanked him for all the help being given by Canadian soldiers. He departed happily that afternoon saying he was pleased with everything he had seen.

He had not raised the question of the age or ability of the majors in the regiment so I brought the subject up by telling him that to take two or three majors away at this stage would create a real problem. One major had been with the regiment for twenty years, he was a sort of father to everyone in his company. He knew the men, their parents and had in fact taught school to most of them. I was sure he would lead them well in their first action and would be a good example. Once he had been in action we could replace him. This applied to two other majors as well, both of whom had been on Montgomery's doubtful list. Each one was a father figure to many of their men. I told him we had a number of good captains who could take over when the time came. He didn't disagree with my reasoning but said, "It's your problem—I hope you are right."

To command an infantry battalion must surely be the most rewarding command of any in the Army. It is the last time in the chain of command that you actually command men whose allegiance is to you because in our system the regiment or battalion is the cell on which brigades, divisions and corps are based. In the Army, loyalty is something that cannot be stretched too far. I do not think you can ask anyone to be "loyal" to a corps, division or a brigade. They may say they are proud to be a part of one or the other, as most regiments were, but there is a difference between that form of pride and the true dedication that 99% of men feel for their regiment. It is something tangible and personal, and a part of them. That is the regimental system that we inherited from the British Army and which has been the basis of our strength in the Canadian Army.

Of all the battalions in the Canadian Army in 1942, I do not think there was one that had a better type of soldier than the Edmonton Regiment. I have always felt that regiments with a high proportion of countrymen, as opposed to city folk, have greater staying power. They may not be quite as 'shiny' as the city regiment but they wear well. The Edmontons had inherited the traditions of the 49th Battalion of the First War which for initiative and downright courage had few equals.

The 49th had been a 'family' and this tradiition had been passed on to the new battalion. There was close continuity between the Militia Regiment of the 1930's and the regiment that was mobilized in 1939—the family feeling was still retained. It was a source of strength.

Countrymen think slowly because they normally have time to think—crops grow slowly, cattle fatten slowly and this becomes the pattern of their lives. But that does not mean they cannot think quickly because when interested, they can size up a situation and make as sound a decision as anyone else.

We had a lot of countrymen in the Edmontons, from farms, small towns and villages. Among them were many of Ukrainian and Polish descent. Some of the officers were teachers from rural communities. These men were a great source of strength.

We also had a fair quota of city folk, many officers were lawyers and government employees. Colonel Stillman, who commanded the regiment in 1939 and had taken it to England, may not have been a great tactician but he paid a great deal of attention to detail in the spheres of military life with which he was familiar. He was also a bit of an actor which is not a bad thing in a commander, so he could use emotion to encourage the family spirit and regimental pride.

Ernie Wilson, who succeeded Bill Stillman, was a wellknown Edmonton lawyer. He continued to build up the regiment, sent parties to the Guards for special training in drill and others to Battle Schools so that they could pass on the new tactics to others in the regiment. Much had been done in two years. A great deal of knowledge had been pumped into the regiment. What it needed now was someone who had enough experience of the Army to put the knowledge gained to good purpose and to steer it in the right direction . I was the lucky man chosen to do this.

To stimulate the officers in their tactical thinking I ran a number of T.E.W.T.'s (tactical exercises without troops). For these I would gather all the officers together in our Mess. We would study a particular type of battle at each meeting. On one occasion we discussed 'mountain warfare' and for this I had a retired Indian Army Colonel as the lecturer. He had taken part in a number of operations on the North West Frontier. After his lecture we broke up into syndicates to solve problems on a cloth model of mountainous country made up for us by the Pioneers of the battalion.

The Pioneers also produced an excellent 'town' model on which we discussed the principles of the attack into a built up area. Ralph Hayter of our Pioneers could do or fix anything.

On another occasion two or three officers put on a short playlet to bring out the differences in new tactics and old. In these and other ways we got the officers thinking about a variety of problems that might arise in action and would require quick solutions.

To make all officers and men appreciate the responsibilities they would have to assume when casualties in action mounted, I turned the battalion into a brigade. Each of the company commanders because battalion commanders, each platoon commander became a company commander and so on down to the newest buck private who had to command a section. These 'brigade' exercises were carried out in the surrounding countryside.

We also sent sections of ten men into the countryside with four or five days rations and told them to enjoy themselves but to act like soldiers. These forays of small groups were greatly enjoyed and of course it enabled the section commander, who would be a corporal, to practice the art of command.

One of the things I noted soon after joining the regiment was the number of NCO's and men who were officer material but who, for a variety of reasons, had given little thought to trying for a commission. Most of them preferred to remain with their 'buddies'; they had joined up together and could not see why they should not stay together. I decided that I would get all the warrant officers and NCO's together and explain just why many of them should become officers.

When they were all assembled I said that I was sure they would normally like to be commanded by Edmonton Regiment officers, someone who had the same spirit they had and who was equally proud of wearing our flashes. I went on to remind them that the average 'life' of a lieutenant in command of a platoon was about ten days. I assured them that this did not necessarily mean he would be killed or wounded by then; he might be promoted, attached to brigade as a liaison officer, sent off on a course, but whatever the reason he would have to be replaced. Based on the expected 'life' we would need about five new junior officers each month or 60 a year.

I told them that we had about eight in the reinforcement stream, enough for two months. After that we might get the cast-offs from other regiments, possibly a flock of subalterns from the Royal Canadian Regiment.

That was enough. In the next few days we had applications from a number of NCO's, many of whom had distinguished records in action with the regiment and in peace in the Canadian Army.

We played as hard as we worked and thoroughly enjoyed ourselves. There were a number of attractive young ladies in Eastbourne and one of them who had us rocking on our heels used to tint a lock of her blondish hair with the blue-grey of the Edmonton flashes. All went well for a while but eventually we noted with regret that the dye had changed colour. It was now red as she had fallen in love with someone in Princess Patricia's Canadian Light Infantry who were stationed nearby.

Relations with the people of the town were very cordial—we helped raise money for a local police fund by putting on 'all in' wrestling matches. People of Eastbourne had not seen 'grunt and groan' artists at work before and were horrified at first to see the terrible things they did to each other. Our wrestlers were mostly in our stretcher bearer section and had been professional wrestlers before the war. Steve Jossul, Tex Wilkins and Goofy McMasters are three names that come to mind amongst others. When they went into action in Sicily and Italy that Happy band of stretcher bearers were a courageous team and saved many lives.

Brigadier Chris Vokes' Brigade Headquarters was in Willingdon only a couple of miles north of Eastbourne and I think that many brigadiers would have been tempted, with such a short distance in between, to visit the regiment more often than they normally should. Chris Vokes, however, was extremely good in this regard. We would submit our training programme to him well ahead—he, in turn, would let us know which parts were of special interest to him. He rarely interfered unless there was good reason for it so he was always a welcome guest.

General Pearkes left command of the 1st Canadian Division in late August 1942. During his two years of command he had transformed an unprofessional division into one that had few equals in Britain. He was tireless in visiting regiments to judge their progress and encourage them and to blast them when necessary. Unfortunately on leaving the division he was only given a few days notice before returning to Canada and it was not possible for him to visit us to say goodbye. We were hurt at the time without knowing any of the circumstances.

During my time with the regiment I am sure we must have been on training exercises at least four days out of ten. Some were laid on by division, some by brigade but, for the most part, they were our own as we rehearsed and practiced manoeuvres to perfect our tactical deployments. Physically we were in superb shape and could march with full loads across country at a pacc not too far from that of a marathon runner. I recall one exercise in particular. We were near a small village called Boreham, about ten miles as the crow flies from our billets in Eastbourne. According to the exercise we had landed on the coast with as much ammunition of all kinds as we could carry. We had completed that part of the exercise overnight, having marched in from the beaches. Brigadier Vokes expressed his satisfaction with the way things had gone and at about 10:00 a.m. said we could go home.

I got the Company Commanders together and told them that we would return through the Pevensey marshes and I wanted everyone in billets within two hours. We had about nine miles to go, the marshes were fields with ditches filled with water between each one. Some of them were four or five feet wide. We had our three-inch mortars with us and the Mortar Platoon had carried as many mortar bombs as possible. Each soldier in the battalion was carrying 70 rounds of live ammunition plus his rifle and full equipment. We distributed the mortar bombs, each weighing ten pounds, amongst the companies. Since the officers were not armed with rifles many of them carried three bombs each.

Every man in the battalion completed the march in under two hours. We were sopping wet from the ditches and had had hardly any sleep the night before. If anyone got a little wearly someone else would carry his rifle for a while. We all took a hand in carrying the 30-pound frames of mortar bombs. After it was over we figured that we had all averaged 70 pounds of dead weight which, of course, included our normal equipment with full pack. But the march was a great test of endurance and I was very proud of what we had done. I phone Chris Vokes shortly after the last man was in to boast about our achievement; his reply was that he would be down to have a drink with us that evening to congratulate us. He did, and stayed for dinner. It was a great night.

One day Chris Vokes asked me to go to his headquarters to sample some gin that he had made. As far as I was concerned this was rather like asking me to drink with the Borgias; however, Chris was very persuasive and, anyway, he was my boss. On arrival at his mess I was shown two or three glass flagons containing a colourless liquid in which was floating a mass of green foliage which looked for all the world like seaweed. Chris assured me that the green stuff was juniper cut from a bush in the garden of the Mess. He had acquired two gallons of alcohol and had immersed the juniper for four weeks in it; that should be long enough to give it flavour. Where had he got the alcohol from? He was sure it came from the hospital. But one of the junior members of his staff was certain it came from the local undertaker.

With great ceremony the cork was withdrawn from one of the bottles which was then passed to Chris Vokes. He sniffed the open bottle, paused and taking in a deep breath, he sniffed again.

"Corporal," he called to the Mess steward who was standing in the doorway, "bring me a scotch and soda and ask Colonel Kitching what he would like—thank you."

Thhat was the end of our 'gin' tasting.

Chris Vokes started a Brigade Battle Drill School close to Eastbourne in a small village called Jevington. To run the school he selected Major Budge Bell-Irving* of the Seaforths and Lieutenant Jim Stone from the Edmontons. They were two completely different people but they had a common aim and the school was first class.

I was not always a great believer in 'Battle Drill' as taught at some of the schools. There was often too much shouting and yelling and not enough thinking. In fact, I did not agree with battle drill at all at one time. To me it was a short cut designed to make people do things automatically because it was thought that there was not time to teach the normal platoon and section tactics. Unfortunately, the early 'battle drill' schools went overboard in trying to produce realism. In one of them the instructors used to get a few quarts of blood from the local slaughter house and splash it around on their students as they slipped and slithered under barbed wire and bullets and through drainage ditches. To me that was nonsense. Our school at Jevington was tough but it did encourage the students to think.

On the 14th of December, the Brigade Commander, Chris Vokes, phoned to say that I was to take over the appointment immediately of G.S.O. I at Divisional Headquarters. I naturally was disappointed; it seemed that I had only been with the regiment for a matter of weeks and I was thoroughly enjoying it. Time had gone past so quickly—it

---

* Brigadier-General the Hon. Henry Bell-Irving, Lieutant-Governor of British Columbia, 1978-83.

had been four and one half months since I had first worn the Edmonton Regiment badges and flashes and yet it seemed like yesterday. I was proud to continue wearing them. I handed over to Major Jim Jefferson.

Chris Vokes commiserated with me when I called on him on my way through to Divisional Headquarters. He had been the G.S.O. I a year before under General Pearkes. I reported to the new Divisional Commander, General Salmon, that afternoon.

The headquarters of the 1st Canadian Division was in one of the many country houses that dotted the countryside in southeast England. Heathfield House, 12 miles north of Eastbourne, was located just south of the small country town from which it took its name. Built entirely of grey stone it had an air of permanency about it, furthermore it had a form of central heating that made it more homelike than some of the vast houses that Canadian headquarters had moved into elsewhere.

It was not a vast mansion but the rooms inside were large and well proportioned. General Salmon and his senior staff did not live in the building, they were in a much smaller house about half a mile away where the General maintained his 'A' Mess. However, all our offices were in Heathfield House.

It was early afternoon when I reported to General Salmon in his office. I had only been notified that morning of my change in jobs; things moved fast and I had not even had time to say goodbye to the officers of the regiment although I was able to do this a few evenings later. General Salmon seemed glad to see me. His office was pleasantly furnished, he even had a carpet. However he soon got down to business. I was to take over the job of GSO I from Lt.-Col. Harry Foster immediately. Foster was already packed. I could move into his room in 'A' Mess that evening but now I was to go and take over the job so that Foster could get away. One thing I was to make sure of—that Foster had amended the "Plans to Defeat Ivasion" (PDI) and brought them up-to-date.

I had got to know Harry Foster fairly well since meeting him back in 1939 in Aldershot. At that time both he and Harry Salmon were majors. Foster had gone on to command and organize the new reconnaissance regiment of the 1st Canadian Division, the Princess Louise Dragoon Guards, a militia regiment from Ottawa. He had done an excellent job and had created an agressive and hard-hitting unit. He must have felt as disappointed as I was to have to leave command and become a Staff officer. He had become GSO I when General Pearkes was commanding the division, he was quite a different boss to General Salmon who had taken over from Pearkes in September. Foster was a cavalryman brought up on horses. To him the quickest way between two points was across country. Salmon was an infantryman, an excellent trainer but a lover of detail, a man who would never go across country without careful examination to ensure that it was the best way.

From the moment I stepped into Harry Foster's office—soon to be mine—I realized that he and General Salmon did not get on too well together.

The office was an enormous room fully 40 feet in length and 20 in width. It was beautifully panelled in dark oak and the glow from two ceiling chandeliers highlighted the deep red of an oriental carpet which covered the floor. Four large windows were doing their best to let in the light of that gloomy wet December day.

Foster's desk was at the end of the room. As soon as I entered he stood up and said:

"Jesus, George, am I glad to see you—come on in and take over this God-damned coffin."

As he mentioned the word 'coffin' he pointed to the panelling. He obviously did not appreciate the texture of the wood! I asked him if there were any special documents or papers that I should take over from him. What about the P.D.I.? Was it fully amended?

He roared with laughter and said he was sure the General would mention them. "Of course, the amendments are all in the book George, they're all there, don't worry."

With that, Harry put on his black beret and walked over to where I was standing.

"We don't need any hand over, you have a good staff here, so I'll just wish you luck, George, you'll need it."

That was the official 'hand over' of the appointment. Harry Foster drove away and a few months later was appointed to command 7th Canadian Brigade which he led so well in the invasion of Normandy on 6th June 1944.

When I opened the official book "Plans to Defeat Invasion" I found a large pile of amendments lying loose inside the front cover. As Harry

Foster had said, they were all there, but he hadn't bothered to stick them onto the pages they were to amend!'' I felt that that was a measure of his respect for Salmon's insistence on detail.

The Author, Field Marshal Montgomery
Kingston, Ontario, 1953

12

Sicily -
The Planning And The Battle

By the end of 1942 the 1st Canadian Division had reached a very high standard. Major-General Salmon, its new Commander, continued the same pattern of intensive training which had been put into practice by Major-General Pearkes. Although I would have preferred to remain with the Edmonton Regiment, I felt that if I had to go to a staff job I was lucky to be appointed GSO I of the 1st Canadian Division.

As General Staff Officer 1st Grade, or GSO I, I was responsible to the General for all operational matters including Intelligence and training. Although other officers at the headquarters were responsible directly to the General for such combat arms as Artillery, Engineers and Signals, and Administrative matters were handled by the Assistant Adjutant and Quarter Master General or AA&QMG, it was generally accepted that the GSO I was the coordinator for most activities and this proved the case when we went into action in Sicily and Italy.

I was lucky enough to have Dick Danby as my GSO II. We had been together at the headquarters of the 1st Division in 1941 with General George Pearkes and later at the Staff College. Dick had great capacity for work and was meticulous in organizing the mass of detail involved when issuing written orders to subordinate formations.

Below the GSO I and GSO II were a number of GSO III's handling the details of Operations, Intelligence and Training. In addition, we had a liaison officer attached to us from each brigade or formation under our command. Their job was to keep their brigade commanders informed of what we were doing or planning at Divisional Head-quarters, and to carry special messages from our General to their com-manders. To do their job effectively they had to be taken into the con-fidence of the General and the GSO I.

The AA and QMG was my old friend, Willis Moogk, now a Lieutenant-Colonel like me. After a period commanding the Royal Winnipeg Rifles, Willis had been posted to the job of AA and QMG. The Commander of the Engineers in the Division was Lt.-Col. Geoffrey Walsh—a man whom I was to get to know well in the years ahead. He was a Regular officer.

Shortly after I arrived at the Headquarters, Lt.-Col. Bruce Matthews was promoted to Brigadier to take over as Commander of Artillery. Bruce was one of many businessmen who had joined the Militia as part-time soldiers and who obtained rapid promotion once we were on active service. They were an excellent back-up for the very small numbers of Regular full-time officers serving in the Canadian Army at the outbreak of war.

The most important man at the Headquarters was, of course, the General himself. Major-General Harry Salmon was one of the most unusual men I have ever served under and I do not think many people, even his close friends, really knew the inner workings of his mind.

He was a Regular officer of the Royal Canadian Regiment, had won a Military Cross for gallantry in the First World War and was general-ly recognized as being one of the best trainers of soldiers in any Army. He was tall, had a good physique and a clipped moustache on a square and rugged face. He had attented the Staff College at Camberley before the war and was a student of military affiars. He was a stickler for detail, which sometimes clouded my opinion of him, but he taught me a great deal during the five months that I served under him.

He was very demanding and I recall how, in the early months of our working together, he would call me into his bedroom-cum-office in the small 'A' Mess building at all hours of the night to discuss some pro-blem which he felt needed a solution before dawn. He would do this for five nights of each week and then with a friendly grin tell me that he was going to take the weekend off but would like me to produce for him on his return a summary of the points that he and I had discussed the previous week!

When I first arrived at Divisional Headquarters the staff were in the throes of completing plans for each brigade in turn to entrain for a week of intensive combined operations in the Clyde area of Scotland. "Combined Operations" was the name given to the whole spectrum of assault landings by sea on a hostile shore. It included the planning, assault, naval and air fire support and, after the landing, the problems of resupply across the beaches.

At this period the British Staff responsible for combined operations had reached a standard far above that of our Allies. For one thing, the British had been studying detailed operations since shortly after Dunkirk with a staff that had been specially assembled and told to do nothing but plan for a return across the Channel.

It was obvious, as we became familiar with the thinking of these planners, that they were deterimined to get the best value out of every soldier, gun, vehicle, aircraft and ship taking part. There was very little 'fat' but once the commander had made up his Plan they did everything possible to ensure its success.

General Salmon, Dick Danby and I together with a number of staff officers went north to largs—a small, lovely town facing west to the Firth of Clyde. It had become a centre for Combined Operations in conjunction with the even lovelier town of Troon about 20 miles south.

The units of each brigade were given instructions in the use of each type of landing craft and practiced loading and unloading under a variety of conditions. Once the units were familiar with the problems of scrambling from the assault craft as they beached, the complete brigade would take part in an assault landing on Arran, Rothesay or on the shores of Loch Fyne. It was a different type of training and I think most of the men enjoyed it although Scotland in December and early January is not the warmest of places.

However, in spite of it, we managed to enjoy ourselves when we could escape. Dick Danby and I got away on New Year's Eve when we were in Scotland where the people celebrate Hogmanay more enthusiastically than Christmas. We had had a small party in our Mess at Troon so perhaps it was a bit late when Dick and I took off looking for

Scottish revellers. We were walking—it was a pleasant night—we had a certain amount of anti-freeze inside us to beat off the cold—all was well with the world—but we could not find a soul on the streets nor could we hear the welcoming sound of a party. Dick was a Seaforth Highlander but after an hour or so of walking even he was beginning to waver in his loyalty to Robert the Bruce, Bonnie Prince Charlie and Robert Burns. We sang all the Harry Lauder songs we could remember—we made noises like bagpipes but we were getting nowhere when we heard the welcome sound of female laughter and the tinkling of glasses. We hurried our pace and turned into the driveway of a house. This was the place—and although we couldn't see into the windows because of the black-out, we could tell there was a good party going on. Female chatter, tinkling glasses and the sound of plates being distributed—we knocked on the door—an attractive girl in uniform opened it.

"May we join the party," we asked in unison.

A squeal of delight greeted our enquiry. In no time at all Dick and I were dragged into the kitchen were we joined five other girls and spent the next hour helping them to wash to dishes left by their officers who had been celebrating Hogmanay in true Scottish fashion! Fortunately there was still a little of "Scotland's Glory" left in the bar so we were able to renew our strength before staggering back to our own quarters in the early dawn.

Back in England during February and March 1943, we took part in a number of interesting exercises. However, we did not take part in the large scale exercise "Spartan" in which General McNaughton commanded an Army of three Corps amounting to perhaps 200,000 men. This was the last large-scale exercise in Britain—the island and its training areas were beginning to fill up with divisions from the U.S. Army and training space became difficult to find. Future exercises were limited to Divisional level or were organized to practice staffs at all levels but without any troops taking part.

Early in April, General Crerar, who was commanding 1st Canadian Corps, laid on an exercise designed to test the commanders and staffs of our Headquarters and the commanders and staff of our three infantry brigades. On these exercises we would move out of our 'static' headquarters buildings and operate 'in the field' just as we would in action.

All went well. General Crerar was satisfied with our operational procedures and ability to handle the problems thrown at us. However, one evening at about six o'clock, he visited the headquarters again and spent some time in our operations tent when I happened to be elsewhere with General Salmon. When I returned to the operations tent a few minutes later, I found a somewhat irate General Crerar who called me over to him.

"Kitching," he said, "I don't know how much liquor your young staff officers in the operations tent have been consuming but I found it very difficult to discuss anything with them—their minds are not on the job. You had better get in there and straighten them out. Report to me later."

The staff officers he referred to were my three GSO III's—all from the Royal Canadian Regiment. They were Ted Price, Peter Bingham and "Klink" Klenavic. The two that Harry Crerar had found so difficult were Price and Bingham. When I entered the tent they were still gazing happily and vacantly into space, a very unusual posture for both of them. "What on earth is the matter with you two," I asked, "you have the Corps Commander in a mood to put you both in irons."

They both broke into happy smiles from ear to ear. "There's nothing the matter really," said Peter Bingham, "it's just that I received a letter half an hour ago that told me I have been left 80,000 pounds sterling by an aunt who has just died—I'm just floating and can hardly believe my luck."

"And I," broke in Ted Price still grinning from ear to ear, "have just had a telegram telling me that Mary gave birth to twins and that she and the twins are well."

It was great news for both of them and I was only too happy to tell General Crerar the cause of their happiness in which alcohol had played no part. He, in fact, congratulated them later that evening.

In England church bells had been silenced, because of wartime restrictions, since 1940. Because of this many celebrations, including Saint George's Day, passed unnoticed but I shall always remember St. George's Day, April 23, 1943. That evening General Salmon had a call from Brigadier Charles Foulkes requesting him to report to General McNaughton at 8:30 a.m. the next day and to bring me with

with him. We were told to be prepared to spend the entire day at Army Headquarters and we speculated at the time why General McNaughton needed to see us. We knew there had been secret discussions with the War Office about the possibility of Canadians taking part in an operation in Northern Norway but our understanding was that those plans had been shelved. Perhaps our headquarters was going to be used as a Planning Organization for the invasion of France, an operation that was bound to come in the months ahead. We thought of a variety of possibilities but we never hit the right one!

When we reached Army Headquarters the next morning we checked first into Charles Foulkes' room. Charles had taken over as Brigadier, General Staff a short time before from Guy Simonds who, after spending two weeks with the 8th Army in North Africa as an observer, had returned to command our 2nd Infantry Division.

Charles Foulkes did not waste any time with us as he indicated that General McNaughton was waiting impatiently even though we were a few minutes early; he had time, however, to warn us that we were going into an operation very shortly.

General McNaughton was poring over maps and papers when we entered his office. He told us that we were going to be a part of 8th Army under General Montgomery and part of the assault force in the invasion of Sicily. We were to accompany him to the War Office where we would have a full briefing. He was to spend an hour or so with the Chief of the Imperial General Staff, General Sir Alan Brooke, but the briefing would continue in his absence as Charles Foulkes would be with us. He warned us not to disclose the reason for our visit to anyone, no matter how senior, as he was still discussing the matter with the Cabinet in Ottawa. He would be going over the outline plan with Alan Brooke to ensure that our assault role was within our capabilities. He did not want another Dieppe.

After a few minutes we went downstairs and climbed into General McNaughton's large Canadian-built staff car. McNaughton and Salmon sat in the back, Charles Foulkes and I sat in the jump seats. As we left the Headquarters, General McNaughton pressed the button that raised a heavy sheet of glass between us and the driver. "Now we can talk," he said.

It was obvious that the Army Commander must have spent a large part of the previous night reading all he could about Sicily, its people, climate, topography and economy. He repeated to us all he had learned that was important. The independent nature of the people could work to our advantage if we guaranteed them freedom from Fascist domination in exchange for their cooperation. We should bear in mind also that although a large part of the population in the interior worked many hours each day on farms, they always returned to the neighbouring towns at night. They had done this for centuries as a means of gaining protection. We should be careful, therefore, about the bombing of these towns by night unless it was tactically essential.

Thse and other points were discussed as we drove into London. To me, it was particularly interesting to note the human side of the Army Commander because generally he appeared to be much more interested in the mechanical side of a problem.

On arrival at the War Office we were ushered into a room that was more like the study of a large house than an office. We were introduced to a number of senior British officers many of whom left the room with General McNaughton for his meeting with the C.I.G.S.

Salmon, Foulkes and I remained and had an excellent briefing on the known enemy forces in Sicily, and on the communication and road systems of the island.

On McNaughton's return we were told to get together a number of our senior commanders and staff officers, brief them on the outline of present planning, swear them to secrecy and then move with them into Norfolk House on St. James Square where we would take over from the commanders and staffs of 3rd British Division.

Two further points were made by General McNaughton. First, he would ensure that the Canadian formation that took part in the Sicily operation was the best equipped one ever to leave the United Kingdom. He had the assurance of the C.I.G.S. on that point. We would get new Sherman tanks to replace the present Rams, new 6 pounder anti-tank guns to replace our 2 pounders, new trucks from Canada and a large number of the new amphibious DUKWS that had been developed and used by the American forces in the Pacific. The second point he made was of a more personal nature. In view of the need for urgency and for great accuracy in our planning, he told me that if there were any members of our staffs who, in my opinion, could not stand up to the strain, they must be replaced immediately. We had carte-blanche and could take anyone we wanted to obtain maximum efficiency.

I had lost Dick Danby during March as he had gone off to another job. His replacement was an able Major from the Maritimes and I think that had he and I been able to work together for four or five months he would have been capable of handling the Sicily planning. However, I had to get Dick Danby back, we had worked together so often, particularly on the Combined Operations planning of the previous months. He returned the next day. Other changes were made at various levels, the most vital of which was a replacement for Lt.-Col. Willis Moogk who was having a recurrence of his stomach disorders

There were a number of cover plans made to explain our absence from Divisional Headquarters in Sussex. It was obvious that we must be planning something, somewhere, so there was no point in hiding that side of our activities but the details of our real intentions were highly secret and, from a Canadian point of view, were only known to the comparatively small group of Commanders and Staff Officers assembled at Norfolk House, perhaps fifty of us all told. A list was maintained of all personnel who had been briefed, together with the date and circumstance of the briefing. I recall two incidents connected with "security."

Harry Salmon used to check details of our methods and plans in a way that used to infuriate me. He did not appear to trust us. I know that when he was commanding the Hastings and Prince Edward Regiment he would inspect the barrack rooms of each Company looking for even the smallest item that was out of place and would go on looking until he found something wrong. The regiment quickly reacted to that type of detailed search and carefully made an obvious error in the layout of some soldier's kit so that Harry Salmon would have the satisfaction of finding the fault after which he would go happily on his way.

On one occasion, shortly after we had moved into Norfolk House, Salmon asked me if I had checked the security arrangements at the front desk to ensure that only authorized personnel were allowed to enter. I told him I had checked it and that the guards knew their business. About ten minutes later General Ramsden, who commanded 3rd British Division, which we were replacing for the Sicily Operations, came in to check that we were getting all we needed from his staff. Harry Salmon immediately asked him if he had had to show his "pass" on entering our area of the building. "No," replied Ramsden somewhat mystified by the question. Salmon immediately turned to me and somewhat peevishly said "George, you told me ten minutes ago that no one could get in here without their pass being shown on entry." Before I could reply General Ramsden came to my aid. He turned quickly towards my General and said, "Salmon, don't get angry with Kitching. He is quite right, because you may not have noticed that my 'Pass' hangs below the left hand pocket of my battle dress. When you asked me if I had had to show it I couldn't understand the purpose of your question and since I didn't have to 'show' it, I gave you the answer 'no.' But the security guards are first class and you need have no worry about that, I can assure you." I was grateful for Ramsden's intervention but a little ashamed that Salmon seemed to have so little confidence in me.

Another security incident involved a senior Security Officer of the British Army. He dropped in to see me soon after we had settled into Norfolk House to ask if I had had a visit from Major-General Guy Turner who had been on General McNaughton's staff since 1939, and who was now McNaughton's official link with "COSSAC."The reason why he asked about Guy Turner, the senior security officer explained, was that he was being unduly inquisitive about the purpose of our planning and was beginning to upset a number of senior officers on the COSSAC staff by trying to get from them the destination of our assault. General McNaughton, in his original briefing of Salmon and me, had stressed that we were not to give any information at all to senior officers of his headquarters other than Charles Foulkes and Dan Spry. Yet here was a Canadian general, trying to gain information to which he was not entitled. "I was asked to help by playing a trick on Turner." I was given a large map of Sardinia which I hung behind the curtains which normally hid the map of Sicily. In addition I was given a book on Sardinia which I was asked to leave in a prominent place on my desk. I ws also asked to position the curtains covering the map of Sardinia so that the letters 'SARD' were fairly obvious although the

---

*"COSSAC" (Chief of Staff to Supreme Allied Commander) was the code name for the staff planning the invasion of Normandy.

outline of the island would be hidden. With General Salmon's assistance, Guy Turner was invited to visit us the next morning. After a short time with Salmon, he came in to see me. I pretended not to notice the way he walked past the map which I had carefully exposed. He started past it a second time and then stood close to my desk so that he could read the title of the book, "Sardinia." I had, of course, hastily put the papers away that I had been working on so that to him it looked as if I had inadvertently left the book on the desk. After a few pleasantries he departed. It was 11:30 a.m. The security officer phoned me at about 2:30 that afternoon with the short message, "Kitching, it worked, well done and thank you." He never told me how it 'worked' but I felt that Guy Turner must have made some reference to Sardinia whilst meeting with his COSSAC contacts at lunch. Harry Salmn was amused but very shaken that Guy Turner, whom he had known for many years, could be so foolish.

The first four or five days in Norfolk House were hectic as our Brigade Staffs moved into London for their first briefing and were introduced to their opposite numbers of 3rd British Division. Unfortunately, the plan for the assault was still not settled at the highest levels so it was not possible to work on the detail of which particular beach we would assault or of our subsequent route. However, we were advised that we would probably be operating in the mountains and that in order to reduce the number of vehicles in such restricted areas, we would probably do most of our moves on foot. How right they were!

We were also told that since we could not be supplied by 8th Army once we were ashore, we had to bring everything we needed for a period of 42 days which meant that we would require 92 ships quite apart from our naval escort. These ships would be divided into various convoys, some fast and some slow, but all designed to arrive at the Sicilian beaches at prearranged times and dates to off-load the stores, ammunition and guns required to fight the tactical battle. We had to do some long-range guessing at that stage because the Army plan was not firmed up until about ten days after we moved into Norfolk House. But more about that later.

In London, we stayed at the Mayfair Hotel where I had a room next to General Salmon. We were advised that we were not to discuss the Sicily operation at all outside Norfolk House so it was not possible to talk 'shop' of that kind in our rooms. The result, from Harry Salmon's point of view, was quite dramatic. He became cheerful and lively and thoroughly enjoyed his meals in restaurants when we had time to get to them. He would stay up at night and have a drink with us even though we might have been working for 14 hours that day. He was a different man and I thoroughly enjoyed his company.

In order that General Salmon could meet with the Corps Commander under whom we were to fight in Sicily (General Sir Oliver Leese), arrangements were made for General Salmon and a number of officers to fly to Cairo. There they would go into the details of our planning.

Harry Salmon decided that I should remain to continue the planning and that he would take with him Colonel Wilson of the 3rd British Division who had been working on the plans for several weeks and who was familiar with the staff of General Leese's Corps. He would also take Lt.-Col. Chuck Finlay with him. Chuck had just taken over as AA-QMG of the Division from Willis Moogk and since he and Salmon had not met before it would give Harry Salmon a chance to get to know him. Admiral Mack, who was to command our convoys and who would be responsible for getting us to Sicily at the right time and place, would travel in the same plane and would take two officers of his staff with him. The plane would leave from Hendon Airport, south of London, early in the morning of 29 April and after gassing up at an airfield in Cornwall would head for Gibraltar.

Having made all these arrangements, Harry Salmon began to change his mind about who should go with him. He felt that our Chief Engineer, Lt.-Col. Geoff Walsh should go and perhaps I should go too. It was the British General Ramsden who persuaded him to take Wilson and not me and who reminded him that the aircraft he would be flying in would probably be a Hudson and that the fewer people he took the more petrol they could take on.

The day before the take-off, General Salmon had a long session with the Brigade Commanders of the Division, with Brigadier Bruce Matthews who commanded the artillery, Lt.-Col. Geoff Walsh, our Chief Engineer and the senior members of our Staff. he told us that as soon as he could get a firm plan from 8th Army in Cairo he would signal it to us, and that we were then to assume that the plan was final. He would stress the need for a final plan with Cairo because we would have to start loading the slower ships of our convoys in the middle of June, only six weeks away.

Our Brigade Commanders were all men whom I had got to know well in our three years in England. The 1st Brigade was commanded by Brigadier Howard Graham. He had served briefly in World War I, had maintained a continuing interest in the Militia between the wars when, as a lawyer, he went into local politics, becoming Mayor of Trenton. He was second-in-command of the Hastings and Prince Edward Regiment when it went over to England in 1939.

The 2nd Brigade was commanded by Brigadier Chris Vokes, a man who became almost a legend before the end of the war.

The 3rd Brigade was commanded by another Regular officer, Brigadier Howard Penhale. "Pen" was originally a 'Gunner' or artillery-man and had served in World War I.

The Commando Brigade which was to operate under our command was commanded by Brigadier Bob Laycock who later took over Combined Operations after Mountbatten went to India as Supreme Allied Comander. Bob had been in the Household Cavalry originally although his Commando Brigade was entirely made up of Royal Marines. Like Lord Lovat he believed that the success of a Commando raid depended very much on the detailed preparation for it. It was very interesting to discuss Dieppe with him during the early days in Sicily. He felt at the time that, quite apart from the cancellation of heavy bombing and airborne troops, he felt we put too many men into the assault. Perhaps fewer units, but more expert in assault landings, could have had greater success. Every man had got to know exactly what was required of him—he doubted if that had been the case with our 2nd Canadian Division.

After his meeting with his Commanders and Staff, I returned to the Mayfair Hotel with Harry Salmon. He was completely relaxed as he packed his bag and organized his personal papers. He didn't expect to be gone for more than a few days so we made arrangements with the hotel to store the uniforms he would not be taking with him.

It was about 7:00 p.m. when he had finished his packing and arranged his papers. He was in great form and in a happier mood than I had ever seen him before.

"George, let's go and have dinner at the Hungaria—just you and I.

Phone and book a table—they know me well there so book it in my name for 8:00 o'clock. That will give us time for a bath and change.''

After a tub and a change into service dress from our normal battle dress, we walked down to Piccadilly and turned left at the Ritz. I didn't know the Hungaria very well but Harry Salmon was greeted as an old friend. I was sure that he must have used it frequently on the weekends when he was in London and I was sweating away at the Divisional Headquarters.

Normally, Harry Salmon was fairly reserved but I had never seen him let his hair down in the way he did that night. He was full of fun, talked about his early years with the Royal Canadian Regiment and the personalities in the Army generally and towards midnight he told me that he was very happy that I was his G.S.O. I and that Dick Danby had returned. He apologized for doubting my word over the security of our building when I had been saved by General Ramsden. He was assured and positive and I was delighted to experience the change in the man.

We wandered back to the Mayfair and turned into bed at about two o'clock. When he said goodnight, Harry said he hadn't enjoyed himself so much for a long time, nor had I. Soon after seven o'clock we left for Hendon Airport where, after the usual civilities, General Salmon, Admiral Mack and their four staff officers climbed aboard the Hudson, a two-engined bomber converted to a transport role. We saluted and waved, wishing them luck and God's speed and the plane took off at about 9:00 a.m. I returned to the hotel with Geoff Walsh who had also gone to see the General off.

It must have been about 11:00 a.m. when I got to Norfolk House and had no sooner arrived in my office than I had a message to go and see Howard Graham in an adjoining room. On entering I noticed that the colour had gone from Howard's face. It was pale and drawn.

''George,'' he said, ''I'm sorry to tell you that Harry Salmon and all his party were killed when their Hudson crashed somewhere in Devon.'' He told me later that the colour drained from my face too. Certainly I could not bring myself to speak for about half a minute and when I did, Howard told me later, it was to ask some silly question like, ''And now what do we do?'' I should finish these memories of General Salmon with this added note. Whilst the senior members of our staff waited for news of Salmon's successor as Commander, Dick

Danby flew down to Devon to the Crash site to recover any papers or documents that might link the Canadian with the operations planned in the Mediterranean. Almost everything had been burned beyond recognition. However, a part of General Salmon's personal folder was recovered and the part that was, read ''Recommended for promotion to Brigadier: Lt.-Cols. Kitching and Walsh.''

I was glad I spent that last evening with Harry Salmon. I had seen him at his self-confident best. His recommendation meant a great deal to me.

General McNaughton did not waste any time in naming the replacement for Harry Salmon. Within a matter of hours General Guy Simonds, who had recently taken over command of our 2 Division, was at Norfolk House as our new commander. He reviewed our plans for our landing and was relieved that he would not have to make changes in the progress we had already made. He left for Cairo immediately, but in case of further accidents we were to follow in a separate aircraft.

Mr. Churchill had heard of the death of General Salmon and made available immediately the spare Liberator which normally accompanied him on his flights. In this four-engined converted bomber were to travel Brig. Chris Vokes, who was Deputy Commander of the Division, our Signals Chief at Division, Lt.-Col. Jake Eaman and myself. It was also decided by General McNaughton that Brig. Warwick Beament and Lt.-Col. Don Tow would travel with us and remain in North Africa to establish the various Canadian elements required to give us full administrative support at the General Headquarters of the Allied Armies in the Mediterranean. We left London by train early on the 30th of April for one of the big R.A.F. airfields on Salisbury Plain about 70 miles to the West, and were airborne in our Liberator that afternoon. At the airfield we were equipped with flotation clothing in case we came down in the ocean and parachutes in case we had to jump. All we felt we needed to guarantee us a safe arrival was to have the blessing of the Pope and the Archbishop of Canterbury!

I do not know what we expected when we were told at the airfield that the plane in which we would be flying was the spare for Mr. Churchill. Comfortable beds? Armchairs? A dining room with attractive WAAF's to serve us? We got a rude shock as we climbed into the main

bay of the converted bomber. It was completely open and the only furniture of any kind were about a dozen mattresses scattered around the
floor. We found that these were to be our beds for the next twenty-four
hours and our food would be haversack rations. It was a bit of a let-
down but we found the mattresses were comfortable and that there
were a number of clean pillows to enable us to prop up our heads to
read or to recline in the Roman fashion.

To be on the safe side the Captain took us on a wide swing into the
Atlantic before turning eastward for Gibraltar where we landed early
in the morning. The new runway which made Gibraltar so vital to the
success of Operation Torch had been partly built by Canadian
Engineers although at the time we knew little about their work.
General Eisenhower went so far as to say that ''without Gibraltar,
Torch would not have been possible'' but there was no indication that
Canadians had played such an important role during their two year stay
on the Rock.

The fighting in North Africa was rapidly coming to a close.
However, on the next leg of our journey we stayed well clear of
Algiers passing over the Atlas Mountains until we saw the Mediterranean again over the site of one of Montgomery's final battles in North
Africa—the Battle of Mareth, 20 March 1943. The pilot of our aircraft
was flying at about 10,000 feet and it was possible to see clearly the
German defensive positions along the Wadi Zigzaou (ZigZag to the
troops) and in Mareth itself. Burned out tanks and vehicles could be
identified and the tracks made by the New Zealanders as they moved
south and west to outflank the German positions. The weather continued clear as the pilot kept slightly south of the coast. We reached
Cairo at about 7:00 p.m. to be met by a number of staff officers from
30 Corps under who we were going to serve in Sicily. They drove our
party into Cairo and to the accommodation which they had arranged
for us at the famous Shepheard's Hotel, which had been taken over by
the British Army early in the war.

The next morning, the 2nd May, we were told that General Simonds
had landed safely in Gibraltar and was then going on to Algiers. He
was expected in Cairo on the 3rd. However, sand storms in
Tripolitania delayed his take off and he did not reach us until the evening of the 4th.

In the interim, Chris Vokes and I had been to 30 Corps Headquarters where the staff were anxious to hear about our state of training and our re-equipment programme. They realized that our tank crews would have to retrain on the Sherman Tank, our anti-tank gunners would have to retrain on the 6-pounder and 17-pounder guns and they wondered if we could do it within the few weeks available. We assured them that all would be well.

Fortunately for us the final plan for "Husky," the invasion of Sicily, was not approved at the highest levels in Algiers until the 4th, the day Guy Simonds arrived. This meant that things were not too hard and fast when we heard the Corps plan at a meeting with General Oliver Leese the next morning. His staff had built an excellent model of the south eastern corner of Sicily which was of great value to General Simonds as he studied the problem of how to deploy the Division so that it could complete the tasks given to it, not only on the beaches but also to secure its ultimate objectives deep inland.

Chris Vokes and I remained with him during these hours at 30 Corps Headquarters. We returned to Shepherd's Hotel where in his room Guy Simonds studied our operational maps. After writing out his 'Intention' he told me to start writing as he dictated his plan.

In his discussions with General Leese, Guy Simonds was concerned about his open left flank. Briefly the overall Allied plan was to land the 8th Army in the south east corner of the island whilst the 7th U.S. Army landed further west with a gap of about 20 miles between the armies. Since our Division was to land on the left flank of the 8th Army, we would have the open flank to worry about. To handle this gap and knock out the enemy coastal guns in that area, we were given the Marine Commando Brigade commanded by Bob Laycock.

During this period in Cairo, I accompanied General Simonds when he visited the General in charge of Administration, General Robertson, and the General commanding the 51st Highland Division, General Douglas Wimberley. In each case, Simonds had known the individual before so that a very easy and informal atmosphere prevailed at the meetings. We found all the authorities in Cairo were anxious to help and arrangements were made for the Chief of Staff of 30 Corps, Brigadier George Walsh, to return to the U.K. early in June and visit us in Scotland so that he could help to straighten out any last minute hitches.

For these and many other reasons, we felt that we were getting a sincere welcome from everyone in 8th Army. We knew that the Australians, who had played such an important part in many of the desert battles, were being withdrawn to fight in the Pacific theatre. We also knew that the New Zealand and South African divisions had had manpower problems after their heavy casualties in North Africa. Apart from our severe losses at Dieppe, we had suffered few casualties elsewhere, our regiments and reinforcement depots were fully up to strength. An Army that did not appear to have a manpower problem was most welcome!

Since we had been told that we could not expect support from any facilities in the Mediterranean area for a period of 42 days, we obviously would have to bring with us enough reinforcements, particularly of infantry, to see us through about 30 days of fighting. The losses in battle, or 'wastage rates' as they were called, could vary according to the intensity of the fighting and since we had at that time no experience of casualty rates, we initially adopted the British rates. General Simonds decided that he would need about 120 reinforcements for each infantry battalion and proportionately fewer for the other combat arms such as artillery and tanks where casualties were generally about 10% of those in the infantry. Furthermore, he insisted that they should be available when requested by regiments and not back on some long supply line from which they might take days to reach their units. This system was followed and proved most effective.

After completing his plans and discussions Guy Simonds decided that we should again divide into two parties for our return to Britain. He was anxious to get back to check into the re-equipment programme that had been promised us, so his party were to fly in an aircraft of the R.A.F. The remainder of us would fly as civilians in a plan of Imperial Airways.

Guy Simonds and his party left early on the 9th of May and did not arrive in London until late on the 11th after a hair raising ten minutes when the pilot of the aircraft thought he was flying along the south coast of Wales only to be told quite forcefully by General Simonds that the country below them was Eire and that the sooner he flew away from it the better.

We did not have quite the same experience in our Imperial Airways aircraft although we had our ups and downs and were very glad when we finally landed in England.

On our return I found that Dick Danby had everything well in hand. The tactical plan for the assault had been made known to the Brigade Staffs who in turn had prepared their own detailed plans. The brigades themselves were in transit to Scotland from Sussex as were all troops who were to accompany us to the Mediterranean area. The movements went off without a hitch in spite of numbers—over 27,000 men and 4,000 vehicles and tanks. We had come a long way from the days of 1940 when the Division was sent only 90 miles to Northampton and ended up scattered through Wales, Lancashire and East Anglia!

The new AA & QMG of the Division, replacing Chuck Finlay who was killed with Harry Salmon, was Lt.-Col. Preston Gilbride. He was not known to any of us in the 1st Division as most of his service had been with the 5th Division. However, it was obvious that he knew his job and in addition he had first-class commanders of the various services—Army Service Corps, Ordnance Corps, Electrical and Mechanical Engineers and others who made up the Administrative team. Major "Ab" Knight, who was his No. 1 staff officer, was a tower of strength to him in the meticulous detail required for such an operation.

General Simonds went north to Scotland to see the troops training on their new equipment whilst we remained in Norfolk House to complete the planning details with the War Office and their various agents in Shipping and Supply. They lived up to their word and there was no doubt in anyone's mind that we were the best equipped force ever to leave the U.K.

The Movement Control organization in Britain was excellent. All we had to do when moving from A to B was to be at the railroad station at the right time. They did the rest.

Mr. Churchill said that the Battle of Britain period in 1940 was Britain's "finest hour." Perhaps it was but I think her 'finest year' was 1943. In that year her people became highly organized—they were no longer on the defensive; all effort was coordinated to one end, the preparation for the great offensive across the Channel. In anticipation, the whole population worked willingly. Their pay was low but the prices of essential goods and meals in restaurants were controlled. The children throughout Britain were being given free and nutritious meals at school, their diets improved with orange juice, milk and vitamins. They ate meat every noon meal whilst adults were rationed to 8 ounces a week. The sweet smell of victory was in the air.

By June 1st final plans for our part in the invasion of Sicily had been completed and committed to writing. When typed and reproduced as a reference document it comprised over two hundred pages of detail including all its appendices. It was the last document of that size that was produced by the Division but it was recognized that the circumstances warranted it. The loading and eventual unloading of 92 ships, the passage of 27,000 men, the carriage of 30,000 tons of stores to last us 42 days, the requirements for the long sea journey, the details of the assault landing and subsequent operations could not be condensed into fewer pages. Sealed copies of these plans were placed on every ship with orders that they must not be unsealed and read until a certain date by which time the ships would be at sea. Moreover, the plans and other 'Top Secret' documents were carried in special containers to ensure their destruction in the event of a ship being sunk or other emergency.

Before embarking for Sicily we went up to Scotland and quickly became involved in the final training. I went to the station in Kilmarnock to meet the Chief of Staff of 30 Corps, Brigadier George Walsh, who had been flown back to England with General Montgomery. George Walsh spent a few days with us and gave us useful information particularly connected with the siting of headquarters and the maintenance of communications. We knew that in the 8th Army the layout of a headquarters of Divisional size was generally the compact grouping of Operations, Intelligence, Administration and clerical, with each part contained in separate truck that had been converted into offices. We practiced this layout in Scotland so that our Camp Commandant, Captain Richardson, would have a good idea of how much terrain would be required in the various locations the Headquarters might move to once we landed in Sicily.

Our final days in Scotland were taken up with last minute preparations for the embarkation of the assault force. The 'slow' convoy had already left the safety of the Clyde and were now in mid-Atlantic. They were the follow-up ships that would not be expected to unload until at least three days after the assault went in.

The 'assault' convoys had been marshalled and loaded and it was hoped we could rehearse our Sicily landing using the actual craft and order of launching that we had been planning these past weeks. But luck was against us as bad weather and heavy seas closed in on our practice beaches.

As we waited impatiently aboard ship an incident occurred that almost cost one of our Regimental commanders his career. General Simonds went from ship to ship as they lay at anchor to wish each one good fortune and to see if there were any problems arising from our enforced confinement to the ships.

On visiting one of the tank-landing ships he found that the commanding officer of the Three Rivers Regiment, the tank unit that was to be with us in the assault, had already opened the Top Secret envelope which contained the information that our landings would be in Sicily. Up to that time no one, except our small planning groups, had any knowledge of just where the landings would take place. All the others knew was that they would be landing on certain beaches at certain times. Once they were all at sea the Top Secret Plans could be opened and studied in conjunction with a model of the terrain and a large number of maps all of which were enclosed in the sealed Top Secret Envelopes and Boxes.

General Simonds was so angry at this breach of security that he left the particular ship immediately and returned to our Headquarters Ship—leaving instructions that the commanding officer who had breached the security was to report to him in two hours time.

As soon as he was aboard our Headquarters Ship, General Simonds sent for me and told me what had happened. He was determined to give the officer concerned a severe reprimand and return him to Canada. He would be replaced by his 2nd in Command.

However, the more we discussed the problem the more obvious it was that the commanding officer had to remain with us since he knew our destination. If he was taken off his ship and returned to Canada he—a disgruntled man no doubt—would have this vital information for about 12 days before the date of landing!

The individual was Lt.-Col. Booth. I had not met him before he became involved in our Sicily operation; however, I was to see a fair amount of him in the next 12 months. He duly came aboard our ship to report to General Simonds and it was obvious that he felt he was for the high-jump. He was a small man physically—only about 5 feet in height—and although he later became suntanned and fit he was shaking like a leaf and quite pale as he staggered up our gangplank. I took him down to the General's cabin and went in with him. I had never seen Guy Simonds in a cold rage before. Everything was ice. For five minutes he told Booth exactly what he thought of his conduct. I was standing behind Booth and at one time thought I would have to support him physically as he wilted from the blast. I think the only thing that saved him was that no one except himself had seen the Top Secret document. I helped him off the ship into the small motor-boat that had brought him over. He told me a month later that his five minutes with Simonds had made him all the more determined that he and his regiment would do well in Sicily. They did.

The Headquarters Ship was H.M.S. Hilary—an unimportant and rather insignificant ship to be given the title "His Majesty's Ship." Before the war Hilary may well have been a coastal vessel or 'tramp.' She was about 4,000 tons, and whatever her original purpose, had been given a complete transformation to make her suitable as a Control Ship. The whole of her centre below the bridge was a large Operations Room into which were fed all the wires and electronics to enable the Staff to communicate with all Naval, Army and Air Force units involved in the Assault.

Accommodation for about 15 officers and 60 other ranks was plain but comfortable and quite separate from that of the crew.

The Admiral commanding our convoys and the man responsible for getting us to the beaches in Sicily at the right time and place was the well-known, bold, destroyer leader Philip Vian. His exploits when rescuing 300 British sailors from the prison ship Altmark in a Norwegian fjord, his chase of the Bismarck when commanding a flotilla of destroyers and his actions when commanding a fleet in the Eastern Mediterranean, were legendary. We found him one of the most silent men in a Service that prided itself on being silent.

During the voyage, I went on the bridge quite often to talk to this remarkable man. He did not talk very much but he did discuss the difference between operating a fleet and operating a convoy such as ours.

A fleet could put up an intense area of anti-aircraft fire when attacked by aircraft. The problem with our convoy was that our escorting destroyers were far ahead or to the flanks, leaving the stern of our convoy very vulnerable to sneak attacks from the air.

We were on complete wireless silence throughout the voyage and so any signal between the ships in our convoy had to be by lamp or by flag—a very real problem in an emergency.

Each morning I would ask General Simonds to draw out of a hat the names of three of the ships sailing in our various convoys. My staff and I would then examine the effect the loss of these three ships would have on our projected plans. We had with us complete lists of who and what was on each of our 92 ships. I was thus able to tell General Simonds the implications of each loss.

On 3rd July, he drew from the hat the names of three ships in our 'slow assault' convoy. They were the City of Venice, St. Essylt and Devis, the three ships on which we had loaded equal portions of our Divisional Headquarters. We had done this in an effort to ensure that we would be able to operate effectively on landing. The chance of all three ships being sunk was a million to one. I asked General Simonds to draw another three names from the hat, which he did.

On the 5th and 6th July, the three ships, City of Venice, St. Essylt and Devis were sunk by enemy submarines—the impossible had happened. We would arrive in Sicily without any vehicles or communications; they had all been sunk. With complete wireless silence we could not inform 8th Army of our predicament. But as we passed Bizerta two days later, we were able to send the information ashore by small boat.

Three other exciting things occurred to keep us on our toes. North of Algiers we received a signal that we were five hours ahead of schedule. We were to turn about and retrace our steps for two and a half hours before turning about again. Admiral Vian made a signal to all ships by lamp and flag that we would all turn about in ten minutes when he hoisted a certain signal.

These ten minutes gave the two destroyers on the outer flanks time to go through their normal drill of exchanging places at high speed and crossing in the rear of the convoy before taking up station on the flanks again.

At the right moment, the signal to turn about was hoisted. Each line of ships swung hard to port, without reducing speed, and turned about. We, in Hilary, resumed our position at the head of the centre line as the great ships churned the seas and the remaining destroyers raced through our columns to regain their protective positions forward of the convoy. It was a beautiful drill to watch from the bridge of Hilary and I was fascinated by the speed at which the Yeoman of Signals ran up the various signal flags to transmit instructions. I wanted to make sure that General Simonds was on the bridge to watch our return turn-about due in two and one half hours.

As the time approached we both went up to the bridge to observe the drill in reverse. Out went the ten minute warning signal acknowledged by all ships. The two flanking destroyers raced at high speed to cross close to the stern of our great ships and there riding high in the wake of our propellers, was the periscope of a submarine. The German U-boat captain had failed to read the orders sent out by flag by Admiral Vian! No doubt at such close range he was debating which ships of the convoy he would sink. His periscope was seen by both destroyers at the same time. They were too late to ram the U-boat as it must have seen them as they closed towards it. It dived and the periscope disappeared from view but each destroyer threw its maximum of depth charges into its wake. The resulting explosions were dramatic. Out of the water emerged the submarine which was lifted a clear 10 feet by the explosions. The whole submarine was visible for perhaps a second before it plunged back into the sea. Signals were run up the mast of Hilary. The convoy altered course before turning eastward again. Admiral Vian left two of our escorts to depth charge the submarine into oblivion whilst we went quietly on our way. The original explosions that blew the submarine out of the water shook Hilary to such an extent that we landlubbers thought she would sink too. If the Admiral had waited for another ten minutes before giving his order to turn about, it would have been possible for that submarine to have sunk three or four of our great ships which might have put an end to our assault on Sicily. It was a close shave.

The second event of interest occurred when we got information by destroyer out of Algiers that the sandbar half a mile out from the beaches on our right brigade front was only two feet below water. Our infantry landing craft would be stuck on it which would mean that the assaulting infantry on leaving the craft would wade into eight or nine feet of water. Plans were immediately made for three landing craft tank (LCT) each with seven DUKW's on board to leave Malta and join our convoy. They were to land our right hand brigade, the big LCT's would hit the sandbar, disgorge the DUKW's which would then swim ashore loaded with assaulting infantrymen. It was essential for the LCT's to undertake the first part of the plan because of heavy seas which would have swamped the DUKW's. It says a great deal for the efficiency and cooperation of all concerned that such an extra force could be sent at such short notice, remembering that wireless silence meant that all communication had to be done by sending destroyers and frigates in to shore installations where messages could be transmitted without disclosing the location of our convoys.

The arrangement went off well although the problems of the LCT's finding the right ship in rough weather, and in the dark, meant some delay. There was also the fact that the troops, having trained to load and disembark from armoured assault craft, now had to load into un-familiar and unarmoured DUKW's which were really trucks with pro-pellers and the ability to float. But the great thing was that many lives were saved by the change.

The third item of unusual interest occurred just after we had passed Malta on our final run north to Sicily. On each side we could see many hundreds of ships and landing craft of all sizes, all heading to their ap-pointed stations.

Our convoy was due at our anchorage shortly after midnight at which point all assault craft would be lowered and proceed to their beaches. The anchorage was about seven miles from shore.

At about eight o'clock, with only four hours to go, Admiral Vian received a message telling him that information had been received from a high Italian source that the area in which we were to anchor was the centre of an extensive minefield which could be detonated elec-trically by the Headquarters of the enemy forces in the capital city of Enna. The message went on to say that although the source of the in-formation was on a high level, it was generally regarded as unreliable.

General Simonds and I were in the Operations Room at the time when a messenger arrived asking Guy Simonds to go up on the bridge to see the Admiral who had received an important message. Simonds sent me up instead and I found the Admiral staring at the message in disbelief. "Kitching," he said, "take this down to your General and ask him what he thinks we should do, but read it before you go so that you can prepare him for some unusual news." I read it quickly and hurried below to the Operations Room.

"Sir," I said, "the Admiral asks what you think we should do about this message." Guy Simonds read it looked up at me and said, "Tell the Admiral that if I were he I would pay no attention to it." I returned hastily to the bridge and gave Admiral Vian the message verbatim. He smiled happily and said that was exactly the way he felt. "In fact, Kitching, please give my compliments to General Simonds and tell him from me that he would make an excellent admiral." No further thought was given to the problem and our great convoy anchored safely at the appointed time and place.

There is no point in my trying to tell the detailed story of the operations in Sicily. They have been accurately and fairly presented in our official histories but I have many personal memories of those hot and dusty days.

To me, the fighting in Sicily showed the Canadian soldier at his best. All our previous training had been based on the drills learned from 'battle schools' in Britain which required the initiative of each soldier to be a part of the automatic deployment of sections, platoons, and companies into positions from which they could take offensive action against the enemy. These drills were based on a battle of movement in which the actions of every soldier were important whether carrying a rifle, a Bren gun, a mortar or a radio. Each was part of a team but each knew that his personal initiative in combat was a critical element. The operations in Sicily, with only one exception, gave the Canadian soldier that unrestricted use of his initiative. The exception was the first battle of Nissoria in which the Royal Canadian Regiment attacked that town behind a timed artillery programme which, as so often happened, galloped ahead of the infantry leaving them without support at a critical time. In Italy, later in the campaign, these programmed barrages were replaced by a system which gave the infantry the fire support they needed when and where they wanted it and restored their initiative.

There were so many examples of the way individuals and small groups of men achieved the impossible that it is difficult to select any one of them as being the most exceptional. For instance in the battle for Leonforte, Pte. S.J. Cousins of the Patricias and an N.C.O., on their own initiative, advanced on two enemy machine-gun posts that were holding up the advance of their company. About 150 yards from the enemy, the N.C.O. was killed in a hail of bullets. Despite the fact that further progress appeared to be utter suicide to the men of his company who were watching this gallant soldier, Pte. Cousins, with complete disregard for his own life, rose to his feet in full view of the enemy and carrying his Bren gun boldly charged the enemy posts. Firing his Bren gun from the hip, he killed or wounded all the German machine gunners, silencing both posts.

An example of a small group of men achieving a great deal was the platoon of the Edmonton Regiment that penetrated the enemy positions at night to a distance of about four miles and placing a number of mines on a road succeeded in destroying three tanks, a tank-transporter and three trucks. In spite of a fierce fire-fight before withdrawing, this platoon, commanded by Lt. John Dougan, also captured 18 German prisoners without suffering any casualties itself.

An example of a large group using its initiative was the capture of the 3,000 foot hill and castle of Assoro by the Hastings and Prince Edward Regiment. Instead of attacking it frontally, the Commanding Officer, Lt.-Col. Lord Tweedsmuir, decided to scale one side of the hill which in parts was almost vertical as he felt the enemy would not have built strong defences there. He was right. When he led his battalion up the escarpment in the dark, he was able to capture the hill and hold it against repeated counter-attacks by a startled enemy.

Until the final days of the Sicily battles, our tanks did not have much chance to display initiative. The mountainous country, cut by ravines with precipitous slopes, and the scarcity of roads, kept them on a one-tank front for long periods.

The Commander of the German 15th Panzer Grenadier Division wrote at the time, ''The Canadians are good soldiers and they fight fairly and in field-craft superior to our troops. Very mobile at night, surprise break-ins, clever infiltrations at night with small groups between our strong points.''

We were able to do this because the control of the battle was with the companies and battalions who were fighting it. They had been told what to do and they generally had lots of room in which to do it. They could, and did, use their initiative and their own resources because, owing to poor communications, they could not always count on tank and artillery support.

Conditions in Sicily allowed the Canadian soldier to develop and use his best qualities and although no soldier likes war I think that all ranks in our 1st Division and in the Three Rivers Regiment enjoyed their time in Sicily.

The sinking of the three ships in our slow assault convoy, with the loss of 50 men, 40 guns, and 500 vehicles, had a decided impact on our early operations in Sicily but the unit that suffered most was our own Divisional Headquarters. None of our vehicles survived nor did any signal equipment. In addition, five of our six special 'caravans' were lost with all my personal belongings and those of our four Brigadiers. The immediate result was that our Main Headquarters had to remain on Hilary for 24 hours longer than we had planned. From the ship we had excellent communication with our Brigades and with 30 Corps and 8th Army so there was no problem of loss of control. We managed to scrounge a jeep for General Simonds so that he could visit the forward troops. We also were given three DUKW's which we immediately gave to Brig. Matthews and his artillery headquarters so that they could control the fire of our three artillery regiments. No sooner had that group left the beaches than they were attacked by German fighter aircraft. Two of the DUKW's were destroyed and there were several casualties, one of whom was the Brigade-Major of Artillery, Major Gus Dyer, of Victoria, who lost a leg. Although there were quite a few German fighter aircraft in our area they confined their attacks to roads and troop concentrations and rarely attacked shipping. The ships were attacked by bombers quite frequently but generally at night. The biggest concentration of German fighter-aircraft that I saw was a squadron of 12 which flew over our headquarters near Leonforte at tree top height. Fortunately they did not think we were a worthwhile target.

Waiting patiently on our headquarters ship, Hilary, we were finally advised that an 'armoured command vehicle' (ACV) would be available in which there would be sufficient radios for us to do our job ashore. We would also be lent three three-ton vehicles for carrying our personnel and stores. We had been used to operating with a communication set-up of about 12 vehicles and an administrative back-up of about 25. It would be interesting to see how we could operate with a total of only four! The ACV turned out to be a Godsend, although at first its bulk frightened us. They had been designed originally as Command vehicles for Armored Divisions, they were armoured on the sides and top with enough armour to withstand shell fragments and bullets and as a result they weighed 18 tons. The interior of what was a long rectangular armoured box was conveniently divided into three areas. One was for radios and signallers to operate them, one for clerks to handle messages and the third for an officer to handle and plot incoming and outgoing messages and orders. Thus, into this one vehicle we were able to put the essential elements of what in our earlier training would have required three smaller vehicles. We had always assumed that it was essential to have two officers working in the Operations Room; now with only room for one we were able to work with greater efficiency and so space the work load that staff officers had a chance to eat and sleep in a more regular pattern than we had been able to do on exercises in England. It was so easy on exercises to have all the staff working, getting in each other's way because they generally only lasted a few days but in action a Divisional Headquarters has to be able to operate twenty-four hours each day for months on end. Fortunately we had three excellent young staff officers who were capable of working the system alone. As a result, Dick Danby was able to rotate them and always be able to assist them personally in moments of crisis. Although we lost our ACV after Sicily, we continued to operate our Headquarters as if it was still with us. We called it the "Elephant" and I have been interested to read since the war that Field Marshal Rommel used one that he had captured as his command vehicle and called it "Mammoth."

We had the U.S. Army on our left throughout the Sicily campaign and for a period we exchanged Liaison Officers in order to coordinate our movements and avoid shelling each other. Our only real problem arose when the Americans were trying to capture Troina, a city about ten miles north of our axis. We had captured Regalbuto which, from the air, must have looked like Troina because on three separate occasions 24 Mitchells of the U.S. Air Force dropped their bombs on our troops by mistake. After the second occasion, General Simonds sent a very strongly worded message to the neighbouring American Corps Commander, General Bradley, asking him to stop the bombing. We were assured it would not happen again. However, the same thing happened a few hours later and we felt it would go on but fortunately the U.S. forces captured Troina which put a stop to it.

General Simonds kept a regular schedule which allowed me to adjust my own activities to conform to his. He would be woken before 6:00 a.m., given a briefing of the night's activities at about 6:30 a.m., and, after a quick breakfast, visit the brigades. By noon each day he would have a fair idea of the way he wanted to develop operations on the next day so I would meet him at some point in the forward area when he would give me advance warning of the probable course of the next day's operations. This allowed me to return to the headquarters and brief the senior members so that they could make the preliminary moves to ensure that their units were able to support the intended plans. With only one road available, its use had to be planned very carefully.

Once General Simonds had made up his mind about a situation or a person, it was very difficult to get him to change it. He was brought up as an artilleryman, or 'gunner,' and he believed that artillery was essential to the success of any battle. He would delay an attack in order that more artillery could be deployed to support it whether or not the battalion commander who was to carry out the attack wanted more artillery or not. He believed sincerely that artillery saved lives and there was no doubt that on most occasions it did when correctly employed, but for quite a period General Simonds appeared to be wedded to the barrage type of support of World War I vintage. This barrage was a successive curtain of artillery shells fired to explode about fifty yards in front of our attacking infantry and timed to keep just ahead of them as they closed with the enemy. It was designed to pulverized the enemy in their defensive positions just before our infantry reached them, and it did when we used massed artillery which included medium and heavy guns. But the 25-pounder field gun, which was the gun in most of our artillery regiments, did not fire a shell that was effective against strong defences or deep trenches although it was a very potent killer when engaging enemy in the open. So, very often the German defenders would take shelter once the barrage started and then emerge quickly, once it had passed them, to engage our infantry as they charged the last 25 or 50 yards and were in the open.

We only tried these barrages twice in Sicily and on each occasion the German defenders were able to interfere with our timed programme and cause the attacks to fail. But instead of looking for other ways of using our guns, Guy Simonds criticized the infantry for not keeping up with the artillery fire. I think that this rather stubborn use of the barrage was about the only thing for which General Simonds could be criticized during the whole Sicilian campaign and I think that his early training as a gunner unduly influenced some of his tactical decisions. I am sure that I could be criticized for much the same thing. I was trained as an infantryman and it influenced me in my tactical thinking.

Once Guy Simonds took a dislike to a person or distrusted him for good reason, I do not think he would ever change his mind. When the fighting in Sicily was over for us, Preston Gilbride produced a bottle of gin and a number of bottles of tonic. He asked us to celebrate with him in our small mess tent. Guy Simonds came in after a couple of minutes and was obviously looking forward to a gin and tonic when he looked at Gilbride and asked where he had obtained the bottles. Gilbride said he had sent a jeep down to the beach area to get them—a road journey of about 150 miles. Without saying a word, Guy put down his glass, walked out of the tent and called for Gilbride and me to follow him. Once outside, he blasted Gilbride for extravagance in wasting the time of a driver and an officer to get a few bottles of tonic. Later, just before we crossed into Italy on 3 September, Simonds gave permission for Gilbride and me to have caravans built from two of our three-ton trucks. I made up a simple plan for mine, and after a couple of days it was produced largely from the lumber taken from the hundreds of packing cases in which stores had arrived on the beaches. It was quite plain but comfortable. Guy Simonds approved it.

But when Gilbride produced his and asked us to view it we were all a bit shaken. One of his staff had looted an Italian home and incorporated some very fine pieces of furniture into the vehicle. When Guy Simonds saw it he went quite white with anger and ordered Gilbride to return the furniture immediately. From that moment forward General Simonds never trusted Gilbride again in spite of the many attempts by

Preston Gilbride to ingratiate himself into Simonds' good books.

Another incident shows Guy Simonds in a quite different light. Early in the Sicily fighting, our 1st Brigade was in action at Grammichele, a sky-line town astride our main axis of advance. Unfortunately, the enemy was able to inflict a great deal of damage to men and material in this, our first action with the Germans. General Simonds was not satisfied with the performance of Brigadier Howard Graham who commanded the brigade so on his return to our headquarters at about six o'clock one evening he told me that I was to take command of the brigade at 7:00 a.m. the next morning. Archie Butlin, my batman, had to do some quick cutting and sewing as he added the two extra pips on each of my shoulder epaulettes and then made Brigadier's Red Tabs out of our Divisional Red patches which we so proudly wore on our sleeves.

When I saw General Simonds the next morning at 6:00 a.m., he told me to wait at our headquarters until he sent for me. Shortly after leaving the headquarters he met General Leese, our Corps Commander, who was on his way forward to see how things were going. Simonds told him of his intention to replace Graham. General Leese replied that whilst he had no intention of interfering in what was entirely a Canadian affair, he would be inclined to give Graham another chance. Simonds agreed to this and sent me a message to remain at headquarters and reduce myself to a lieutenant-colonel again! I was glad because Howard Graham was a good friend. The rest of this incident shows that Guy Simonds could forgive, forget and be generous as well.

Only three days after the Grammichele fighting, the 1st Brigade were involved in two days of heavy fighting before capturing their objective, a town called Valguernera. On the day we captured Valguernera, General Simonds sent for Brig. Graham. The latter had had little sleep for two days and nights and when he arrived at our headquarters he was obviously very tired, a condition that was aggravated by the thick film of dust that covered us all. I saw Graham arrive in his jeep and walked over to the road to greet him. I congratulated him on the success of his brigade's capture of Valguernera but I had a feeling that he felt he was going to be relieved of his command and that Guy Simonds was just looking for an excuse to get rid of him. I took him over to the General who was standing under one of the trees that lined a near-by dried-out water course. I knew what Guy Simonds was going to say to him but moved away to allow the meeting to be a more personal one.

After congratulating him for the capture of Valguernera, Guy Simonds told him that he had recommended him for an immediate award of the Distinguished Service Order (D.S.O.) for his courageous leadership.

Howard Graham was a different man when he left the headquarters. The weariness had left his face and I, for one, realized that Guy Simonds could be human after all.

Shortly after our part of this campaign was over General McNaughton, then the General Officer Commanding-in-Chief 1st Canadian Army, visited Sicily and spent several days speaking with the men of each unit. There was no doubt that he was popular with the troops, his rugged features and pleasant smile were well known to them and further more they liked to hear from a Canadian. It was to be his only visit to an active theatre.

One final note about our Sicily operation. During our planning days in London a decision was taken to include in our establishment an "historical" officer and a war artist. The initiative for this came from Major Charles Stacey who was the Senior Historical Officer in the Army Overseas. He was determined that the course of operations would be documented as accurately as possible and that the daily War Diaries of units were properly maintained—and not filled in a week after the event. One of our GSO III's, Captain Gus Sesia, was appointed to do the job of Historical officer—he must have pleased Charles Stacey because he promoted him and gave him greater responsibilities as the war progressed. Like most of us at Divisional Headquarters, Gus Sesia had a problem with transportation as jeeps were at a premium. However, I recall seeing him hurtling around corners in a requisitioned Italian car which a few days before had been my only means of transport.

Captain Will Ogilvie was the Official Artist with us and I think his watercolours and drawings are some of the most beautiful and accurate records of our time in Sicily. Will accompanied the troops on foot across some of the toughest countryside in Sicily. His drawings of the men of the Edmonton Regiment during the assault on Hill 736 are the work of a true war artist.

13

The Invasion Of Italy

The decision was made that early in September we would take part in the invasion of Italy under the command of 13 Corps commanded by Lt. General "Bimbo" Dempsey. Our partners would be 5th British Division. We would cross on the 3rd September.

General Simonds selected our 3rd Brigade to lead the assault which was to go immediately north of the City of Reggio, Calabria, and, once having established a beachhead, drive eastward into the Aspromonte hills. Our Intelligence predicted only light opposition and they were right. The assaults went in as planned and the only discomforts suffered by our troops as they climbed into the mountains was the climb itself and the cold, damp nights that were such a change from the warmth of Sicily.

German demolitions were as effective as we expected but it was surprising how the individual battalions, trudging along the mountain highways could overcome the problems, at least on a temporary basis. Jeeps and motorcycles, the former sometimes carrying ten or twelve men, took up the forefront of the advance.

On the 6th September, three days after the landings, our Division was told to develop a thrust up the east coast of Calabria. The absence of large German forces in the Italian toe made it all the more important that the Division hasten up the coast instead of climbing through the mountains. Whilst Gen. Simonds went forward to see the Brigade Commanders who were by this time heavily committed in the mountains, he told me to assemble a force, to be known as 'X' Force, which would be under command of Lt.-Col. Cy Neroutsos of the Calgary Tank Regiment.

Force 'X' was assembled in a great hurry, Cy Neroutsos ending up with a squadron of his own regiment, two companies of the Carleton and York Regiment in lorries, a squadron of armoured cars of the Princess Louise Dragoon Guards and a strong supporting group of heavy mortars, machine guns and anti-tank guns. After collecting his force, Neroutsos took off with great speed and determination, reaching Locri, in spite of demolitions, and covering 45 miles in only twelve hours. In the next three days elements of this force charged ahead taking Catanzaro Marina and then Croton, a further distance of nearly 100 miles. It was a great example of cooperation as the force comprised various segments from several regiments.

Lt.-Col. Pat Bogert who commanded the West Nova Scotia Regiment was also given a special force. It was called "Boforce" and with it he was ordered to advance into the hinterland and capture the town of Potenza, a distance of about 125 miles. In spite of demolitions, Pat Bogert reached the outskirts of Potenza after only three days and captured the town the next day. General Simonds preferred the creation of these "special forces" because it gave the full responsibility for action to one man; furthermore, with only one road on which to operate there was no room for larger forces. In fact, throughout the early months of the Italian campaign the commanders of battalions were frequently fighting their battalions as almost independent groups. The initiative lay with them and they took full advantage of their opportunities. Until we reached Potenza we rarely met the Germans head-on but from there to Campobasso battalions met with increasingly stubborn resistance; it was then that the tactical drills and battle procedures that they had developed in Sicily, and in the approach to Potenza, began to pay handsome dividends. Cooperation between the artillery, armour and infantry became almost automatic; each got to know what the other wanted under a wide variety of battle conditions and each gave their all to help the other. The 1st Canadian Division and the 1st Armoured Brigade, in spite of losses, had built up a strong hard core of 'battle-wise' veterans who proudly fought their way forward, through Motta and Decorata to Campobasso and through the Biferno and the upper Sangro, until they were decimated, winning two of their greatest battles, the crossing of the Moro River and the capture of Ortona.

In September, shortly after our landings in Italy, we had a number of changes in the staff at our Headquarters. Dick Danby went off to be the Second-in-Command of the Carleton and York Regiment and was replaced by Major Trumbull Warren of the 48th Highlanders who rapidly became a part of the operations team. In retrospect, it was remarkable how quickly and effectively a trained staff officer could fill an empty position on any staff and often without any period of 'hand over.' We had all been trained along the same lines and had a good idea of what was required of us, whether it was on the Operational or Administrative side.

Unfortunately, Guy Simonds became ill at about the time we reached Potenza. He tried to remain on the job, working from a sick-bed in his caravan, but after a week he was evacuated to a British hospital in Bari. Chris Vokes was appointed acting commander of the Division and re-mained in that appointment for over two weeks during which the Divi-sion fought a series of widely separated battalion battles against an enemy of Panzer Grenadiers and Paratroopers. Bert Hoffmeister of the Seaforths was appointed to command the 2nd Brigade in place of Chris Vokes and succeeded in winning a number of objectives by careful deployment of his battalions. The Germans fought hard although, where possible, they tried to withdraw from each position before our main attacks hit them.

Whilst Chris Vokes commanded the division he maintained much the same pattern in his briefings and visits to brigades and units as General Simonds. He had a far more outgoing personality than Simonds and, when at the Headquarters, would often drop in to the Operations Centre or in to my caravan for a chat. He soon got to know the staff and they appreciated his interest although one or two were a little frightened of him. He could look very ferocious with his large moustache and strong square face and he used some awful language on occasion, but, underneath the gruff exterior, was a warm and understanding personality.

During the weeks that the 1st Division was fighting its way to

Campobasso and beyond, the Three Rivers Tank Regiment, which had been with us in Sicily, took an important part in the defence of a coast town named Termoli when the British 78th Division and a Commando force, who were in and around Termoli, were threatened with an attack by a strong German Panzer Division. At that time the British force only had six tanks, so the arrival of the Three Rivers Regiment with its 48 operational tanks, not only ensured the defence of Termoli but also allowed the British to attack so successfully that they defeated the Panzer Division and forced it to retire.

I was particularly interested in the Termoli battle because it was the first time I realized that we, on the Allied side, had such a good knowledge of German Army plans. Termoli was captured on the night of October 2nd by British Commandos who landed from the sea. The 78th Division was rushed forward by land and sea on October 3rd and 4th to reinforce them. But early in the morning of the 3rd October, only a few hours after the Commandos had landed at Termoli, Brigadier Wyman, of our Army Tank Brigade, was ordered to send the Three Rivers Regiment to Termoli to help the British. He was told then that this was to counter a German Division which was on its way to recapture Termoli.

That same morning, General Dempsey, who commanded 13 Corps of which we were a part, came to our Divisional Headquarters. He had hoped to see Brigadier Vokes but the latter was forward with one of the brigades, so instead he gave me a verbal message which he asked me to pass on to Vokes when he returned. The message was that Termoli had been captured by Commandos, 78th Division was moving forward to reinforce them and he had ordered our Three Rivers Regiment to join the 78th Division. The reason for this urgent reinforcement, he said was that 8th Army Intelligence had reported that 16th Panzer Division was on the move to regain Termoli. General Dempsey hastened to add that he thought the knowledge of the German moves was the result of air reconnaissance reports. I remember thinking at the time that the air reconnaissance must have taken off very early, but not knowing any of the mysteries of higher Intelligence, I accepted his surmise. In retrospect I am sure that the information of the German move must have come from Ultra because the loss of Termoli quickly reached the ears of Hitler himself who personnaly ordered its recapture. Whether

General Dempsey, as a Corps Commander, would have any knowledge of Ultra is doubtful as the existence of that code-breaking apparatus was known to very few, and certainly it would not be known to commanders who might fall into the hands of the enemy.

The only other time when I wondered about our knowledge of enemy movements occurred fourteen months later when I was Chief of Staff at Headquarters of our 1st Canadian Corps in the north of Italy. On that occasion the Chief of Staff at 8th Army Headquarters, Brigadier Sir Harry Floyd, asked me to go and see him. On arrival he told me that two German divisions were on their way south, having travelled by train through the Alpine tunnels which our Air Forces were doing their best to block. Harry even named the divisions and the number of tanks they had since it was important that we should know what we would be up against if the German divisions were deployed in our area.

I thanked him for the information which I promised would be confidential and passed only to my Corps Commander, and asked him how we could gain such information and the extent of its reliability. I knew that a number of Partisans, mostly Communists, were operating on our behalf behind the German lines but, to me, it would be a very clever Partisan who could count the number of tanks with each division, particularly when it would take several trains to accommodate the many thousands of men and tons of equipment on their move through the mountains.

After a while Harry Floyd said, "George, I'll let you into a secret which you must not pass to anyone except your Commander. When 8th Army overran Rommel at Alamein they captured, intact, a vehicle in which were special wireless sets and all the codes of the German High Command. There were two operators in it, one of whom tried to destroy the ciphering system. He was shot dead on the spot; the other German put his hands up and has been with us ever since. We never originate messages because Rommel reported to his superiors that the vehicle had been destroyed together with all codes. However, we listen and can decipher all messages to and from Kesselring, the German Commander in Chief, and that's why we know about the arrival of the two divisions."

It was a plausible story and I thanked Harry Floyd for taking me into his confidence. But now, after so many books on Ultra and the information it gave us, I am sure that Harry cooked up the story of the German vehicle in order to satisfy my curiosity. As Chief of Staff of 8th Army, he was probably one of the very few people in Italy who might know of the existence of Ultra. He certainly fooled me!

General Harry Crerar arrived in Italy in November together with parts of the Headquarters of 1st Canadian Corps. We know now that another Corps Headquarters was the least of Montgomery's requirements. What he wanted were two or more infantry divisions to fight in the mountains; and a variety of landing craft to enable him to mount small seaborne operations, like the one that captured Termoli, in order to avoid having to fight for every river that the enemy cared to defend. Instead he got General Crerar's Headquarters and was told he would be getting the 5th Canadian Armoured Division. He immediately suggested to Crerar that Simonds should take over command of the 5th Armoured Division to broaden his experience, and that Crerar should take over the 1st Division to gain some experience of command in battle. The Corps Headquarters would remain, well out of the way, in Sicily!

For some reason - false pride, perhaps - Crerar would not accept the idea of demoting himself, even for a temporary period. I think it was a great mistake on his part because it was his one opportunity to establish himself as a real Commander. Instead, I think it is fair to say, he remained just a kindly figurehead. At the time I knew very little of the politics behind the arrival of the Corps Headquarters and the Armoured Division. Simonds perhaps knew as much as anyone because he was close to Montgomery and the latter deferred to Simonds' opinions on purely Canadian matters. However, with Simonds in hospital, I don't think Chris Vokes wanted to be mixed up in the Montgomery-Crerar affair.

Guy Simonds had only been back with 1st Division for a day or two when he told me that he was going to command the 5th Armoured Division and that I was to be promoted to Brigadier to command the 11th Infantry Brigade, the infantry component of the armoured division. He told me that the division was due to leave the U.K. in about two days time for Naples. We would leave the 1st Division Headquarters on the 1st November so as to greet the 5th Armoured Division who were scheduled to land there on the 5th or 6th November.

The 1st Canadian Division had been my home for nearly four years and I was genuinely sorry to leave it even though I was to be promoted. Chris Vokes was appointed to command in place of Guy Simonds and got a well-deserved promotion to Major-General. He directed the division through its toughest battles during the next twelve months, earning himself the well-deserved title of the ''War Lord.'' My place as GSO I was taken by an old friend, Lt.-Col. Malim Harding.

We had to wait a week before our troops were due to arrive, a week that was mostly taken up with visits to the headquarters that would be responsible for arranging the re-equipment of our regiments and, in addition, making a reconnaissance of the areas in which they would have to bivouac. An arrangement had been made between Canada and the U.K. that we would take over the tanks and vehicles of 7th Armoured Division, the famous Desert Rats. After the handover, that Division was to return to the U.K. to be re-equipped for the cross-channel invasion. Whoever represented Canada in this take-over plan had obviously never seen the condition of tanks and vehicles that had been a part of the desert fighting for many months. Furthermore, the maintenance on all types of tanks and transport had been neglected and the condition of many of them was disgraceful. In the end, we refused to take any of their tanks and accepted only enough of their vehicles to make us mobile in the training period before going into action. But the whole incident left an unpleasant taste in our mouths and our opinion of the efficiency of the British Army slumped several points.

A characteristic of Guy Simonds was that when he had real problems on his hands he would withdraw for hours on end during which time he would remain in his caravan or room. He would avoid contact with anyone, unless it was urgent, until he had reached a solution of the particular problem. He had great powers of concentration.

Unfortunately, mostly unbeknown to me, he was having real problems with Harry Crerar who had arrived in the theatre with his 1st Corps Headquarters. The dishonest way Canadian and British politicans planned for the Corps Headquarters and 5th Armoured Division to be sent to Italy without consultation with Generals Eisenhower, Alexander or Montgomery, and, even more serious, behind General McNaughton's back, was bound to cause friction.

To Simonds it was disgraceful that, as the senior Canadian officer in the Mediterranean theatre, he had not been given any information on the move. I am sure he felt that General Crerar had been working hand-in-glove with the politicians in Ottawa and London at the expense of General McNaughton.

Although at the time I was not familiar with the details of how the arrangement to send this large increase in Canadian troops was made, I certainly feel now that the Chief of the Imperial General Staff, General Sir Alan Brooke, was delighted to agree to it as it would reduce the 1st Canadian Army Headquarters in England in importance. It would now only control one Corps (the 2nd Canadian) which could mean the beginning of a movement to do away with the Army Headquarters entirely. The 2nd Canadian Corps would then be placed under command of a British Army just as our 1st Canadian Corps was under command of the British 8th Army. We would be split into two parts with a decreasing say in the development of strategy, the deployment of subordinate formations, and our administrative back-up. It took General McNaughton's strong will to prevent the break up of our Canadian Army Headquarters.

General Crerar was always very kind to me and on occasion had gone out of his way to help or encourage me so perhaps I should not be unduly critical of him. But there was no doubt in anyone's mind that he was not an inspiring commander, and, unfortunately, he was becoming increasingly jealous of Guy Simonds' success as a commander and also of his close contacts with Montgomery and other senior officers of the U.S. and British Armies.

General Simonds, of course, became involved in the problems of our re-equipment in 5th Armoured Division and I know that he was very disappointed when General Crerar insisted that some 3,500 new trucks and other vehicles of Canadian manufacture were to go to the re-equipment of Corps troops and not to us in 5th Armoured Division. Crerar said it was because, if he had allotted the vehicles to us, the British would not have produced the trucks to make his Headquarters operational. They would produce excuses to delay the time when he would be ready. To me this made no sense at all - it was the tail wagging the dog and it resulted in my brigade having to operate for two months with inefficient transportation. Our tanks did not arrive until January and February 1944, nearly three months after the arrival of the regiments. We had been promised 50 or 60 new Sherman tanks each week from 1 December. However, only a token shipment had been made by early January. It was a frustrating period because we, in the Infantry Brigade, did not have any tanks to train with from our arrival in Italy until we went into action in mid-January north of Ortona supported by an armoured squadron that we had not known before.

I think that one reason why Crerar did not let our division have the transport was to make Simonds sit idle for some ten weeks and thus not be able to to command the division in operations. If we, in the Infantry Brigade, had had our vehicles in mid-December, I felt at the time that General Simonds would have asked for his H.Q. and my Infantry Brigade to be sent into action on the 8th Army front. He would have 'borrowed' one or two armoured regiments so as to give him an armoured brigade equivalent. Whilst he would not want to throw this new division into the cauldron of the Moro River Battle he considered we could usefully be employed with the New Zealanders in the Orsogna sector.

In spite of the fact that 1 Corps Headquarters and its two Canadian Divisions did well in Italy in all their battles, and was finally linked up with 1st Canadian Army in March 1945 in North West Europe, I think we should have sent only one more infantry division to Italy in 1943. We could then have demanded that both divisions be returned to the U.K. well before the cross-channel invasion in 1944. This would have given us a strong 1st Canadian Army of two full Corps for the invasion of France. I should add that this opinion is not all hindsight; at the time, in December 1943, neither General Simonds nor I could understand why a Corps Headquarters and Corps troops had been sent out. To us it made it all the more certain that the Corps would remain indefinitely in Italy. Furthermore it was not essential for a complete Corps Headquarters to have 'battle experience' before becoming efficient. Our 2nd Canadian Corps Headquarters functioned well in France in 1944 without having had 'battle experience' - it was much more important that the divisions have that experience.

There were many other problems between Crerar and Simonds at that time although I had very little knowledge of them. One of Crerar's moves during this period was to question Simonds' stability and his fitness for promotion. He wrote to General Montgomery telling him that he felt Simonds was too intense and needed a long rest before being given any further command. I have not read Montgomery's reply but I understand he wrote that Simonds was an excellent commander who, after further experience, would be suitable to command a Corps.

The 11th Canadian Infantry Brigade arrived in Naples on the 8th November and both Guy Simonds and I went aboard to welcome them. The battalions in the brigade were the Perth Regiment commanded by Lt.-Col. Bill Rutherford, the Cape Breton Highlanders commanded by Lt.-Col. Jim Weir and the Irish Regiment of Canada commanded by Lt.-Col. Bobby Clark. The artillery regiment, the 17th Field, was commanded by Lt.-Col. Bob Armstrong. The Support Group equipped with 4.2 inch heavy mortars and Vickers machine-guns was from the Princess Louise Fusiliers and commanded by Maj. Bill Reid. In addition, of course, we had anti-tank and anti-aircraft batteries, a squadron of Engineers, a company of the Army Service Corps, a Field Ambulance and a Brigade Workshop. We were complete except for guns, vehicles and the other heavy equipments. We were to take these over from the 131st Infantry Brigade, commanded by Brigadier "Bolo" Whistler, which was part of the 7th Armoured Division of the British Army and until we had these items we were told to bivouac in an area about five miles to the west of Naples.

I was very proud of what I saw coming off the troopships in Naples. The men were smart in appearance and looked fit, their discipline was good. It must, therefore, have been a terrible shock to them to be taken by trucks to the somewhat damp fields in which we were to spend the next two weeks.

General Simond's headquarters was in a very unpleasant looking group of houses in a neighbouring village. Mine was in a couple of equally battered houses on the edge of the highway. If we had been in action it would not have been too bad because one expects to be uncomfortable under those conditions but to remain under canvas in waterlogged fields without much to keep us busy presented the units with quite a problem: Their ability to overcome this and still keep fairly cheerful says a great deal for their high standards of discipline.

The Brigade Staff was headed by Major Jotcham of Montreal. "Jotch" was a very good organizer and made sure that he knew all aspects of a problem before taking action or making a recommendation. He also had a good sense of humour, was consistent and did not 'flap' in a crisis.

In late November, after taking over what we could from 7th British Armoured Division, we left our sodden fields for the rocky uplands of Altamura, a substantial town some 28 miles from the large port of Bari. Here the troops were able to move into huts where they could dry out and clean up. In the first days of December, the Minister of National Defence, Colonel Ralston, visited our brigade. As many troops as possible were brought into Altamura where Colonel Ralston addressed them. He promised that he would do everything possible to get us Canadian made four-wheel drive trucks. He was particularly struck by the smart appearance of the men and I remember that I was just as proud of them as he was. We had not yet been in action so that our uniforms were neatly pressed and our equipment shining as if we were Trooping the Colour for the King. Col Ralston spoke well and I know that the men were impressed by his sincerity and concern for their future welfare. He had been an inspiring battalion commander in the First World War and, being a Nova Scotian, the Cape Breton Highlanders knew him well.

He was very concerned about General Crerar's decision to equip his headquarters and his Corps Troops with the new trucks from Canada instead of giving 50% of them to us in 5th Armoured Division. I can clearly remember him saying that ''he could not understand the attitude of a man who would look after the tail before the teeth.'' Another problem of concern to Col. Ralston was the future of the reinforcement stream for the infantry. He told General Simonds and me in private conversation that when our five divisions were all in action and the losses of infantry equalled the casualties forecast in the existing 'wastage rates' he would find it difficult to maintain the fighting strength of units. He said that, on his return to Canada, he would recommend to the Government some form of conscription and, as a first move, would increase the allotment of infantry positions at our recruiting stations. The heavy fighting in which our 1st Division became involved during December on the Moro and in Ortona would have strengthened his arguments on his return to Ottawa. One important result of his visit to Italy was his insistence on the publication of a Canadian newspaper to give the troops up-to-date news of home. Dick

Malone, who had been on the Minister's staff in 1940-41, was promoted to Lieutenant-Colonel and became editor of the new "Maple Leaf." It was given top priority so that it could be distributed to the troops wherever they might be - in action or at rest. It was a great booster for our morale and I think "Herbie" cartoons were as welcome as the sunshine and appeared much more frequently!

The Altamura region was an excellent one for training and we were able to arrange for extensive areas to be cleared of the civilian population so that we could use live ammunition including artillery and heavy mortars. Fortunately it was winter when the farms were lying fallow so we did not disturb the villagers too much. In addition, our troops, who followed up our use of an area in order to compensate the farmers for real damage, were always generous with their cigarettes and chocolate - items that were in short supply for the civilian population.

The commanding officer of the Irish Regiment was Lt.-Colonel Bobby Clark whom I knew well from our R.C.R. days together. The Cape Breton Highlanders were commanded by Lt.-Col. Jim Weir who was originally with the Black Watch from Montreal; but together with several other members of that regiment he was posted to the Cape Breton Highlanders shortly after the men of that regiment indicated fairly strongly that they had little confidence in their senior officers. Their way of showing their displeasure was a 'sit-down' strike when they had refused to leave their barrack rooms to go on parade.

When the Black Watch team arrived peace was declared and the men got on with their jobs. The team included the R.S.M. and, amongst others, Majors Boyd Somerville and Aird Nesbit. I was told that one or two of the ring leaders of the strike, on being paraded before the commanding officer, were given the option of a number of days 'detention' or ten minutes of fisticuffs in the yard with the second-in-command, Major Somerville. One of them—a fairly tough soldier—opted for the fight with Somerville. When Boyd Somerville had finished him off, carried him to his barrack room and laid him on his bed, the attitude of the trouble makers changed. A few minutes with Boyd was worse than having four teeth out without an anaesthetic. Perhaps the most important thing about these punishments was that there was rarely a grudge or any ill-feeling between them.

Boyd was of average height with broad powerful shoulders, a voice that sounded like falling gravel, an infectious grin and a heart of gold. In October 1983 he died in Toronto and I am sure that Cape Bretonners who served with him will remember him with affection. I do.

Bill Rutherford, who commanded the Perth Regiment, was a very capable officer in whom we all had confidence. His regiment was recruited mostly from south western Ontario. It had a Scottish tradition and its Regimental cap badge bore the Cross of St. Andrew. However, they did not have the 'glamour' of the Irish Regiment with its green 'Cawbeen' or of the Cape Breton Highlanders with their heavy Gaelic content. I made a mental note that I would employ the Perths in the first attack that our Brigade would make. They deserved a slight boost.

Guy Simonds attended most of our exercises and expressed himself as being well satisfied with our progress. However, the absence of tanks made some of the exercises a little unreal since the cooperation between armour and infantry is such a critical part of any battle, particularly one in which an armoured division is engaged.

Guy Simonds also ran a couple of Tactical Exercises without troops (T.E.W.T.) in one of which the commander of our armoured brigade, Brigadier Bradbrooke, ran afoul of Simonds. "Brad" lost command of the brigade about six weeks later. What happened was this. The situation in the TEWT was that the armoured brigade had reached its objective and was anxious to push ahead whilst the enemy was disorganized. Simonds laid down that the armour should pause, reorganize on its objective and then wait until the artillery had caught up with them before advancing any further. "Brad" disagreed strongly with this policy and went on to commit 'hari Kari' by saying "Why should I wait for another 24 guns when I've got over 150 of them in my tanks. I don't need the artillery to shoot me on to anything and I can get there quite well by myself."

You could not have heard a pin drop at the time because the TEWT was being held in an old barn with a mud floor but the atmosphere became instantly electric. Guy Simonds was an artillery man and to a 'gunner' this was heresy of the worst kind. Simonds was not at all amused and laid down that we would always wait for the artillery in such situations. "Brad" remained unconvinced and lost his command. Another change at the time was in the command of the artillery. Brigadier R.O.G. Morton was the incumbent but there was no doubt that he was a somewhat nervous individual and a little frightened of Simonds. His place was taken by Brigadier "Sparky" Sparling whom I got to know well later.

Just before Christmas we began to visit all units to wish them the usual "Merry Christmas." On one occasion I went with Guy Simonds to the small officers' mess of the head of our Divisional Medical Services, Colonel "Bill" Coke. Bill had taken over the ground floor of a fairly substantial house and, as so often happened, the Italian family remained in possession of the second floor in which they normally lived. The servants and chickens and other livestock usually occupied the ground floor and would move back again once the military had departed.

After the season's greetings had passed between us all, Bill Coke offered Guy Simonds and me a drink which, in the absence of whisky, had been based on some of our issue rum. There were a number of other ingredients in it, too, and we had a second glass. It was very tasty and Simonds congratulated Bill Coke on the mixture. "What was in it? Formaldehyde?" "No," said Bill, "but you will be interested to know, sir, that the Contessa who owns this house had a drink of it last night and approved of it. But, poor soul, she died this morning." We almost dropped our glasses with fright but Bill put us out of our misery by telling us that the Contessa was very old and had had a terminal illness for some time. She was dying when he had given her a pain killer and a small tot of his rum mixture to help her on her way out. She had been grateful for his help. I don't think we finished our drinks before departing!

Early in January I was told that my brigade would probably move north and would be under command of the 1st Canadian Division. That division had suffered very heavy casulaties in fighting its way across the Moro River and in capturing Ortana, and we assumed that we would take up defensive positions alongside them as a powerful reinforcement to compensate, temporarily, for their heavy losses as their own reinforcements were being absorbed effectively into their units.

The distance between Altamura and Ortona was about 200 miles by road so we arranged to move by easy stages with the regiments bivouacing on the way. I went forward with the commanding officers and with my Brigade Major "Jotch" and two or three officers of the staff. We stayed with the headquarters of the 1st Division that night before going forward to take over the defensive sector of the 3rd Brigade. Chris Vokes told me that he was hoping to take a few days of well-earned leave but he did not envisage any problems ahead; the brigade sector we would be taking over was on the coast, and the critical point of the sector (Point 59) on which stood the remains of a stone tower, had been captured on the 4th January in a well planned attack by the Carleton and York Regiment commanded by my old friend, Dick Danby. It had been defended by paratroopers of the German 1st Para Division; 40 of them were killed in defending it and were buried on the site.

The 3rd Brigade was commanded by Brigadier Graeme Gibson and from the upper floor of a badly damaged farmhouse on the forward edge of his defended localities, Graeme pointed out to me the buildings and features of ground on which the enemy was basing his defences. Between our forward positions and those of the enemy ran a small stream, the Riccio. Like many others of its kind in this part of Italy the level of water rose and fell with each rainstorm but although we had our share of damp, cold rain and wet snow, the river bed was dry.

The take over from 3rd Brigade went off without a hitch on the evening of the 13th January. To make sure that the Perths would have the honour of being the first of the three battalions to lead an attack, should one be necessary, I arranged for them to be held in reserve. The Cape Bretons took over on the right and the Irish on the left and both these battalions became active in their patrolling of the river valley below them and the forward slopes of the ridge on which the enemy defences lay.

The night after taking over, Bobby Clark of the Irish arranged for a slit trench to be dug just forward of his leading defences from which the Pipe Major would serenade the enemy with his rendition of "Lilli Marlene," then the favourite song of the German Army. When all was ready Pipe Major Pape went forward and in no time at all we heard the stirring strains of the Irish pipes as he warmed up and broke into the unmistakable lilt of "Lilli Marlene." There was no doubt that the enemy heard it and there was no doubt that they didn't like it because after about five minutes, during which they must have made an accurate fix on the Pipe Major's exact location, they mortared the area.

All would have been well had the Pipe Major been in his slit trench, but as he said later, "You can't play the pipes standing still, you have to march up and down." The result, unfortunately, was that he received a piece of mortar bomb in his backside and had to be evacuated!

Whilst we had been told that our role would be one of holding and patrolling only, I was surprised to hear on the 14th that two or three nights later my brigade was to take the lead in a major attack on the enemy on our front. The order for this attack had come indirectly from 8th Army which was now commanded by General Sir Oliver Leese who had taken over when Montgomery left to prepare for Normandy.

General Leese, requested to "keep up the pressure" on his front by General Alexander, then ordered the two Corps Commanders of his Army to mount attacks that would keep the enemy from moving any of his divisions away from our front. The result of this order was that the Corps Commander of 5th Corps in which we were then serving seemed to think that he should plan my brigade battle. He obviously had little else to do because, in fact, the brigade plan evolved from his ideas that with immense artillery support we would succeed "with the minimum of casualties." At the time I did not know that the Corps Commander, General Allfrey, had been cautioned by the Army Commander NOT to undertake our attack if heavy casualties were likely. How on earth Allfrey expected a brigade, which was going into its first action, to take on two battalions of 1 Parachute Division without having heavy casualties, I do not know. The veteran battalions of our 1st Division were grimly aware of the cost of taking on 1 Para. Division and I am sure that Allfrey must have known of that cost because on the 3rd January, General Vokes had written personally to Allfrey that the battles of the Moro River and Ortona had cost his division over 2,300 casualties and that he could not maintain the "sharp fighting edge" of his infantry battalions, each one of which had suffered 50% casualties in its rifle companies. Certainly Allfrey never asked me if I thought we would succeed without heavy casualties and I am sure he never mentioned that side of his directive to General Vokes.

The decision to attack initially with only one of my battalions and then follow some hours later with another battalion was the direct result of Allfrey's instructions to concentrate all available artillery in the Corps to assist each battalion in turn. I must accept the blame for agreeing to that plan when it seemed at the time that it might be better to disperse the enemy's counter fire by attacking with two battalions. I agreed because I felt that the overwhelming fire support of sixteen artillery regiments would neutralize the enemy during that critical period when our leading companies would close with him. I was wrong.

In fact, the barrage got away from our leading troops who had to fight their way forward using their own weapons. I think that the leading companies of the Perth Regiment did well and, if they had received the full support of the tanks which were supposed to accompany them, they might well have succeeded in gaining the important objective which one of the company commanders was trying to capture when he and the six soldiers with him were killed.

Only one tank had been blown up on a mine and yet it was obvious to me that none of the others in the squadron had any intention of trying to cross the Riccio to go to the aid of the Infantry. The squadrons that were supporting us were from the Three Rivers Regiment which had done so well in Sicily and at Termoli. I was angry that they were not going to the aid of the infantry and sent for the commanding officer, Lt.-Col. Booth. The later must have been off duty because a Major came forward in his place. I ordered him to instruct his squadron commander to give the infantry all possible support by crossing the Riccio and getting into the fight. He tried his best but without success at the time, although in the afternoon, in a further attack by a company of the Perths, several tanks crossed with the infantry and gave them much needed fire support both during the attack and the subsequent withdrawal.

As usual, communications broke down between platoons and companies, companies and battalions, and even between the battalions and brigade headquarters. Jim Weir, commanding the Cape Bretons, had had a trench dug on the forward slope of his defences into which he and his signallers moved as soon as the Perth Regiment attack began. He was determined to be well forward so that he could accompany his own leading companies. Fortunately we had arranged a telephone cable to be run forward to his trench so that I was able to speak with him at any time and also, luckily, the cable was not cut by shell or mortar fire. At about 9:30 a.m., Jim Weir phone to say that he was having a difficult time with his radios because every time he put up the antennae he received a burst of machine-gun fire! He demonstrated his point by raising an antenna and then putting the telephone receiver on the parapet of the trench. I heard the immediate response, the sharp crack and whine of bullets as they passed over him or splayed the ground around him. In their anxiety to be sure that Jim Weir was really well forward, his men had dug his trench rather closer to the enemy than he had wanted.

By using this telephone I was able to discuss with Jim Weir a possible change in the timing of his projected attack and in its initial direction. Having got his agreement, it was then easy for his second-in-command, Major Boyd Somerville who was with me, to brief the company commanders concerned since it would have been impossible for Jim Weir to do it as he was stuck in his trench.

It was almost impossible to see what was happening on the Perth Regiment front; the smoke, dust and debris all floated slowly back towards our positions masking all accurate observation from the crest of our ridge and the same fickle breezes interfered with plans to help the Cape Bretons forward with a heavy smoke concentration when it was their turn to attack.

Bill Rutherford of the Perths worked tirelessly all day to get accurate information of what was happening and to organize further attacks, particularly on his left where Major Macdougall's "C" Company had had some success. "D" Company went in late in the afternoon and were supported for most of the way by their tank squadron but the battalion had taken fairly heavy casualties and was badly disorganized as were the Cape Breton Highlanders who, after some success with their leading companies, reported that they were pinned to the ground by heavy machine-gun and mortar fire. I therefore gave orders both battalions to withdraw as soon as it was dark.

Whilst our regiments were upset that they had not succeeded in their attacks, both Rutherford and Weir were anxious to try again the next day and, as the evening wore on and stragglers and the wounded came back, they became more confident that in another attack they could succeed. However, they both stated they would prefer a silent attack and not the heavy barrages of that morning. In killed, wounded and missing, we lost that day about 185 all ranks, and of these over 130 were from the Perths. A young officer, Lt. Chamberlain of the Perths, was recommended for a Military Cross. He had led the first company in its attack that morning, had held his position throughout the day and returned in the darkness with the men who had fought beside him.

I immediately discussed with Bobby Clark a plan to employ his Irish Regiment in a further attack the next day. He would be supported by the Cape Bretons. However, at midnight the Corps Commander called off any further action and ordered the brigade back into reserve. I am quite sure, that after he reported to the Army Commander that it looked as though we had nearly 300 casualties (as originally reported) General Leese would have been very angry and blamed Allfrey for permitting such losses. Only two weeks later the Hastings and Prince Edward Regiment of the 1st Division put in a well planned attack a little to the left of our original attacks. It also was to be carried out behind a heavy barrage and as usual the barrage gave away the direction of the attack. The battalion of 1 Para. Division, who were defending, fired back into the barrage causing heavy casualties and confusing our men who thought that our guns were firing short. After further gallant attempts, the attack was called off. The regiment suffered over 90 casualties in killed and wounded in this attack which was one of the last where troops moved behind a barrage in the 1st Canadian Division. General Allfrey had personally directed that this attack should go in -the second under his direction which had resulted in heavy Canadian casualties without any corresponding success. He was not a popular commander from our point of view.

The 11th Infantry Brigade was taken out of the line early on the 18th January to give us a chance to absorb our reinforcements and assess our mistakes.

To us, at the time, our biggest disappointment was the lack of vital close support from the tanks of the Three Rivers Regiment in the early stages of the Perth attack. I had built up the name of that particular armoured regiment because of its actions in Sicily and at Termoli and there is no doubt that our battalions expected their special close support since they were the veterans and we were the novices. The degree of cooperation between infantry and tanks, particularly in an armoured division, is frequently the measure of success or failure. My brigade had not been able to train with tanks during December because there were no tanks available for the armoured regiments and, of course, we had had little opportunity to train with the Three Rivers Regiment before going into action alongside them. So the need for much closer cooperation between armour and infantry was the first of our lessons. We also discussed the pros and cons of the artillery barrage and whether it might have been better to do our initial attack on a two battalion front instead of one.

During this period I had a visit from Guy Simonds, who was about to hand over command of the 5th Armoured Division to Major-General Burns. Tommy Burns came with him and both generals discussed with me the lessons learned from our attack. Burns had been able to go into the planning details of that operation and I think it is fair to say that he felt there had been undue pressure by the Corps Commander, General Allfrey, to accept his views.

At this meeting, General Simonds took me aside and asked if I would return with him to the U.K. to be his Chief of Staff at Headquarters of 2nd Canadian Corps. His promotion to command that Corps was to be announced shortly. I told him that I would be happy to be with him again but that I would like to remain with 11th Brigade for as long as possible.

We remained in reserve for two days and then took over a part of the front from a brigade of the 4th Indian Division. This division was commanded by Major-General. Tuker and we remained under his command for about nine days. Our 'front' was not a planned one—it happened to be the high water mark of the New Zealand attacks of late December when their infantry dug in both to the east and the south of Orsogna, a city that remained in German hands and dominated our positions as long as we remained in that sector. General Tuker's division were ordered to plan an assualt on Orsogna shortly after we joined them but these plans were cancelled, leaving the German garrison of that town the advantage of overlooking two-thirds of our brigade front. A further problem was the absence of any roads to service two of my battalions. This meant the construction of nearly four miles of new road, one-third of which lay in a soggy valley. The New Zealanders started the road and the engineers of 4th Indian continued the work. From a jeep track it slowly advanced to becoming a good one-way road with occasional widening to allow overtaking and passing for priority vehicles.

All three of my battalions were in the line because of the unusual shape of our front. The Irish on the right and the Cape Bretons in the centre were based on the 'new' road with supplies being taken to them by jeep. The Perths were on the left covering the Orsogna Road and the ridge that rose gently towards that town. My only reserve was a company of the Perths which Bill Rutherford loaned me as his front was the shortest of the three. Brigade Headquarters was established in a very battered group of farm buildings in rear of the Perths. Fortunately, the enemy in our sector were not capable of strong offensive action as they had been greatly reduced in numbers to reinforce their divisions facing the recent allied landings at Anzio. However, they had enough artillery to disturb us and produce accurate counter-battery fire on our artillery regiment that put its left-hand guns up against the battered building in which Jotch and I had hoped to be able to sleep. One night about 24 shells landed amongst our farm buildings of which about 75% were duds and one of them hit the front end of my caravan-truck, shattering the engine. Armourers who examined a couple of the duds the next day told me that the fusings must have been sabotaged during production. I offered up a prayer of thanks to the man or woman who, in the impressed ranks of slave labour in German-occupied Europe, had had the courage to be the saboteur.

During these last few days of January a number of divisions were being sidestepped so that as many Canadian troops as possible could be moved towards the coast where they would be taken under the wing of General Crerar's 1st Canadian Corps Headquarters. My brigade was sidestepped from our Orsogna positions to about three miles to the north-east where we took over the defensive sector held by 8th Indian Division covering the small town of Arielli.

General Tommy Burns visited our brigade frequently. On one occasion I took him to an isolated stone house which was occupied by one of the forward platoons and used as an observation post by our artillery. From the top floor we had a superb view of enemy country from a large hole through which we looked from behind a thick screen of empty sandbags. The Sergeant of Artillery who was on duty told us that the use of binoculars in front of the sandbags brought instant accurate rifle fire. The enemy must have had snipers watching throughout the daylight hours. As we walked back from the house we passed through a well-entrenched platoon of heavy 4.2 mortars of the Princess Louise Fusiliers. Just beyond the mortars were their latrines, a series of 'one holers' in front of which was strung a canvas screen which gave only about 30% privacy. The heads and feet of the occupants were clearly visible. As we went by, a young soldier, who was seated, suddenly saw us. He leapt to his feet, stood to attention and called out "Good Morning, Sir." After returning the compliment, Tommy Burns said quietly, "That's Regimental pride for you."

I enjoyed my walks and talks with Tommy Burns during those first few February days. Although I knew him by reputation, this was my first opportunity of getting to know him personally. He had won a Military Cross in the First War, had a first class brain and had written a number of articles for military journals. He had developed new techniques in map-making and map reproduction, and been on McNaughton's staff of the 1st Canadian Corps. As I got to know him better I realized that Tommy was not only a quiet man but that he had great difficulty when trying to encourage and enthuse any large group of men. He just could not 'sparkle' and continued speaking in the same tone of voice whether he was talking about a victory or a defeat. His nickname was "Smiler" because he had the reputation of never smiling although, when in conversation with friends, he seemed to smile as much as anyone else. But I must confess I never heard him let go a real belly laugh!

During the first week of February our brigade was visited by General Price Montague who was head of our Military Headquarters in London. He was accompanied by Tommy Burns and Colonel Beverly Matthews who was then the AA&QMG at Headquarters of 5th Armoured Division. We showed Price Montague round part of our sector but he was trying to cover all the Canadian brigades in one day and did not stay long. But before going he said he would like a photograph of himself with me against the background of a badly damaged building! We obliged very easily as there were few buildings near my headquarters that were not in ruins. The photo shows the four of us—with ruins—and everyone is smiling—even "Smiler" Burns.

Shortly after Price Montague's visit Tommy Burns phoned to ask me to have dinner in his Mess and to arrive a full half-hour before dinner time. I arrived at the appointed hour and we went to his caravan which was camouflaged and drawn up under a group of trees. Once inside I assumed and hoped that he would give me a drink. Instead, however, he handed me an envelope saying, "I'll leave you for a few minutes whilst you read the contents." He then left the caravan. The envelope was marked "Secret and Confidential" and "For the eyes only of General Burns and Brigadier Kitching." I assumed it was to tell me that I was to return to the U.K. to be Guy Simonds' Chief of Staff. Instead, it said in so many words that the Cabinet in Ottawa had approved my promotion to Major-General to command 4th Armoured Division which was a part of Guy Simonds' Corps. If I had not been seated at the time I would have fallen down. My knees would have given way.

I read and reread the message ten or fifteen times to make sure I wasn't dreaming and then staggered out of the caravan to be greeted by Tommy Burns who said very quietly, "Congratulations, that must have been a nice surprise." It was. He then reminded me that I was not to mention this to anyone until an announcement was made a few days later just before I was to leave Italy. After the announcement I hardly had time to say farewell to anyone.

I was to be at the landing strip on the beach at Vasto at 9:00 a.m. the next morning - it was about 25 miles south of us. Archie Butlin did some hasty packing for me and I made sure that he would be following me to the U.K. People like him were a rare breed.

Next morning I duly reported to the R.A.F. air strip on the beach at Vasto. There was a Dakota waiting, with its engines turning over. I went aboard to find about twenty or thirty others already seated on the canvas strips that made up our uncomfortable seats. I think many of the passengers had just climbed aboard for the ride to our first stop at Naples. We were a mixed group with everything from private to brigadier—Canadian, British and Indian.

From Naples we flew on to Rabat in Morocco and spent one night there in a small but exclusive hotel. Shortly after breakfast we boarded another Dakota - and an equally uncomfortable one - for the long flight to the U.K. We took off about 8:00 a.m. and were in the air for ten and a half hours sitting upright with no opportunity to relax. On arrival, I found a message from General Simonds inviting me to spend a couple of nights with him at his headquarters. After arranging for a staff car, I went to see my old friend, Miss Miller, in Hobsons. The last time she had 'fixed me up' with new buttons and badges had been in July 1942 when she changed me overnight into a member of the Edmonton Regiment. When I told her that I wanted to be converted to a Major-General wearing the green flashes of 4th Canadian Armoured Division, she closed the door of her office, pulled out a bottle of excellent sherry and toasted me! She sent for the tailor and asked him to measure me for a new khaki barathea uniform which she said was to be 'on the house' and would be ready in two days. Meanwhile, she converted the battle dress I was wearing from Brigadier to Major-General and sewed on my green flashes.

I was delighted to find that Guy Simonds had his Mess in Gravetye, the splendid Elizabethan mansion five miles southwest of East Grinstead, which was the Mess I had lived in two years before when Major Eric Smith fought his way upstairs with his revolver blazing.

I had a long talk with Guy Simonds who made me feel very welcome. I told him how surprised I had been when I read of my promotion in Tommy Burns' caravan. Marshal Stearns was with him as his A.D.C. and had been promoted to major. Amongst other old friends were Bruce Matthews and Geoff Walsh, who commanded the Artillery and Engineers respectively. Elliot Rodger was the Chief of Staff and the senior Administrative Officer was Darrel Laing. The head of Signals was Fin Clark. It was a good group and I was to work with many of them in the later years of peace.

14

"Totalize," "Tractable" And The Gap

The Headquarters of 4th Canadian Armoured Division was in the Ashdown Forest area of Sussex with most of the units billeted within ten miles. It is a beautiful part of England much favoured in peacetime by picnickers but in wartime we had it to ourselves.

General Worthington, from whom I took over command, was the father of the Armoured Corps and a man of intense energy. It had been this energy, coupled with his resourcefulness, that had obtained our first tanks from the UK and US, in 1938/39. There were only a few of them, and the American Renault's were obsolete, but they were a start. "Worthy," as he was known to everyone, gave birth to the Ram Tank - the first tank to be built in Canada and I understand that the U.S. Army used some parts of it in the design of their famous Grant and Sherman tanks.

I spent two days with Worthy during this 'hand over' of command. On the first day he went to say farewell and introduce me to the troops. It was emotional because he had commanded the division since its formation and in my remarks I said I was sure that Worthington's departure would leave a gap that would be difficult to fill.

On the second day we spent the morning in his office on one wall of which was a huge chart showing the organization of the division by brigades, regiments and corps. Included in detail on the chart were the names of all officers of the ranks of major and above, listed with their particular regiments and squadrons. Starting with the Division Headquarters and going through each unit in turn, Worthy gave me his impression of every officer named. He appeared to know them all and went into great detail about some of them. I was most impressed.

During the afternoon, I met with the G.S.O. I (Lt.-Col. Eddy Ganong) and the AA&QMG (Lt.-Col John Proctor) to discuss the set-up of the Headquarters. I told them I wanted everyone to start operating as if they were in action - to move out of offices and start to function in the field. In discussing this, I said I was sorry that the huge chart showing regiments and squadrons and their commanders could not be located in a vehicle or tent as it was too big. John Proctor laughed and said, "Oh, I wouldn't pay any attention to that chart, it's completely out-of-date as half the people on it left us some months ago!"

I was fortunate in having with me in 4th Division a number of officers who had been in action in Sicily and Italy and who were mostly given a promotion on being transferred. Jim Jefferson, who had commanded the Edmontons, was promoted brigadier to command the 10th Infantry Brigade. Leslie Booth took over the Armoured Brigade and Herm Lane the Artillery. The latter was an outstanding officer who would have gone to the top had he not been killed in action later that year. Amongst the squadron and company commanders who came from Italy were Ned Amy, Snuffy Smith and Bill Cromb—each of them to earn well-deserved promotion and decorations in the months ahead. I had met Ned Amy on the Orsogna front when his squadron of the Calgarys supported us. Both he and Snuffy Smith had won Military Crosses during the fighting in December which culminated in the capture of Ortona. At my headquarters it was soon obvious that John Proctor. the senior administrative officer, was the driving force. He had had a good military grounding at R.M.C., was physically strong and a hard worker. He knew what was wanted.

During March I visited most of the units in the division with the intention of speaking to the officers. Unfortunately, we were not allowed to hold any divisional exercises with everyone participating and I think that was what was needed. Whilst the individual regiments had reached a good standard of training, the essential cooperation between armour, infantry and artillery had not been practiced to the extent it should have been. Nor had the brigade and divisional headquarters had enough experience of command and control, on exercises of some duration, that would have taxed their resources and taught them lessons. We rehearsed our communications on Corps map exercises and so improved our battle procedures but it was not possible to create the 'fog of war' that engulfs a unit in its first actions.

Whilst we trained as best we could, our routines were interrupted almost each week with visits from very important people.

First, was His Majesty the King who spent the day with 2nd Canadian Corps. He visited 4th Armoured in the morning and lunched at Guy Simonds' Mess before visiting 2nd Infantry Division in the afternoon. It was quite a day. The plan was to greet him with a Guard of Honour of the Governor-General's Foot Guards after which he would meet my staff and other senior officers of my Headquarters and then inspect the units of the division which would be drawn up on each side of the road. Since the inspection would take about an hour and the King would have breakfasted early that morning, I was asked to provide coffee in a suitable tent at the halfway point in the walk through and also arrange for a latrine in the area "just in case."

The Guard of Honour was excellent and the King was very pleased with them except that, in accordance with new Canadian and British protocol, we had drawn up the Guard in three ranks. The King said he liked Guards to be in two ranks and did not appreciate the new protocol at all. He was quite correct, of course, because with three ranks the inspecting officer ended up on the wrong end of the Guard.

After this inspection I took the King to meet my senior officers. I introduced each in turn by name. As we walked away the King turned to me and said, "Kitching, when you introduce someone to me you must tell me at the same time just what he does, then I can talk to him intelligently. But when you just say 'This is Colonel Smith,' it doesn't help me at all." The King spoke in a kind way. I remembered his remarks and from then on, always used that technique.

After inspecting the first half of the division we went to the refreshment tent for coffee. All was going well and the King chatted happily with a number of officers. After a few minutes I went over to the King's Equerry, to ask if the King would like to go to the latrine before starting off again. He said, "I've no idea, go and ask him!" This was not very helpful but I summoned up my courage and approached the Monarch. "Sir," I said, "would you care to use the latrine?" "No," replied the King, "but am I supposed to use it?" I was completely floored by his directness but recovered immediately and told him that one of our men had built a superb 'throne' for his use in a nearby tent and, although he had no desire to use it, would he mind having a look at it. The soldier, who had painted a magnificent Coat-of-Arms of Canada on the back of the throne, was standing at the entrance to the tent and as the King arrived he saluted and held up the flap of the tent for the King to enter. He went in, had a look at the painting on the 'throne' and on his way out said to the soldier, "Thank you, that is a fine piece of work and I'm sorry I can't christen it!" The rest of the King's inspection went off without incident. He was pleased at the appearance of the men and remarked on the material of our battle dress which was not as coarse as that of the British.

Following our inspection I drove to Guy Simonds' Mess for lunch. Charles Foulkes was there before me and, of course, asked a number of questions about the King and his remarks during his inspection of 4th Division. Charles was being inspected in the afternoon and was already just a little nervous. After a few minutes, the King walked in and we were presented to him by Guy Simonds. When Charles was introduced the King immediately said, "When I inspect your Guard of Honour, will you please have them drawn up in two ranks?" "Certainly, sir," replied Charles Foulkes and was about to move away to phone his headquarters about the Guard change when the King said rather sharply to him, "Why are you wearing a different uniform to the one your men wear?" Charles was wearing a battle dress made of barathea cloth instead of the regulation material. Charles was completely at a loss for words so the King went on to the next introduction. Charles then beat a hasty retreat to the phone to tell his AA&QMG (Lt.-Col. Larry Dezeil) to be sure that the Guard was in two ranks and also to arrange somehow for a normal battle dress to be rushed to Simonds' Mess so that he could change.

I don't know what went wrong but when the Monarch arrived at the 2nd Division's Guard of Honour it was in three ranks and, to one side, was Charles Foulkes' batman with a change of battle dress! The King turned to Charles and said, "They don't seem to pay much attention to your instructions, General, do they?" It was an unhappy day for Charles and he told me later that the reason why Larry Deziel had not carried out his order was that he thought Charles had possibly had a couple of drinks with the King and was confused! Poor Charles, he hadn't even had one.

We had visits from Generals Eisenhower, Montgomery and Crerar. Each had a different approach in the way they talked to the men. Eisenhower walked along the ranks chatting to perhaps a dozen of the men before climbing on a jeep to speak through a microphone. Montgomery climbed on his jeep and then asked the men to gather round him. He spoke slowly without a microphone, repeating himself when he wanted to emphasize a point. Harry Crerar was a little more formal but the troops listened and liked what they heard. He was not inspiring but he was a Canadian and commanded the Army.

Perhaps the most unusual visitor was Prime Minister William Lyon Mackenzie King. I was given about a week's notice of his visit, made a quick plan which called for the Prime Minister to walk through the ranks in much the same way that the King had done, after which we would have a formal march past of Infantry and Armour. Crerar and Simonds were both skeptical about letting Mr. King walk along the ranks of the men; he had been booed by 2nd Division on one occasion a couple of years before and Simonds was determined not to have an incident of that kind on this occasion. After speaking with many of the commanders in our division I assured Guy Simonds that there would not be a problem. Somewhat reluctantly he agreed and we went ahead with our plans. We were determined to show him the power of an armoured division which meant grouping all tanks and weapons at certain places so that he could have an impression of our strength. To march the tanks past him in line of squadrons, we flattened an area of Ashdown Forest using 36 bulldozers with 24 water carts in continual procession to dampen down the clouds of dust thrown up by the dozers.

Wednesday, the 17th May, was the great day and the Prime Minister arrived at 2:00 p.m. and stayed two and a half hours with us.

The men were drawn up three abreast on each side of the road and Mr. King should have been most impressed as they were as fit and healthy a group of men as one could wish for. I couldn't help but feel though that he saw them as potential voters and not as soldiers.

All went well. After his walk through the ranks without incident the men formed up in six ranks and marched past him along the road. We then moved over to a small bleacher that had been built from which he would take the salute of the tanks. I sat on the Prime Minister's right as General Simonds felt that he might want to ask questions about the division. However, Mr. King said nothing. In a few minutes the serried ranks of armour appeared with squadrons in lines about a hundred yards apart. To reduce the dust they travelled at only three miles an hour. Mr. King stood as the first few squadrons rolled past, their guns dipping in salute. He raised his hat to each in turn but then, to my surprise, after only ten minutes, he sat down. Harry Crerar, who was on the Prime Minister's left, leaned across and asked me if I could speed up the march past. I told him it was impossible, not only because of the heavy dust that would cover us all, but that the tank dispersal area was small and on the edge of a ravine. To try and speed them would invite trouble. Mr. King remained seated and nothing was done by Crerar to get him to stand and acknowledge the salutes.

I leaned over to Mr. King and, by way of conversation and in an effort to make him appear interested, said, "Sir, each one of these lines of tanks costs about half a million dollars." He shot out of his seat, took off his hat and remained in that position until the parade was finished. He could not have moved with greater speed if I had told him that in each line there were a thousand Liberals! However, the effort had apparently exhausted him because he said he must leave without inspecting the artillery whose guns had been drawn up in impressive array just behind the reviewing bleacher. Nor would he have tea with us in the large tent that had been put up for the purpose. We never received any message from Mr. King, not one word of thanks or appreciation in spite of the many extra hours of work everyone had put in to make the event the spectacle it was.

Some weeks before the invasion of Normandy, I attended a most interesting and significant gathering at General Montgomery's headquarters in St. Paul's School in London. To this gathering General Eisenhower summoned all the Division, Corps and Army Commanders who were to take part in the Normandy operations together with their counterparts in the Navy and Air Force. There must have been about 100 of us for a briefing of the plans which had been made for the airborne landings, the offensive and defensive naval support, the air support by thousands of aircraft, the assault across the beaches by six divisions and the incredible plans for the instant creation of harbours where none presently existed.

General Eisenhower spoke first, then Montgomery, Admiral Ramsay and Air Chief Marshal Leigh-Mallory. Montgomery outlined his overall plan to reach the line of the Seine and Loire by D-Day + 90. General Brereton gave us his plans for the landing of three airborne divisions; General Bradley followed with his plan for the landing of three U.S. divisions and General Dempsey concluded with his plans for the landing of the 3rd Canadian Division together with two British divisions and additional commandos. We were listening to the culmination of over four years of the most detailed planning for the launching of the greatest Combined Operation in the history of the world. Amongst the many present was General George Patton, flamboyant as ever and making rude noises throughout the period of Montgomery's remarks. I understood that had it been possible, Mr. Roosevelt would have attended but instead he was represented by Mr. Harry Hopkins. Mr. Churchill came in shortly before noon puffing his big cigar which he waved in the direction of Montgomery's big "No Smoking" sign. Shortly after that the King arrived and was greeted with the same enthusiastic applause that had greeted Mr. Churchill. It was a day in a lifetime and I only regret that a photograph was not taken to record the event. I sat beside General Rod Keller who commanded our 3rd Division and who would be taking part in the assault on D-Day. We returned to our rooms at the Dorchester Hotel and had a drink together before dinner. As we went down in the elevator all he said was, "Christ, it's going to be quite a day." He, of course, had been familiar with some of the D-Day planning but was greatly impressed by the magnitude of the whole plan that had been unveiled that day.

A sight I shall always remember was the continual stream of shipping in the Channel once the invasion had begun. General Simonds had moved his headquarters temporarily into Dover Castle and from its walls, 400 feet above the sea, we stood and watched the precession of ships of all kinds moving in orderly lines whilst being fired on by the huge German coastal guns that were located on the Calais shore. Not one ship was hit during the two hours that I watched. Our own heavy guns, mounted on rails or firing from concrete emplacements, engaged the Germans but we could not see how effective they were as the French coast was very indistinct. The duel continued day and night, we were told, for about a month. The Germans must have wondered initially what on earth the huge concrete buildings were that were being towed past by tugs; they were soon to realize that they were the breakwaters and docks of the artificial harbour being created almost overnight on the Normandy coast.

Looking down from the castle walls and off to the right was the dock at which we, in the R.C.R., had loaded the "Canterbury" on that day in May 1940 when we were destined for Calais. What an incredible change there had been in our fortunes in those four years. In 1940 we were defeated by the seemingly unconquerable German Army; and now we had the upper hand and that unconquerable Army was in turn about to go down to final defeat.

After the landings in Normandy on the 6th June were successful I started a round of visits to all units of 4th Division. I took with me each day the official report on the progress of the divisions that had landed in the initial assault and also the build up of new divisions as the endless stream of landing craft criss-crossed the Channel, bringing in tens of thousands of men and thousands of vehicles and tanks each day. During the first month after D-Day over one million men and 100,000 vehicles had been landed safely - an incredible feat. The more I spoke with the units and told them what was happening the more they wanted to get into the fray and it was a genuine disappointment to us all when there was a delay in our departure date. The requirement in Normandy was for infantry divisions and so there were several changes in the priority of departures. More armoured divisions were not required until the bridgehead was expanded and so we sat and waited.

Shortly after D-Day, the German V.1 'doodlebug' pilotless aircraft started to arrive over Britain - mostly over the south-east coast and directed on London. Unfortunately one feel short, landing in one of our units and causing a number of casualties. While the new fighters of the R.C.A.F. and R.A.F. engaged as many of the V.1s as possible in an effort to explode them in flight, every heavy and light anti-aircraft regiment that was mobile and available was moved into position on the south east coast where they engaged the V.1s as they came in from the

Channel. They generally flew at between 500 and 1000 feet and at over 400 miles an hour, a speed that was greater than many of our fighters. Our anti-aircraft regiment, commanded by Lt.-Col. Eric Cormack of Edmonton, went into action not far from hastings and did yeoman service, firing more ammunition at the 'doodlebugs' than they had ever fired in all their training. They claimed three hits which exploded the bombs and a good many near misses that deflected the oncoming bombs from their set course.

In the three months since taking over command I had many opportunities to get to know the staff of the division and the commanders of regiments and services. Shortly after arriving, I was lucky enough to find an excellent A.D.C. from the Edmonton Regiment. Captain Ken Scott had been with the regiment in Italy and proved to be a first-class staff officer and aide.

Before the end of July, Lt.-Col. Fred Wigle replaced Ed Ganong as my G.S.O.I. and he soon established a system that brought more life to the General Staff. Fred was young, capable and full of enthusiasm; there is no doubt he might have become a brigade commander before the end of the war if he had not been killed leading his battalion in an attack early in April 1945. John Proctor remained as the senior administrative officer and was a tower of strength as well as a good friend. He was ably supported by a number of exceptional men who ran the Services including Lt.-Col. Leo Brennan and Charlie Gossage. Lt.-Col. Bill Shireff and Dick Oakes ran a good Signals Organization. Bob Fell commanded the Administrative Group; Clarence Campbell (of hockey fame), Clarence Shepard (later Chairman of Gulf Oil, Canada), Mike Dare (later Vice-Chief of Defence Staff), Red Paradis (who, unfortunately, left the Army in 1951) were majors or captains on the staff. It was a powerhouse of talent.

Brigadier Herm Lane who commanded the Artillery and Bob Jones who commanded the Engineers, were both very able officers. Jim Jefferson, who commanded the Infantry Brigade, was an old friend from my Edmonton Regiment days. He was a quiet spoken man who gave the impression of being 'slow on the uptake' because he always mulled over a question that was put to him before replying. That period of thought and his slow-spoken replies fooled many people, including Montgomery. In 1942 Monty said that Jefferson was "too slow—not a leader'' and recommended that he not be given command of a regiment. When Montgomery visited our division I introduced him to Jim Jefferson who, by this time, was a brigadier and had won two D.S.O.s for his leadership of the Edmonton Regiment which he had taken over from me. Later that day I reminded Montgomery of his earlier assessment of Jefferson. He thought for a moment and said, with a grin, ''Well, I do make mistakes occasionally—but very occasionally.'' Jefferson remained in command of his brigade right through until the end of the war. Two of the best commanders he had in Normandy initially were Lt.-Col. ''Swatty'' Wotherspoon of the South Alberta Regiment which supported him with its tanks, and Lt.-Col. Dave Stewart who commanded the Argyll and Sutherland Highlanders of Canada.

The Armoured Brigade was commanded by Brigadier Booth known as Boothie. I had known him since our early planning for Sicily. He was ably supported by Lt.-Col. Bob Keane who commanded the Lake Superior Regiment but the outstanding regimental commander in the armoured brigade was Lt.-Col. Don Worthington of the British Columbia Regiment. He was the youngest, full of energy and quick to seize an opportunity.

Early in July we had definite news that we would be crossing the Channel in the middle of the month. Some parts of the division, mostly wheeled vehicles, would go through the Pool of London but the remainder would be directed through the complex of docks and 'hards' in the Portsmouth area. The 'hards' were concrete roads built in large numbers which allowed tanks and other tracked vehicles to cross the beaches and climb aboard the tank landing craft through their bow-ramps which were lowered to receive them.

Our headquarters was to cross from the Portsmouth area and as we went through the check points of the movement control and embarkation organization we could not help but marvel at the efficiency of the system. From all over Britain, convoys of vehicles and train-loads of tanks were converging daily on a dozen ports and distributed to waiting craft for passage to Normandy. In addition, tens of thousands of tons of stores of all kinds were lifted each day in small ships for discharge across the Normandy beaches.

Once we were ashore in France and had set up our headquarters, I went to see General Simonds. He invited me into his caravan where he was in conversation with General Dempsey who commanded 2nd British Army. I knew Dempsey from Italy and although he greeted me very pleasantly, it was obvious that he was under a considerable amount of strain. His first words, after greeting me, were "Are your tanks petrol or diesel?" When I told him they were petrol, he seemed disappointed. I did not understand the significance of his remark until after he had gone when Guy Simonds told me that only two days before over 150 tanks of three British divisions had been knocked out during an all out attack to gain the high ground south of Caen. Since many of the tanks were petrol-fueled Shermans they had caught fire more easily and more rapidly than those fueled by diesel. General Dempsey wished that our tanks were diesel and, as we became involved in battle, so did we.

The Headquarters of 2nd Canadian Corps became operational early in July with under its command our 2nd and 3rd Infanty Divisions and our 2nd Armoured Brigade. In its first battles the Corps was under British command, however at the end of the month it came under command of General Crerar of 1st Canadian Army.

General Simonds was under a great deal of pressure from the time his 2nd Corps Headquarters became operational. The expansion of the bridgehead had not gone as fast as Montgomery had hoped. Simonds was ordered to enlarge it in conjunction with an onslaught on his left by three British armoured divisions. The experienced 3rd Canadian Division did well and cleared the factory areas around Colombelles and Cormelles according to plan.

However, 2nd Canadian Division, recently arrived and new to battle, ran into difficulties owing partly to lack of cooperation and understanding between infantry and tanks, and partly due to the fact that they were attacking against the elite 1st SS Panzer Corps. Shortly after, Simonds was ordered to mount another attack east of the Caen-Falaise road and west to the Orne River, in a further effort to hold as many of the German SS and Panzer Divisions on our front as possible while the U.S. 3rd Army under General Patton prepared to break through the Avranches, sixty miles to the south-west. To give General Simonds as much support as possible in what he knew would be a fiercely contested battle, General Dempsey placed under his command for this operation, code named "Spring," two British armoured

divisions and an additional armoured brigade. But the brunt of the battle was to be fought by the two Canadian infantry divisions and the
Canadian armoured brigade.

I attended two or three meetings between General Simonds and the
commanders of divisions and it was quite obvious that Keller and
Foulkes were concerned at what lay ahead. The battle was a 'holding'
one, designed not so much to strike deep into enemy territory but to
keep his forces pinned to the area. Everyone knew that a 'holding' attack is only mounted when the enemy has powerful forces in the area
which must be prevented from being moved elsewhere. To this extent
"Spring" succeeded because the Germans still kept the SS and Panzer
Divisions facing us during the period of the American breakthrough at
Avranches, but our casualties, particularly in infantry, were far high
than anticipated and the attacks were called off. Only the RHLI from
Hamilton, commanded by John Rockingham and supported by a
squadron of British tanks from the 1st Royal Tank Regiment, were able
to hold the ground they had won in the battle. The attacks elsewhere
were a failure. Later reports estimated that the cost to us totalled approximately 1500 casulaties of which 500 were fatal.

To me, two things seemed uppermost in Guy Simonds' mind on that
day. First, we had to find some way of getting the assaulting infantry
through the forward enemy defences without their having to take such
heavy casualties and second, he must get rid of General Charles
Foulkes who, in his opinion, did not have the right qualities to command our 2nd Division. Brigadier Ben Cunningham was being relieved
of his command of 9th Brigade because of his failure to take the small
village of Tilly, as were two of his battalion commanders. But on at
least three occasions Guy Simonds confided in me that he was going to
get rid of Charles Foulkes. I can only assume that General Crerar must
have intervened and insisted that Charles remain because nothing happened.

On the more vital problem of how to get through the enemy
defences, Guy Simonds came up with a solution which had been in
people's minds for centuries but lacked practical application in modern
war. The Romans developed the Testudo or Turtle. They used the
cover of hundreds of shields to protect a moving phalanx of soldiers by
giving it side and overhead cover from enemy spears and other

projectiles as it moved through the enemy lines. Leonardo da Vinci in the 15th century drew a picture of his invention - a wheeled version of the Testudo with permanent roof and sides of armour but propelled by the soldiers inside it.

At the time when Simonds was wracking his brain on how to produce a modern Testudo, four of our Canadian artillery regiments were changing over their guns from self-propelled 105 mm's to the 25 pounders which were in normal use in the Canadian Army. The 105 mm's were U.S. Army weapons mounted on a Sherman tank chassis. Having seen these self-propelled equipments in action, Simonds knew that the area taken up by the gun, its crew and its ammunition was a large one. If the gun and ammunition racks were removed, there would be accommodation for up to 14 soldiers. This, then, was the answer. The armour on the sides and front would, with small additions, be sufficient to protect the infantry during the critical 'breakin' battle which up to now had caused so many casualties.

Simonds obtained permission to remove all the guns and modify seventy of these equipments and they became the first 'armoured personnel carriers' (APC) used in modern war. It meant that infantry could now accompany tanks wherever they went and the APC is now standard equipment in all armies. But the concept came from the innovative brain of General Guy Simonds and they were first used in the great battle code named "Totalize" which started on the night of 7th-8th August.

Prior to "Totalize," 4th Armoured Division took over the defences manned by our 3rd Division which had been in action continually since they assaulted the beaches on the 6th June. They were badly in need of a rest. I spent three hours with General Keller when we took over from his division; a part of the time we went across the front on foot or in a scout car towards the villages of Hubert Folie, Bourguebus and Four which were our advanced defensive positions. We were also able to see plainly from the raised railway embankment the ruined hamlet of Tilly-la-Campagne occupied by soldiers of the 1st SS Division. Rod Keller's 9th Brigade had failed to capture Tilly and his advice to me at the time was "leave it alone—try somewhere else." Unfortunately, pressure from General Montgomery forced Simonds to make two further attacks on Tilly and units of 4th Armoured Division took part in both attacks, neither of which were successful.

Tilly was originally a hamlet of about eight farm houses each built of stone and surrounded, as is the Norman custom, by high stone walls enclosing a small orchard, a garden and a large barn. Each house, within its walled area, was itself a fortress and by the time the Germans had prepared them for defence they were almost impregnable. The first thing they did was to strengthen the basements of the houses to withstand heavy pressure from above, then they dynamited the walls so that they collapsed inwards forming a pyramind of stone on top of the basements. These pyramids were sometimes ten feet thick and could withstand the heaviest shelling. Next, they prepared the basements just like a concrete dug-out with weapon slits at ground level for machine-guns which were sighted to fire along the narrow gravel roads that ran between the walls enclosing each farm house. Any attacker on entering the hamlet would be greeted with a cross-fire of bullets from each basement fortress and heavy mortar fire, from which the defenders in their basements were immune. In addition, heavy tanks, hidden in the woods behind the hamlet, would move forward to prepared positions from which they could destroy the tanks that accompanied our infantry.

Although, numerically, we were far superior in numbers of tanks to the Germans, they had the big advantage of a more powerful gun in their Panther and Tiger tanks and also large numbers of 88 mm guns which could be used in both an anti-aircraft role and as anti-tank weapons. Furthermore, while we generally were always attacking and therefore exposed, the enemy was on the defensive and hugged the ground. He would hide or camouflage his tanks and anti-tank guns so that they were often difficult to detect even when they opened fire. Their more powerful guns could engage our tanks and destroy them before we could get close enough to make our guns effective. In Normandy we started with most of our tanks armed with the 75-mm gun - a good weapon in its day but no match for the German long barrelled 75-mm or the very powerful 88-mm. However, we were learning. In Normandy, four tanks in each of our squadrons were equipped with the excellent long-barrelled 17-pounder anti-tank gun and as the months went by this gun became the main armament of most of our tanks.

To make the Germans think we had a tank larger than anything they had ever produced, I got the commander of our Engineers, Lt.-Col. Bob Jones, to build a huge dummy tank which was to be mounted on one of our Shermans. The Sherman tank weighed approximately 32 tons - the heaviest German Tiger weighed 56 tons and this new phoney tank would look as if it weighed over 100 tons! Our engineers went to work with a will. They produced "Foni," as we called it, in a couple of days, made almost entirely of wood and tin plate. Its size can be judged by the fact that the 'gun' sticking out in front was a hydro pole and on the rear of the turret were three 40-mm. wooden Bofors gun for anti-aircraft protection. With its camouflage paint it looked very real at fifty paces and it attracted a great deal of attention from passing soldiers as it lumbered along a road towards the open fields. As our Signal Regiments had laid hundreds of miles of cable to ensure good telephone service we had a soldier perched at the end of the 'gun' barrel to raise overhead cables before they became ensnared in "Foni." Unfortunately by the time "Foni" was ready for 'action' I had become very involved with Guy Simonds in the final planning for "Totalize" so I could not accompany it on its trial run. However, John Proctor, my AA&QMG and Bob Jones went along in a jeep to observe the enemy's reaction. From what they told me, his reaction was fairly violent as he engaged it with 88-mm. fire. However, "Foni" was not hit and returned to base unharmed. Its dimensions were 45 feet long, 12 feet wide and 10 feet high. Quite a tank!

The preparations for "Totalize" were on an enormous scale. Apart from the size of our forces and the novelty of using APC's for the first time, Bomber Command of the RAF finally agreed to give us close support by employing heavy bombers to obliterate five defended villages only one mile ahead of our advancing troops. That it was possible to make this attack by night shows the degree of excellence of our staffs at this period of the war. Seven hundred guns were to support our attack and they required over two hundred thousand shells to do the job. Hundreds of thousands of gallons of petrol had also to be brought forward to top up the tanks and vehicles. Planning went on for two days and the final details were not completed until eleven hours before the attack was to begin. It was a triumph of staff work and I was very proud of the staff at my divisional headquarters. The battle named "Totalize" was to be fought in two phases. The first phase was the night attack using tanks, infantry in armoured personnel carriers and other armoured vehicles, charging en masse supported by the heavy bombers and seven hundred guns.

It was successful and the use of APC's reduced the number of our casualties dramatically. My division did not take part in that phase; we, together with the Polish Armoured Division, were kept in reserve to play the leading parts in Phase II.

Phase II had major changes made to it only twenty-four hours before the attack. The most important was the introduction of the Polish Armoured Division and the elimination of our 3rd Infantry Division. Right up to the morning of the 6th August the break-out battle of Phase II was to be fought by our veteran 3rd Division and my own division, the 4th Armoured. I was very happy about this and told General Keller how much I was looking forward to working with him. His division was to 'make the hole' through which I would pass. With the change to the Polish Armoured Division, a problem immediately arose. Not only were our two armoured divisions to 'make the hole' ourselves but each one of us was limited in our flexibility by being forced to attack on a very narrow front. My division was given a frontage of only 1000 yards and my 'start' line was supposed to be clear of the enemy some hours before we were due to cross it. The Polish Division had about the same frontage, complicated by the fact that they had heavily wooded areas on their front and flank.

Both General Maczek, who commanded the Poles, and I asked General Simonds to extend our frontage to give us room for manoeuvre but he would not agree as it would mean changing the objectives of one of the assaulting divisions in Phase I. This he would not do. This was unfortunate, not only because it gave us no room to manoeuvre, but also because the enemy commander would quickly appreciate that our attacks were coming on a very narrow front and would then concentrate his smaller forces to deal with them. That is exactly what happened. Another problem that I discussed with General Simonds at the time was the long pause of about eight hours between Phase I and Phase II. General Maczek was present at that time and was also concerned. The long pause was essential, General Simonds felt, in order that heavy bombers could be used against the enemy's second line of defence which his Intelligence officers told him might be manned by the formidable 1st SS Division. In fact, that division had been withdrawn on the nights 4/5 and 5/6 August and was in action against the Americans on the 7th. Canadian Corps Intelligence was quite wrong in its assessment of the enemy second line of defence and I think this made Guy Simonds overly cautious; as a result we lost the momentum of the attack, the very thing that General Crerar had warned against. The tanks and APC's that had penetrated the first line of enemy defences so well halted short of their objectives to reorganize when the enemy was already withdrawing in panic. German General Meyer said it was "like stopping to water the horses in the middle of a cavalry charge." Only comparatively weak German forces occupied their second line of defence.

General Meyer, who commanded 12th SS Division, had half his division watching for a possible British break-through about ten miles to his left at Brieux and the other half astride the Caen-Falaise Road. Because of the long delay between Phase I and Phase II of the Canadian Corps attack, he was able to concentrate his division to oppose us and even to mount counter-attacks.

Prior to the beginning of "Totalize," 4th Armoured Division was concentrated south of Caen, the infantry on the right, armour on the left. From there we were to move in two columns along a series of tracks up to our start line. Although there had been a number of changes in the Corps Plan for the Division, my staff were able to deal with them effectively.

My memory of those early days in Normandy as we prepared for "Totalize" is very clear about the units of the division and the men in them. I had not seen finer soldiers anywhere, they were well disciplined in a cheerful way and had the skills of trained soldiers. I was very proud, and the evening before the great battle I prayed as I had never prayed before.

Phase I of the attack took off before midnight to the thunder of a thousand heavy bombers as they obliterated five defended villages with three thousand five hundred tons of bombs; and, as the armoured columns felt their way behind the bombing, seven hundred guns sent a continuing storm of shells to give them further support.

The attack succeeded in getting through the enemy's forward defended localities and with a minimum of casualties, but the momentum slowed after first light and it was not until early afternoon that their final objectives were taken. At the time, my division was accused of being slow in getting to our start line. However, the painstaking research of historians has shown that most of the delay was beyond our control. In fact, the infantry brigade, led by the Argylls and the South Alberta's tanks, were on their start line on time but were held back because elements of another division were still involved in a battle in the area. Once our brigade got the all-clear, they advanced with great courage and determination to their objectives.

Our artillery moved to an area which we had been assured was clear of the enemy. It was not. The guns had to be deployed whilst they were under machine-gun and mortar fire which resulted in a number of casualties.

Our armoured brigade was to attack up the left side of our boundary and, because of our very restricted frontage, had only had about 500 yards in which to manoeuvre. This was the normal frontage for a squadron to operate in, and so the great power of an armoured brigade of about 160 tanks was represented by a single squadron of about 14 tanks! Since the enemy had been able to concentrate his heavy tanks and 88-mm. guns against our narrow frontage he had the advantage in our initial attack. As a result our armour was slow to get moving.

The bombing by heavy bombers of the U.S. Air Force had not been as effective as we had hoped, causing very few casualties amongst the Germans. However, a number of the Flying Fortresses mistook their aiming marks and dropped their tonnage amongst our own troops causing many casualties. Over 65 were killed and 250 wounded, amongst the latter was General Keller. Over 50 vehicles, five heavy guns and many tons of ammunition were destroyed. The reason why we always suffered heavy casualties when bombed by our own air forces was that we were generally moving in vehicles or out in the open. The Germans on the other hand, being on the defensive, were in trences or in the basements of buildings.

The wounding of Rod Keller was a blow to the Canadian Army. He had done well since landing with his division on D-Day and would, I am sure, have taken over the Corps had anything happened to Simonds. Another loss earlier that day was Brigadier Bob Wyman, commanding our 2nd Armoured Brigade. Bob was standing in the turret of his tank when he was hit in the shoulder by a sniper's bullet. It was shortly after this that General Simonds, who was cruising around the battlefield, came to my tactical headquarters and, in the course of a discussion on the battle, asked me whom I would like to command my armoured brigade in the event that Boothie was hit. I told him that of the commanding officers in the brigade I felt that Worthington of the B.C. Regiment was the most able and he could be a stop gap for a short period. We discussed Jim Roberts of the Manitoba Dragoons, George Robinson and Bob Moncel as possible brigadiers to command the brigade on a permanent basis and we finally settled on Moncel who was a lieutenant-colonel on Simonds' staff. He could be available immediately if anything happened to Boothie.

It was strange but at about the time that Simonds and I were discussing that problem I became convinced that Boothie had a premonition that he would be killed. He certainly was not the same keen and cheerful man of the year before in Sicily. When his brigade was held up at the beginning of our Phase II, I looked for him to hear what was wrong. I had the greatest difficulty locating him and he would not answer calls on the radio. When I finally found him he was nearly two miles away from the battle and fast asleep in his tank. I peronally had to climb up on the tank to wake him and tell him to go and see what was happening. I was so angry that I ordered him out of the tank and gave him a tongue-lashing for five minutes. He was almost in tears when he went forward.

That evening at about 6:30, General Simonds ordered me to continue our operations through the night to secure Point 195, an important feature about four miles south on the way to Falaise. I called my Orders Group to meet me at Brig. Jefferson's headquarters (the Orders Group always consisted of the brigade commanders and commanders of Artillery, Signals and Engineers and my two senior staff officers). At about 8:00 o'clock, I gave orders to Brigadier Booth to push through the night, to capture the village of Bretteville-le-Rabet and then Point 195. Jim Jefferson's brigade were to follow up the armour and assist them after the capture of Bretteville-le-Rabet by occupying two villages astride the Caen-Falaise Road, Langannerie and Grainville.

The Canadian Grenadier Guards and the Lake Superior Regiment captured Bretteville-le-Rabet shortly after first light. The B.C. Regiment and the Algonquin Regiment, given the task of capturing Point 195, swung to the east to avoid the battle then going on at Bretteville-le-Rabet. Moving in the dark in strange country and with no prominent features on the skyline as a guide is a very difficult operation when it involves tanks and other tracked vehicles. The clouds of dust created by the leading tanks blind those following them; and with a total of 100 tracked vehicles the resulting dust cloud is not unlike a sandstorm in the desert. As Col. Don Worthington, commanding the force, continued to swing southeast he must have crossed a road which he mistook for the main Caen-Falaise highway because he then continued on until he saw high ground ahead and assumed it was his objective, Point 195. He reported being on it at 7:00 a.m.

In fact, the Worthington force had swung much too far to the east and was about five miles northeast of Point 195. Without knowing it Worthington had captured one of the Polish Armoured Divisions' objectives. But the tragedy was that we did not know where he was; he insisted he was on 195 but we knew from observation he was not there. We fired artillery smoke shells onto the real 195 and asked him to tell us where he was in relation to the smoke but he said he could not see it. We then thought that he must have swung behind the enemy's main position towards the town of Potigny. Brig. Lane of the artillery went up in a small spotting aircraft to see if he could locate the group but without success. We heard the thunder of gunfire over to our left but we assumed it was connected with the Polish Armoured Division who were supposed to be keeping up with our left flank.

I don't know what went wrong with the Poles on those two days, the 8th and 9th of August, but they certainly were no help to us. They hardly moved an inch on the 8th, so much so that General Rennie of the 51st Highland Division complained to General Simonds about their inactivity and the fact that they continued to pour vehicles and men into his area without making any moves forward to ease the congestion. They were not much better on the 9th when Worthington captured one of their objectives at 7:00 a.m., thinking he was on his objective, Point 195. I formed a poor opinion of the Poles in that battle. If they had been as aggressive as Worthington had been they would have been there to relieve him of some of the fierce pressure that was put on him all day by the heavy tanks of 12 SS Division. As we know now, Worthington's force almost over-ran the enemy headquarters without realizing it; if they had gone another 1000 yards to the south they would have been behind the enemy's main defences. I won't attempt to tell the story here of the very gallant fight put up by Don Worthington's force. It is told in detail by Colonel Charles Stacey in his official history, "The Victory Campaign" and by Professor Roy in his "1944, Canadians in Normandy." They document the happenings of that day and give full credit to the courageous leadership shown by Don Worthington and the resolute way in which his men fought until overwhelmed. It was a triumph and a tragedy; a tragic example of incorrect map and compass readings which led to the loss of nearly 100 lives, including Don Worthington's who was killed late in the afternoon, and Lt.-Col. Don Hay of the Algonquins who died of his wounds later. Nearly 120 others were wounded or taken prisoner. Forty-seven out of a total of 55 of the B.C. Regiment's tanks were destroyed and the Governor General's Footguards lost an additional 20 tanks in trying to go to their assistance when they radioed in the morning that they were at Point 195 and needed help.

To all of us who were in senior positions of command it was a day that we could not forget. But that night our spirits were lifted high again by the actions of the regiments of the 10th Brigade. Led by Lt.-Col. Stewart, the Argylls silently occupied Point 195 during the night and the Lincoln and Welland Regiment came up on their right to protect that flank. It was a daring move which took the enemy completely by surprise; he reacted violently at dawn when he realized what had happened, but our troops held on, supported by tanks of the Governor General's Foot Guards and the Canadian Grenadier Guards who then tried to seize another feature about two miles to the south. However, the enemy had been alerted by our successful occupation of 195 and had moved in a number of his famous long-range 88-mm. guns. After losing a number of tanks, the regiment was ordered to withdraw. I felt that the division had done well in its first large-scale battle - a little slow off the mark on our left at the outset but we had made up for it except for the tragic losses of Worthington's force. Our division was withdrawn to prepare for our next operation, codenamed "Tractable."

"Tractable" took place on the 14th August and should have been one of the outstanding assaults of the Normandy campaign. It was a mass attack by two armoured brigades and four infantry brigades. Each armoured brigade had about 150 tanks drawn up in three ranks of about 50 in each rank and only fifteen yards between tanks. Each of the two blocks of 150 tanks represented a solid phalanx of armour about 1000 yards wide and 200 yards deep. Beside them and in the rear were the infantry regiments, some in tracked or wheeled vehicles, and some ready to move forward on foot. The whole force was to move in daylight behind a wide smoke screen which would be fired just ahead of us as we went forward.

About 18 hours before the attack was to begin an officer of another division drove by mistake into the enemy defences. He was killed but he had on him a marked map giving all details of "Tractable." The enemy was therefore able to reorganize his defences in an effort to deal with the juggernaut that would hit him the next day. As if that was not enough to make us wonder whether "Tractable" would be as successful as we hoped, 77 heavy bombers of the R.C.A.F. that were scheduled to drop their bombs on the enemy as our attack went in dropped them, instead, amongst our headquarters and artillery. They dropped about 350 tons of bombs and as most of our troops were in the open, the Corps suffered over 100 killed and 250 wounded. My Tactical Headquarters was in the area of the bombs as General Simonds, who was also close by, said he saw one stick of bombs straddle my headquarters but, although we had no casualties, the radios in the tanks and on the jeeps were badly effected at the most critical time and our signallers had difficulty regaining communications with our brigades.

But by far the worst thing that happened that day occurred a few minutes before the bombing. Brigadier Booth's headquarters had lined up with the tanks of his regiments and at about 11:30 a.m. he reported all was well. Jim Jefferson also reported that his brigade was formed up and ready to move. At the appointed time the artillery fired thousands of smoke shells to conceal the first lines of tanks and the whole force moved forward. Within a few minutes the clouds of dust thrown up by the many hundreds of tanks and other vehicles made it difficult to maintain direction. Whoever was navigating for Booth's headquarters group swung far too much to the right so that without any warning they were engaged by enemy tanks, Brig. Booth, his Intelligence Officer and a Liaison Officer were killed as were some of the tank and vehicle crews in his group. Since all their radios were put out of action there was no way that I could be told of the tragedy. The Brigade Major, Gerry Chubb, was able to lift Booth's body on to a tank and drive away from the carnage but it was over three hours before we realized the full impact of the ambush. I immediately ordered Lt.-Col. Murray Scott of the Footguards to take over the brigade whilst the staff set about rebuilding the headquarters. When I phoned Guy Simonds with the bad news I asked for Bob Moncel to come up and take over the brigade on a permanent basis as agreed between us.

Before discussing the details of Operation "Tractable" I want to mention three factors which are of the greatest importance in battle and which affected our operations in Normandy. I do not mention them to provide an excuse for what may have gone wrong but they did have a decisive affect on our ability to operate well as a coordinated division. The three factors are Command, Casualties and Communication.

Command in the Army is a very personal responsibility within a regiment or battalion. When one, as a corporal, commands a section of 8 or 9 men; or, as a lieutenant or sergeant, commands a platoon of 30 men, you are their leader. You must inspire them to the extent that they will follow you no matter how unpleasant the job may be. This feeling of personal loyalty and trust between soldiers and their leaders extends to the company level of about 120 men and to the battalion of 800-900 men. But it stops there. That is about as far as loyalty of that kind will stretch. In the Canadian Army the regiment or battalion is the most important component; and formations such as brigades and divisions are made up of a number of these components mixed together. Artillery, Armour, Infantry, Engineers, Signals, Service Corps, Ordnance Corps, etc., etc.—each has its special regimental spirit which it contributes to the whole. Command, then, within these regiments and battalions is a personal relationship between soldiers and their leaders and if the pattern is disturbed and diluted too frequently, it will affect the performance of that regiment. This is particularly true when it happens to a regiment in the shock of its first battle and before it has had any opportunity to work out its battle procedures.

CASUALTIES

When one reads in Professor Reg Roy's book, "1944, The Canadians in Normandy," about the number of our tanks that were destroyed each day, imagine the impact this must have had on the squadrons and troops to which they belonged. When a tank was hit perhaps two of the crew of four or five escaped unhurt. When a replacement tank came forward with a replacement crew, no one, perhaps, would know much about that crew and yet they were supposed to be able to go straight into action as if they were as good and as well versed in the squadron's procedures as the tank crew that had been knocked out.

Extend such thoughts about the problems of new tanks and new crews to the terrible losses suffered by the British Columbia Regiment on the 9th August. On that day they lost 47 out of their 55 tanks and half their crews including the commanding officer and all three of the squadron commanders; and yet, they were in action as a regiment only four days later. But, of course, it could not be quite the same regiment until it had time to shake down and until the new squadron and troop commanders had a chance to practice their drills even if they had to do it in action and under fire. The other two armoured regiments in the Armoured Brigade had also lost over twenty tanks each in their first two days of battle; and, on occasion, in the succeeding ten days of the Normandy battle had to group their remaining tanks into two squadrons as they did not have enough to make up the third. The Infantry had also suffered severe casualties, particularly the Algonquin Regiment which was reduced for a number of days to only two companies instead of four.

COMMUNICATIONS

The radios of World War II, or wireless sets as they were then called, were nothing like as efficient as they are now. Walkie-talkie's were unknown to us in Normandy so that communication between the platoon commander and his sections was by voice, hand signals or a runner. The platoon commanders and company commanders each had a somewhat cumbersome set carried by an orderly but since the antenna had to be extended upwards for good transmission it was easily spotted by an alert enemy sniper. To carry the radio was, therefore, not regarded as a sinecure. Furthermore, nearly all transmissions became dead during the hours of darkness. So, reporting on a battle was a hit and miss affair if one relied on radios, even at brigade and divisional level. Instead, whenever possible, the Royal Canadian Corps of Signals laid telephone line and hoped that enemy action or careless tracked vehicle drivers would not cut it.

The minute by minute operations logs, kept at each headquarters, give a fair idea of our communication problems with their "Where are you?" "Fetch Sunray," "Say again," "Can't read you—only strength 3," "Where are leading troops?" and so on and so on. Without reliable communications, even in daylight, the 'fog of war' descended, and in darkness it was frequently quite impossible to find out what was happening. Fortunately, the Forward Observation Officers (F.O.O.'s) of the artillery required more powerful sets to communicate with their guns and were often able to fill in the gaps in the flow of information. Our Corps of Signals were not to blame for any failure in our sets. We were a small user compared to the size of the British forces and as we operated with them we adopted their sets with certain modifications. It was not until the summer of 1945 that we were issued with the U.S. Army walkie-talkies and their more modern equipment. So communication, or lack of it, was a significant part of our problem.

The combination of so many casualties amongst my senior officers; the frequent changes of command of regiments, squadrons and troops; the loss of so many tanks and tank crews; the breakdown of communications and our inexperience of battle were factors that greatly affected our ability to function as a division in our first few days of action. I do not think these factors were appreciated sufficiently by General Simonds whose vision was focussed on the horizon and whose thoughts were often a day or two ahead of us.

Apart from the tragic loss of Brigadier Booth and his tactical headquarters, the first day of "Tractable", for the Armoured Brigade, was marred by the difficulties they encountered when they reached the Liaison River. We had been told by Corps Headquarters that the river would not prove to be too much of an obstacle but, in fact, its steep banks and approaches forced the regiments to find crossings at Rouvres and other villages to the north-east where tanks were lined up for two hours amid scenes of great confusion. However the Infantry

Brigade had secured the village of Olendon and the woods to the south and were patrolling well forward.

During the night we rebuilt the headquarters of the Armoured Brigade which then moved south to join up with the acting brigade commander, Col. Murray Scott. Until their arrival, Scott had tried to command the brigade from his own regimental headquarters and had given orders for the Grenadier Guards and the B.C. Regiment to advance and capture the high ridge which was our divisional objective. This ridge dominated not only our own front but also the city of Falaise lying only a mile to the south. For that reason the enemy had decided that he must hold the ridge at all costs as long as he held Falaise. Our infantry brigade continued its good work and had cleared three further villages by the afternoon of the 15th when our two armoured regiments, the Grenadiers and the B.C. Regiment, appeared to be nearing their final objective.

I had attended one meeting with General Simonds that morning at the headquarters of the Polish Division and at about 3:00 p.m. I was told he was having another meeting that evening at Corps Headquarters. My tactical headquarters was near a small series of woods about a mile north of Olendon and fairly close to Brigadier Jefferson. I went to see him and at about 4:00 p.m., standing on his jeep south of Olendon, we thought we could see tanks of our armoured regiments almost on their objective. But there were a number of vehicles and tanks milling about to our west. They were a part of our 3rd Division and 2nd Armoured Brigade which had also done well, in fact, it looked as if we would both be converging on the same objective. I returned quickly to my tactical hedquarters and on arrival was told that the Armoured Brigade had in fact captured our objective. I was elated and then depressed a few minutes later when Murray Scott came to tell me that his ankle was broken and he would have to get medical attention. It was then that I appointed Lt.-Col. Bill Halpenny to be the acting commander of the brigade. Soon after, I left to attend the meeting at Corps Headquarters near Bretteville-sur-Laize. General Simonds was delighted to hear we had captured the ridge dominating Falaise and after he had issued his orders for the next day's operations he invited me to stay for dinner. I, of course, had told him about Murray Scott's ankle and the fact that the brigade was now commanded by Bill Halpenny. I asked once again for

Moncel and told him that if I had known that Murray Scott had been injured before I appointed him to replace Booth, I would not have bothered with him at all. I would have taken over the Armoured Brigade myself rather than have it go through three commanders in thirty-six hours. He did not think that would have been a good idea because of the rapily changing battle which forced him to meet with divisional commanders once or twice each day. I got back to my headquarters at about 10:00 p.m. to be told that our armoured regiments had not captured our objective at all but had turned back to wait for additional support. This was the worst possible news because General Simonds' plans for the next day had been based on the assumption that we had captured it. I phoned him immediately, told him the bad news, and apologized for it. I then told him that I was arranging for a battle group in tanks and armoured personnel carriers to take off at first light to capture the ridge. General Simonds was naturally upset by my news. He hated being woken up at night but, in view of the moves then being made by 2nd Division near Falaise, he said I was not to take any further action to gain our original objective unless he personally authorized it. During the night we organized the group in case it was needed but at dawn we were ordered to stand it down. There was to be a complete change in the Corps plans as it now looked as if Falaise would be taken by our 2nd Division.

At 9:00 a.m. I went to see General Simonds at the headquarters of our 3rd Division. He gave us all the details of the new plan which directed 4th Armoured to seize the small town of Damblainville on the Ante River and from there strike down the west side of the River Dives and capture Trun. I was also to prevent any enemy from breaking through between Damblainville and Trun as it was then thought he might use this as an escape route by his armies which were in the process of being surrounded. Our attack was to start at dawn on the 17th so we spent the next eighteen hours organizing our operation. The Infantry Brigade was to capture Damblainville and then occupy the hills on our right between that town and Trun. The Armoured Brigade would head straight down the valley for Trun, some ten miles to the southeast.

Damblainville lay in a valley with hills on each side rising about 200 feet above the village. Unfortunately the sides of the hills were bare of woods for about a mile on each side. Perhaps the attack by our infantry took the enemy by surprise because they were able to clear the village by midmorning. However, the enemy then made it plain that they would not let them advance any further without having to fight hard for every yard. We sent other units down into the valley to strengthen our attacks but with fields of fire of over 1,000 yards of open grassland the enemy was taking a heavy toll. In addition, he was shelling and mortaring our columns on the other slopes as they moved down to the village on tracks that were plainly visible to them.

I had moved my tactical headquarters at first light to the edge of a wood about 2,000 yards northeast of Damblainville and we were just starting to enjoy a late breakfast (cooked by a British officer on my staff) when the enemy started to shell the two tracks nearby down which our troops and vehicles were moving towards the village. We finished our breakfast sitting in a ditch and then went to see what was happening. Although we had captured Falaise, which was only three miles to the west, the enemy was obviously holding us off as long as it was necessary for the remainder of his force to escape on the roads running southeast from Falaise.

Fortunately, on the previous evening Brigadier Jefferson had sent a patrol off to his left to seize a bridge in the small village of Coeliboeuf. The patrol found the bridge intact and stayed to defend it. When we told General Simonds about that bridge and the fact we were having trouble in the Damblainville area he immediately ordered me to cease any further action around Damblainville and switch the whole axis of my advance to go across the bridges in Coeliboeuf and an adjacent village and then head for Trun on the east bank of the Dives. Although the B.C. Regiment and the Lake Superior Regiment of the Armoured Brigade had already been committed and were about to go into action at Damblainville, the other two armoured regiments were on the narrow country lanes that threaded their way through the woods about two miles north of the village. I gave orders to Lt.-Col. Halpenny to turn the armoured regiments eastwards, head for the bridge at Coeliboeuf and, once across, go as fast as possible to Trun. The Infantry Brigade was ordered to hand over its positions in Damblainville to units of our 3rd Division and then follow the armour across the bridge. Once across, it was to guard the bridges and fords over the Dives to prevent the enemy from using those roads as an escape route.

It wasn't easy to change our plans and move from one side of the Dives River to the other. The units of 3rd Division which were to relieve us at Damblainville did not arrive until late in the afternoon and the route of withdrawal for our regiments was up a hill in full view of the enemy. However, it was accomplished in spite of heavy shelling and attacks by enemy aircraft. Amongst our casualties was the new commanding officer of the Algonquins, Lt.-Col. Bob Bradburn, who was wounded.

It is not normal for armoured regiments to advance through enclosed country without being accompanied by infantry. That is the purpose of having a strong unit of infantry (called a Motor Battalion) with the armoured brigade. Tanks are not designed to search out woods and hedges where they are very vulnerable to well concealed infantry who can destroy them with hand-held anti-tank weapons. In such country, platoons and companies of the Motor Battalion were used to clear suspicious looking areas covered, where necessary, by the powerful weapons in the tanks. Since much of the Motor Battalion was already committed in Damblainville it meant that the two armoured regiments that were ordered to turn and cross the bridges at Morteaux Coeliboeuf went without their normal infantry component. I do not think for one moment that Crerar or Simonds had appreciated the problems that would face us with the sudden change in plans. The Canadian Grenadier Guards whom we were all cheering on to capture Trun that evening would have done so if they had had infantry with them; but without infantry support the commander decided to cover the town by fire but not to enter it. The commander, because of casualties amongst more senior officers, was now Captain Baylay, a young officer who a week before had been second-in-command of a squadron. The Governor-General's Foot Guards were in the same position as they moved through the enclosed country to their objective. An unfortunate incident that happened to my own headquarters tanks is a good example of what can happen to tanks in wooded areas.

On the morning of the 18th at about 6:30 I met with my Orders Group in a small quarry near the village of Noney-en-Auge. Although our own armoured regiments had gone through the area the previous evening, I took the precaution of ordering my four 'protective' tanks to accompany me to the meeting. Whilst we were discussing our planned operations for that day, Brigadier Lane, who commanded our artillery, asked if the commander of a British artillery regiment (Lt.-Col. John Oswald) could use two of our 'protective' tanks to make a reconnaissance of an area about two miles west in which he was hoping to deploy his regiment. He climbed into the tank with the dummy gun (used by me as a mobile command post) and, preceded by a tank with a real gun, went off up the road. Ten minutes later he ran into an enemy strong point. The leading tank was hit and disabled and, with only a dummy gun, there was not much John Oswald and the rest of our crews could do but surrender. Oswald escaped two days later. We had heard the shooting but never dreamed the enemy could be that close and assumed the tank crews were having a little shooting practice on the side. With an infantry escort scouting ahead the tragedy might not have happened.

At ten o'clock that morning General Simonds held his Orders Group at my headquarters. My old friend, Dan Spry, attended this meeting, his first as the General commanding our 3rd Canadian Division. At the meeting General Simonds changed our orders again. Instead of the armour going for Trun it was now to deploy in an area about two miles north of it. The infantry, instead of guarding the crossings over the Dives, were now to take Trun and the villages between it and Chambois - the latter being a Polish objective. Change in plans become more exhausting as they go down the chain of command. At the regimental level they must have wondered why I couldn't make up my mind.

The final battle of Normandy which resulted in the destruction of the Fifth and Seventh German Armies as they fought to withdraw through the gap between Trun and Chambois has been documented by historians with accuracy, based on the operations logs and war diaries of the units taking part. But during that three day battle the 'fog of war' descended and remained with us throughout. Just imagine an area four miles by four miles of lovely rolling countryside interspersed by small villages, farms and woods. We, in the Canadian Corps, were in possession of three sides of the square and faced inwards because the fourth side of the square was partly controlled by the enemy who was fighting fanatically to get through to the other side as it was his only way to get back to Germany. About 70,000 Germans made their way towards this narrow gap, mostly on foot but supported by perhaps twenty tanks. Facing them on the 18th August were the Polish Division and our own 4th Armoured Division with a combined total of approximately 5,000 infantry, 300 tanks, 100 anti-tank guns and 180 artillery pieces. On the 19th August an addiitional infantry brigade was placed under my command bringing the total of infantry to about 7,000. We could have done with double the number since infantry are the essential element in preventing large scale enemy infiltration by night.

On the two final days of that battle some of the Germans who were trying to escape concentrated their efforts by trying to get through the Polish Armoured Division which held a part of the square. In spite of being attacked from front and rear, the Poles hung on and fought a great defensive battle.

Estimates vary about the number of Germans who were able to get through in these 48 hours but there is no doubt that over 40,000 were killed or captured. The German dead and dying lay thick on roads and fields and close to them lay their dead horses, the only reliable means of transport that had been left to them. As Charles Stacey wrote in his history, "The Victory Campaign," "From this appalling charnel-house there arose to offend the heavens a stench that was strong in the nostrils even of people in light aircraft far above." On the roads and lanes leading to, and through, their escape route a total of over 3,000 vehicles and guns had been destroyed. An indication of the tremendous losses suffered by the German Panzer Divisions are the strength figures of official reports on the 12th SS Panzer Division that had fought against the Canadians in almost every action in Normandy. On 'D' day it had 20,540 men and 150 tanks. By the 25th August it was reduced to "300 men—10 tanks—no artillery." 1st SS Panzer Division—Hitler's Own Division—was reduced to "weak infantry elements, no tanks, no artillery"!

A German General, captured as he tried to escape with his men through our lines, told me that one reason why so many of his men were fighting desperately to get home was the fear of what the Russians would do to their families when they reached Prussia, east Germany and Austria.

Bob Moncel finally reached me at noon on the 19th - five days after Booth's death—and took command of the Armoured Brigade. At that time we were trying to extract the armour and infantry of the Division so that they could go all out to the Seine River. It was difficult to extricate them when they were in close contact with the enemy. As our war diarist wrote on the 20th August, "Due to heavy fighting, Germans attacking from both the east and the west, and the numerous calls made on the division to seal off any German escape routes, the units are mixed up and it is difficult to define any particular brigade areas." On the 20th August, General Simonds changed our instructions once again and ordered us to go to the aid of the Poles. As far as I was concerned this did not make sense and I said to General Simonds words to this effect: "To hell with them. They have run out of food and ammunition because of the inefficiency of their organization; our people have been fighting just as hard but we have managed to keep up our supply system." That was about as far as I got because he peremtorily ordered 4th Armoured Brigade to rescue the Poles immediately. The Canadian Grenadier Guards reached the Poles on the morning of the 21st, having dealt with several German tanks on the way for the loss of four of their own. They found the Poles in desperate shape with many hundreds of wounded on their hands and hundreds of prisoners.

On the 21st of August General Simonds sent for me and told me that he had decided to replace me as Commander of the 4th Armoured Division and Harry Foster would take over from me that evening. I was naturally very shocked and emotionally upset so I can remember very little of our meeting except that there were no harsh words spoken between us. But I can recall two points that I made in my defence. First, the long delay in sending me Bob Moncel to command the Armoured Brigade - Moncel's job at Corps Headquarters was a comparatively unimportant one. Simonds did not give me an answer to that. Second, the Division had had too many changes in orders over a period of ten days and had taken very heavy casualties in commanders, soldiers and tanks in its first battles. In spite of this, it had been able to emerge as a good fighting division.

It is interesting to recall now the meeting between Charles Foulkes of the 2nd Division, Dan Spry, who had just taken over the 3rd Division, and myself on the 18th of August after we had attended an Orders meeting with Guy Simonds. Charles, Dan and I were all from the Royal Canadian Regiment so we had a drink to the Regiment and to the fact that it was the first time three generals from the same regiment had commanded divisions at the same time. Charles was quite sure then that he was going to be relieved of his command because he said he felt Simonds was 'on the warpath' and was going to fire someone! I told him that as the commander whose men had just captured Falaise, I felt he was pretty safe - he was a hero. Dan Spry joined in and said he didn't think he was going to be fired because he had only just taken over the division that day and hadn't done anything yet! I don't think any one of us thought that I would be the one to get the axe three days later.

When Harry Foster arrived to take over from me his opening remark was "What the hell's gone wrong, George—you and Guy Simonds were so close?" I don't think I gave him an answer at the time as I was still upset by events. However, I feel I must try to answer the question now.

I was close to Simonds in the way soldiers are to each other. I had great confidence in him, he was an outstanding commander and although he was aloof and distant with some people he was always kind and considerate with me. I was told by a mutual friend that I bore a resemblance to Guy's brother who was killed while a test pilot in the 1930's—perhaps that was a part of his regard for me. Anyway, I thoroughly enjoyed his company and we went together to a number of dinner and lunch parties given by civilian friends and neighbours as we waited for "D" Day.

Perhaps Guy Simonds had too much confidence in me - perhaps he thought that I could swing armoured divisions around in the enclosed countryside of Normandy in the same way that they had been swung around in the desert when he was visiting 8th Army. Anyway, he told me that he was not satisfied with my performance and that I must go. That was that.

Had I been an experienced armoured divisional commander with six or eight months of tank battles to my credit, I believe that matters might have developed quite differently in Normandy. With that kind of experience to back me up Guy Simonds would have listened more seriously to changes I recommended at times to his plans. But both Maczek and I were commanding armoured divisions in action for the first time and Simonds preferred to rely on his own experience and judgement.

Under the circumstances I don't think anyone else could have done much better with the Division than I did. The grievous casualties in commanders, crews and tanks within the Armoured Brigade were not foreseen; that Brigade is the spearhead of an armoured division and when it is crippled by severe casualties a great deal of the punch is gone. The individual regiments fought well under adverse conditions and without firm direction. Perhaps I should have taken over the Armoured Brigade in spite of General Simonds' objections - certainly I would have done so if I had known that Moncel would not be available for those five hectic days. With the 20/20 vision of hindsight I realize now that my Commander of Artillery, Brigadier Lane, could have done the job well. I should have sent him forward to take over the Brigade on a permanent basis. I am sorry I didn't.

As far as both Simonds and I were concerned the problems of Normandy were soon forgotten. A month later, I received a letter from him wishing me well in my new job and during the rest of his life I received many warm and congratulatory letters from him.

Guy Simonds died in May 1974 and I was very proud to be one of the eight pall-bearers at his funeral.

15

Italy Again,
And On To Holland

Before leaving Normandy I spent the night of August 21st at General Crerar's Headquarters and the following morning, had a brief talk with him in his caravan. He was kindness itself. I was then 34 years of age and Harry Crerar was about 55; he treated me as an uncle might treat his favourite nephew except that he rarely used Christian names. "Kitching," he said, "you look tired." I told him I was tired, having had little sleep for 72 hours before leaving the division. He then told me how sorry he was that I had lost command of 4th Armoured Division. He said Simonds had discussed my performance with him and he had reluctantly agreed that I should go. But he did not want me to think that it was the end of my Army career. He was arranging for me to take over a training brigade in Yorkshire for a while and went on, in his nice avuncular way, to tell me that he was having trouble with Montgomery. He said that Monty kept phoning him to do this and that and, when he was not available, he knew Montgomery was dealing with Simonds directly and giving him orders! This was not the way things should be done; it was important to keep to the channels of command or otherwise things could go wrong. He went on to say, "If it's any comfort to you, it may not be long before Montgomery tries to remove me!"

On my return to England I took over command of the 13th Canadian

Brigade in Helmsley, Yorkshire. With our five divisions and two armoured brigades now heavily committed to battles in Normandy and Italy the number of casualties among infantry units exceeded the reinforcements available. This was foreseen in December 1943 by Colonel Ralston, then Minister of Defence, who had recommended some form of conscription on his return from Italy. But for political reasons no action was taken by the Prime Minister at that time.

Although the stream of infantry reinforcements was drying up, other Corps in the Army had not experienced anything like the anticipated casualty rates; their reinforcement depots were full. Special appeals were made to the men in these Corps to change over and become infantry. The main task of the 13th Brigade was to retrain these "volunteers." Many of them had been in the Army for three or four years, had reached warrant or sergeant's rank and were well qualified technicians. It was a brave decision on their part to change over and we had to ensure that they were qualified as infantrymen before sending them forward into infantry regiments.

On the one hand the Divisions in action were pleading for more infantry while on the other they were asking for only trained men. They could not have it both ways because many of the men who came to us had not experienced much weapon training since joining up in 1940; in fact very few had ever seen a hand grenade or a mortar. Every man was given three or four weeks' intensive training. The system was effective but it was a "band-aid" approach to the real problem of infantry reinforcements which by the fall of 1944 was reaching serious proportions.

My stay with the Brigade was short. In October I was warned that I would be going to Italy as Chief of Staff of our 1st Canadian Corps and later that month I left for Rome where I met General Burns, the Corps commander, who was there on two or three days leave.

The Corps had just been withdrawn into reserve after nearly three weeks of continuous action on the Adriatic coast on the right of 8th Army. Once the problems of staff and communications which had bedevilled its early operations in the Liri Valley had been overcome, the Corps had established a reputation for aggressiveness and success which was second to none in the 8th Army.

At our meeting General Burns told me in some detail what had happened since I had left Italy the previous February. We must have talked for at least an hour, he was in great form - quiet as usual - but full of confidence. After our talk, arrangements were made for a good driver with a station wagon to take me on the long and winding roads which traversed the centre of Italy between Rome and the Adriatic city of Rimini. Tommy Burns bade me farewell and said he would be back at Corps Headquarters the day after I got there.

As the crow flies the distance from Rome to Cesenatico, where Main Corps Headquarters was established, is only about 200 miles but by the roads and diversions then usable it was over 500 miles. After a brief sleep in a small Italian village we finally arrived at Cesenatico late on November 5th.

In the morning I was joined by the man I was taking over from, Brigadier Desmond Smith. After the usual greetings I said that I had spent a couple of hours with the Corps Commander in Rome and he had indicated he would be returning to the Headquarters that day. Des Smith turned to me and said, "Which Corps Commander?" It was his tone of voice that surprised me as much as the remark itself. He went on to tell me that General Burns had been relieved of the command of our 1st Corps and General Vokes was now the Corps Commander. Des Smith was obviously pleased at the change.

Whilst I was delighted that Chris Vokes was to be my new boss and would get a well-deserved promotion, I felt very sorry for Tommy Burns. Having been away from the Italian front for eight months I was out of touch with command problems that might have arisen. But I am quite sure that Burns did not know he was about to be fired when he and I had talked only two days earlier.

When I reported to Chris Vokes he greeted me like a long lost brother but when I asked him what had gone wrong he said he did not want to discuss it. As far as he was concerned, the matter was closed.

As the majority of the Corps was officially out of the line and in rest areas, Main Headquarters moved back to the town of Rimini where we established ourselves in the grounds of a sizeable house adjacent to a hotel. One evening - it must have been about the 14th November - General Vokes received a personal signal from Field-Marshal Alexander congratulating him on his appointment to command the Corps. This was the first official news we had received that Chris would get command and promotion. It called for a dinner to celebrate the occasion. About fifteen of us sat down to dinner; mostly senior officers of our Headquarters and the brigadiers from the 1st Division, including Paulo Bernatchez who was commanding 3rd Brigade. It was a happy and relaxed occasion.

Chris Vokes had commanded the 1st Division for over a year and guided it through some of the fiercest battles of the Italain Campaign. Everyone in the Corps assumed he would take over from Tommy Burns. In the morning following our dinner, Chris Vokes took off on a round of inspections and planned to be away until late evening. I spent most of the day looking around the Headquarters. At about 5:00 p.m. I was handed a message marked "Top Secret. General Vokes eyes only." It was also marked "Operational Immediate." In accordance with the procedure at the headquarters, I opened the envelope and was horrified to read that Chris Vokes was not going to be promoted but was to move to North West Europe and take over command of 4th Armoured Division from Harry Foster. The man named to command the Corps and to receive a promotion was General Charles Foulkes. I had nothing against Charles Foulkes but I felt that to promote him at this time was Army politics of the worst kind. Chris Vokes was senior to him, had four times as much operational experience, was well known to our troops who had confidence in him. and he was well known at 8th Army Headquarters. I could not help but feel that this was General Crerar at his worst. He did not want Simonds or Vokes to be Chief of the General Staff after the war; they both had strong opinions and personalities. Charles Foulkes would be more amendable to the politicians.

Chris Vokes returned from his visit at about 7:00 p.m. and went straight to his caravan. Before he climbed the three steps leading into it, I handed him the Top Secret message and, at the same time, told him that I was sorry it contained very bad news. He took it, went into the caravan, and closed the door. I waited for about ten minutes and was about to turn away when he opened his door and called me over. "George, who else knows about this?" I assured him that I was the only officer who had read it. He was obviously trying to recover from the deep personal shock of the message. After a couple of minutes that seemed like hours he said quietly, "Ask the senior members of the staff to be in the Mess at 8:15 when I will talk to them. Let me know when they are all present.''

A number of phone calls soon alerted the senior members of the staff, I went over to Chris Vokes' caravan and told him all were present. He had had time to freshen up and was quite composed. ''George, when you lost command of 4th Armoured Division did you consider resigning your commission?'' ''No,'' I told him, ''that never entered my mind although there was a time that day when I thought I might shoot myself.'' He grinned and we walked over to the Mess. When he entered the room everyone rose from their chairs but Chris motioned them to be seated and, having asked me to ensure that the doors were closed, he said words to this effect: ''You are having a new General to command this Corps. He is Charles Foulkes. I am leaving to command 4th Armoured Division. I want you to give General Foulkes the same support and loyalty that you have given me. He may be a stranger to many of you but I know that if you continue to work as you have done in the past this Corps will continue its unbroken record of victories.'' He paused a moment and then turned to where Preston Gilbride and I were standing. ''George and Pres, I want the best possible Guard of Honour with full band and a red carpet to be at the airfield when he lands. And I want every senior officer of the Corps, down to and including full colonels, to be at the airfield to meet him. I will introduce them to him and I want it to be a first class reception in every way. We will then return to this Headquarters where he will take over officially from me. Is that clear?''

The dinner that night was a sombre meal and after it was over Chris Vokes phoned Bert Hoffmeister to tell him personally of the change. I sent out the necessary orders to those concerned to be at a certain airfield at 3:00 p.m. on the great day. The airfield mentioned in the signal from Allied Forces Headquarters on which General Foulkes would land was between Rimini and Cesenatico and both Pres Gilbride and I made sure that the rather small and dilapidated airfield reception building was spruced up for the occasion. By 2:30 p.m. the Guard of Honour of the Royal Canadian Regiment (Charles Foulkes' unit in peacetime) was drawn up and looking as smart as fresh uniforms could make them. The band was there in the rear of the Guard and 30 or 40 senior officers waited patiently to one side. When General Chris Vokes arrived I think everyone was hoping he would be given a General Salute by the Guard. However, Chris had insisted that this was to be Charles Foulkes parade and nothing was to be done to interfere with it. Three o'clock came and went but there was no sign of the aircraft. By 3:30 we were all getting a little impatient as the damp and cold November weather made us stamp our feet to get the circulation going again. Shortly after 4:00 we had an urgent phone call from the Chief of Staff of 8th Army, Sir Harry Floyd. He told me that General Foulkes was then at 8th Army Headquarters and was hopping mad because no one was at the airport to greet him. He suggested we get to Army Headquarters as soon as possible to escort him to Corps Headquarters. I have forgotten what Chris Vokes said when I gave him the message but on our drive to 8th Army Headquarters he vented his anger on the crew of the aircraft that had obviously taken Foulkes to the wrong airfield. They had spoiled the excellent arrangements he had prepared for the new Corps Commander and he could appreciate Charles Foulkes' reactions on arriving at a strange airfield with no one to meet him. We went directly to the Army Commander's Quarters when we reached 8th Army Headquarters, and found a somewhat reserved Charles Foulkes waiting impatiently for us. General Sir Richard McCreery then commanded 8th Army - a tall, capable and unpretentious cavalryman. He realized what had happened and had done his best to explain matters to Charles Foulkes. However, our ride in the staff car back to our headquarters was a very silent one. Charles Foulkes and Chris Vokes sat beside each other whilst I sat beside the driver. I don't think there were a dozen words said on the whole thirty-minute drive.

On arrival at Corps Headquarters, Chris Vokes took Charles to the Corps Commander's caravan and said, "Charles, I'll let George explain what happened this afternoon. There is no need for an official handover. Everything is in good shape. Good bye, I'm leaving now. It's all yours." With that he climbed into a car and disappeared into the night. It was the last I saw of him until we met again in Holland.

We had arranged for a soldier to look after Charles Foulkes so his caravan was warm and comfortable when he first went into it. He asked me to give him about five minutes to clean up and then return to his caravan for a talk. It was about 6:30 p.m. so I phone all our senior officers to stand by in the Mess at 7:00 to greet Charles Foulkes. Then I knocked on his caravan door.

Charles greeted me with, "George, what's the matter - why weren't you at the airfield to meet me? I had a hell of a time after the captain of the U.S. Air Force Mitchell left me on the runway; I'll tell you about it later but now you tell me what went wrong." I explained everything to him and repeated almost word for word what Chris Vokes had said about giving him our full support and loyalty. I told him that I had the senior staff standing by in the Mess and everyone could be relied on to give him their full cooperation. We walked over and I introduced him to the assembled group after which he said he was honoured to command a Corps with such a great reputation and how much he looked forward to working with us. He was completely relaxed by this time and realized he was amongst friends.

After dinner, I went back to his caravan where he told me of his experience on arriving at the airfield that afternoon. The captain of the Mitchell aircraft had not told him that he was landing at a different airfield to the one ordered. The plane taxied to the end of the runway and then, rather unceremoniously, the crew door was opened and he was left on the small road that ran round the circumference of the airfield. His baggage was left on the road and he walked over to a small hanger nearby in which Canadian soldiers were working on a vehicle. It was an L.A.D. (Light Aid Detachment) of our 1st Division, the NCO in charge being a corporal. He called him over and told him his name was Foulkes and that he was the Corps Commander and needed transportation. The corporal who knew Chris Vokes well, having seen him many times told him that he was sorry he could not help him because he certainly was not the Corps Commander. Of course the corporal was confused by the similarity in pronunciation of the two names. Vokes and Foulkes both rhymed with "Oaks." The corporal was polite but firm—he assumed Charles was playing some part in a deception plan and wanted nothing to do with it. Charles walked over to the main highway where, fortunately, the first vehicle that stopped was a jeep from the Provost Corps. He had much the same problem with the Provost Sergeant but he finally convinced him of his identity. After picking up his baggage he asked the driver to take him to 8th Army Headquarters. He admitted being in a towering rage as he was quite convinced that our failure to meet him was deliberate, that it was our way of showing him he wasn't wanted! The footnote to that story is that, when interrogated later, the Captain of the Mitchell said he decided to land where he did because the field on which he was supposed to land was too close to the enemy! A rather casual way of complying with an order.

The staff at 1st Corps was a very competent one which included men who went far on their return to civilian life after the war. Brigadier "Johnny" Plow became Lieutenant-Governor of Nova Scotia - he was the Commander of our Artillery. The Commander of Engineers, Brig. Colin Campbell, had been a Cabinet Minister in the Liberal Government of Ontario - one of the most sensible and likeable men I have ever met. Brig. Clarence McKee commanded our Signals -his name became well known in Ontario in connection with the Annual Horse Show. Preston Gilbride, who was the staff officer responsible for administration, later headed Global Life in Toronto. The Provost-Marshal was Colonel Nicholson, the future well-loved head of the RCMP.

Shortly after his arrival General Foulkes spoke to all Lieutant-Colonels and senior Commanders in the Corps. There must have been about 125 present, many of whom had never served with him or known him before. In that sense it was a very important introduction from his point of view and I told him before the meeting that I felt it would be a good thing if, in his opening remarks, he praised the fighting qualities of both our 1st Infantry Division and our 5th Armoured Division. They had established an excellent reputation and were proud of being a part of 8th Army.

For some reason or other Charles Foulkes took an opposite tack. Instead of praising them he implied that the tactics used by the formations in Italy were a little out of date and would have to change in order to make use of the new equipment which the Divisions were using in Belgium and Holland and which would be made available shortly in Italy. He remarked that we were crossing the same rivers that Caesar had crossed and were using the same equipment as he had.

I watched the faces of his audience as he spoke and it was obvious to me that he had failed to win their enthusiastic support. As soldiers, of course, they would go about their duties as well as they had in the past, but there was no sparkle in Charles Foulkes' remarks and there was little interest in the eyes of his audience. He missed a great opportunity. He also had to eat a great deal of humble pie in the weeks ahead when both of our divisions, without the aid of the promised new equipment and employing the tactics they had mastered in earlier battles, fought for and won crossing after crossing of rivers and canals in fierce battles and skillful manoeuvres which earned the praise of both the Army Commander and the enemy. In eight weeks of close combat when, frequently, only the bank of a river separated friend from foe, we only had one severe setback. It occurred on the 5th December at the Lamone River and involved the units of our 1st Infantry Brigade.

The story of that battle is told in accurate detail in Colonel Nicholson's Official History "The Canadians in Italy." After a successful crossing of the fast running and icy-cold Lamone, the Royal Canadian Regiment had, by 3:00 a.m., gained a bridgehead over 1,000 yards deep. That was the information passed by 1st Division Headquarters to us at Corps Headquarters. I went over to General Foulkes' caravan to give him the good news. After studying the map for a moment, he told me to drive as fast as I could to 1st Divisional Headquarters and order Brigadier Smith to ensure immediately that 6-pounder anti-tank guns were rafted or dragged across to give the infantry the necessary support in case of a German counter-attack.

As I was leaving his caravan he stopped me and said that, as time was vital, I was to phone the Divisional Commander and give him the message directly. I did this from the Corps Commander's caravan - there was no time to waste. I spoke personally to Brig. Smith, who was the acting commander of 1st Division, and gave him the message at about 4:00 a.m. As I spoke to him General Foulkes, who was sitting up in his bed, nodded his head to emphasize my remarks. "Get the anti-tank guns over immediately and let me know the minute they are over."

No 6-pounder anti-tank guns crossed the river that night and before mid-day German counter attacks had driven our men back to where they had started. General Foulkes was furious and in a matter of days the commanding officer of the battalion had been replaced, as had the brigade commander. In later years General Foulkes told me, and also General Burns, that he should have also replaced Brig. Smith. The only reason he had not done so was that General Foster was due to arrive in Italy three days later to take over the 1st Division at which time he would put Smith to command the 1st Brigade. Harry Foster assumed command of the Division on the 9th December. He settled in quietly and took over firm control.

During the six months that I was Chief of Staff to General Foulkes I always felt his tactical plans were sound and sensible and I do not think anyone could fault him for them. I often wondered why General Simonds had such a poor opinion of him in our early days in Normandy because the more I worked with Charles Foulkes in Italy the more I respected his judgment in tactical matters, and I know that the staff at Corps and the Divisional Commanders had the same confidence.

On the operational side of our Corps Staff, I was lucky enough to be able to get Lt.-Col. Dick Danby to head the group as G.S.O.I (General Staff Officer 1st Grade). He replaced Lt.-Col. Jack Eaton who, after a short while at the Headquarters of 1st Division, went to command the New Brunswick Hussars, an armoured regiment in the 5th Armoured Division. On the administrative side Preston Gilbride also had a first class group of officers on his staff, amongst them handsome, tall, John Bassett who seemed to spend a great deal of his time, as did many others, standing patiently outside Gilbride's caravan waiting to be summoned into the presence.

The Chief of Staff of 8th Army was Sir Harry Floyd, an excellent soldier and staff officer and also an active business man who later headed one of London's best known auctioneering firms. Shortly after my arrival in Italy, Harry sent for me and in a very personal interview said that he hoped in future "if we had any dirty linen, would we please wash it ourselves and not involve the Army Commander in purely Canadian domestic problems." I gathered from him that someone on our staff had been disloyal to General Burns when he commanded the Corps and had been inclined to involve the Army Chief of Staff and the Army Commander in a matter that should have been handled more properly by General Weeks, the head of Canadian administration in Rome. Harry Floyd would not enlarge on the subject or name names but he just said "draw your own conclusions." I understood later from General Foulkes that he had had a similar discussion with the Army Commander. Whilst on the subject of disloyalty, Charles Foulkes told me that when he was appointed to command 1st Corps and heard that I had just taken over as Chief of Staff, he had some doubts about whether we would get along together. We had been equals as divisional commanders for six months during which I used to pull his leg unmercifully. However, once the memories of his unpleasant reception had faded, we got on well together. I admired his ability as a tactician and he got on well with the Army Commander and with the various divisional commanders who served under him. But Charles Foulkes was not at his best when addressing a large group; for some reason he always seemed on the defensive, as if he had a chip on his shoulder which he was determined to unload on his audience.

In the fall of 1944 the Italian Army, loyal to their King and on our side, raised five 'Gruppa' or light infantry divisions. One of these, the 'Cremona Gruppa,' was placed under command of our 1st Corps. It was commanded by General Primieri, a capable and courageous General. The Cremona Gruppa took over part of our defensive line early in January 1945 and, in order to give them more confidence, arrangements were made for a number of our tanks to move into some of the farm buildings and make them into small fortresses.

Each of these tanks were supported by a section of eight or nine infantry from one of the Canadian regiments. This small nucleus of tank and infantry strong points was, in fact, the backbone of the defence because as soon as the Germans knew from radio interception that they were now faced by Italian troops they mounted a strong attack against them. The attack came in at night after a fairly intense mortaring and shelling of the area and, unfortunately, a great many of the Gruppa left their foxholes and trenches and ran to the rear. They were, of course, caught in the open and suffered many casualties. The tanks and Canadian infantry teams remained in their small fortresses and beat off the enemy attack without much trouble and the Germans must have been quite surprised to find them there. It was a good lesson for the Italian soldiers when they saw that 90% of their casualties were amongst those that had left the comparative safety of their slit trenches to run to the rear across open ground. When the Germans put in another attack a few nights later, the Italian soldiers stayed and fought them off. We noted that during the first battle, General Primieri moved amongst his troops as they ran to the rear and stopped a great many from joining in what could have developed into a rout. He apologized to General Foulkes and said it would not happen again.

The cooperation between the Desert Air Force and the troops of the 8th Army was very close indeed and, considering the thousands of sorties flown, there were few instances in which they bombed or straffed our own troops. Many young pilots would ask to join an infantry unit to get a better idea of the targets offered by the enemy and also so that they could judge, from an infantry point of view, the effect of their support. I must confess that very few stayed with the infantry for more than a couple of days; a beaten up, damp and roofless building that seemed paradise to the infantry was a leaky sieve to an airman and a place to be avoided. In the same way, those infantry officers who were lucky enough to get a short attachment to the RAF and fly on a medium-bomber mission were only too happy to get back to the comfort of their beaten-up, damp and roofless buildings. It was the close support given by the fighter-bombers of the Desert Air Force that was the deciding factor between success and failure on many occasions when our men were clawing their way across swollen rivers without the close support of armour; but the weather in December prevented the Air Force from flying more than two or three days each week and it was noticeable that German counter-attacks were mostly at night or in periods of low cloud and rain when our Air Force could not operate.

Most of the heavy bombing in the Mediterranean theatre was strategic and directed against communications, factories, shipyards and concentrations of material. What had been developed by 8th Army and the Desert Air Force was the 'cab-rank.' When the Army was to make an attack or if the enemy was expected to, we would ask for three or four fighter-bombers to be in the air over the battle for a period of perhaps two hours. The Air Force would then arrange for relays of aircraft to be available for the whole of the required period. These fighter-bombers would circle at about 5,000 feet and be 'talked' on to particular targets, such as houses or tanks, by the air controller below. If no targets were given to them before it was time for them to return and be replaced by other aircraft, they were at liberty to attack any target they could find in enemy territory. It was a very effective system which allowed the fighters to engage targets only a hundred yards ahead of our own troops.

Early in the morning of the 17th December I had a call from Harry Floyd asking me to see him as soon as possible and soon after I left for 8th Army Headquarters. The news he gave me was not good. On the previous day the German Army had launched an attack through the Ardennes forests in considerable strength and had overhwelmed two new American Divisions which had been given the responsibility of defending very wide frontages in the belief that the enemy was incapable of large scale offensive operations. In a matter of 24 hours it looked as if the Germans had achieved a dynamic success. Certainly it took everyone by surprise and the reason Harry Floyd wished to see me was to get us, at 1st Canadian Corps, thinking about what we would do if the enemy in our area suddenly mounted an offensive, however, suicidal it might turn out to be. There is no doubt that we had become very offensively minded; we were always planning for the next jump ahead and I don't think we ever thought the Germans were capable at that stage of mounting a three or four divisional attack. Certainly we did not have much in the way of a reserve in our rear areas as most of our fighting strength was in the shop window deployed along the rivers and canal banks.

On my return to Corps, I spoke with General Foulkes about Harry Floyd's concern. He and I sat round a map that evening in his caravan and discussed the various ways in an enemy might try to get at us. The problem was complicated, and also eased by the fact that at that time the units of our two divisions were in the middle of a series of successful attacks which carried them across the Lamone River and the series of canals on which the enemy had based his main defences. The overall plan for the attack by our two divisions was made by Charles Foulkes in consultation with Major-Generals Hoffmeister and Foster who commanded our 5th and 1st Divisions respectively, and Charles did not want anything to interfere with the progress of the well-planned battles being fought by brigades and battalions. He was convinced that the enemy were incapable of mounting a large-scale attack in our area and decided that he would not burden the divisional commanders with the additional problem of considering such a possibility. He was right as events proved but only a few days later a German force of about 1,200 assault troops succeeded in penetrating a distance of six miles down a valley on the other coast of Italy close to the important port of

Leghorn. The 8th Indian Division was immediately sent to the area and quickly restored the situation. The enemy must have regretted that he had not attacked with a stronger force which might have enabled him to destroy the harbour installations in the port.

During these battles of the rivers, there was frequent exchange of propaganda leaflets between ourselves and the Germans. These were enclosed in shells fired by the artillery and distributed rather like air-burst shrapnel. I remember one clever German leaflet which was fired at us shortly after the Royal Canadian Regiment's battle at the Lamone River. It was a copy of the front page of the then popular American magazine "Life." On one side, under the title "Life," was an appealing and partly undressed blonde whist the reverse was entitled "Death" and showed the bodies of three of our soldiers who had been killed in the battle.

An amusing exchange of leaflets occurred when the Commander of the Artillery of our 1st Division, Brigadier Bill Ziegler, sent out invitations for a party he was planning to give at a time when the division was out of the line. He gave the time and place including a detailed map showing the location of the building in which the party would take place. Unfortunately, one of the invitations fell into the hands of the enemy because a day or two later a shower of leaflets descended on the building. The leaflets were in the form of a letter addressed to Brigadier Ziegler and went something like this:

"Thank you kindly for your invitation to attend your cocktail party on the 23rd at 1900 hours. Unfortunately, owing to circumstances beyond my control, I will not be able to attend in person. However, I will send you some special greetings at the time."

It was signed Heinz Ziegler, General of Artillery, German Army.

Needless to say, the Canadian Ziegler changed the venue of his party as he expected a storm of shells to greet his guests. All that arrived at the original site were leaflets saying "have a good party."

Bill Ziegler was the only Commander of Artillery in the 8th Army in Italy who had ever called for, and obtained, a 'William.' A 'William' called for every gun within range in the whole Army to engage a special target for a minimum period of one minute. It was a priority and would mean that all artillery regiments would have to switch their fire on to the 'William' target at a specified time. The target on that occasion had been a German force of tanks and infantry which was concentrating prior to launching an attack. Thirty regiments of artillery responded to the call including nine Medium and two Heavy Regiments; their 670 guns fired nearly 100 tons of shells onto the target simultaneously. The enemy counter-attack was broken up before it could even get started.

One of the problems of operating an Armoured Division in Italy was that there were never enough infantry to maintain the momentum of the advance. General Bert Hoffmeister got around this by creating a second infantry brigade in his division. He put into it the Motor Battalion (which was normally a part of the Armoured Brigade) and two regiments that had been converted to infantry, the Princess Louise Dragoon Guards who were normally the Reconnaissance Regiment with the 1st Division, and his own Light Anti-Aircraft Regiment which was almost unemployed in its normal role owing to the absence of enemy aircraft. There was a certain amount of weeping and wailing in the two regiments when they were told of the change but they rapidly settled down and were soon as good as any other infantry unit. There is no doubt in my mind that if an Armoured Division with only one infantry brigade is going to have to use it in the break-in battle where it has to fight hard to make a hole for the armoured brigade to pass through, it will have used up all its infantry before it really gets going. The British overcame this problem in Italy by having two Independent Infantry Brigades which could be attached to their Armoured Divisions when needed. Bert Hoffmeister did well with his 5th Armoured Division and I was delighted at the way my old brigade (the 11th) had gone from success to success under the able leadership of Brigadier Ian Johnston. Brigadier Sparky Sparling had been a tower of strength as the commander of the Division's Artillery as had Brigadier Ian Cumberland who commanded the 5th Armoured Brigade. Bert Hoffmeister had had many complimentary messages from Army and Corps Commanders during the past six months. He was proud of his "Mighty Maroon Machine."

During the battles for the rivers my main task at Corps Headquarters was to think about and plan for the major assaults which we would deliver once the weather permitted the start of the Army Group's offensives for the destruction of the German Forces in Italy, and the

pursuit into Northern Italy, Austria and Yugoslavia. We assumed that
our Corps would operate across the shallow Comacchio Lagoon using
the armoured amphibious carriers known as buffaloes - an extension of
the APC's we had used in Normandy, modified to be able to move
through swamp and flood. The Comacchio Lagoon was a formidable
obstacle some twenty miles long by seven miles wide which formed the
left flank of the enemy's defences forward of the Po River line. We
were just putting the finishing touches to our plan when, at the end of
January, General Foulkes told Gilbride and me, in strict confidence,
that he had been advised that our 1st Canadian Corps would be moved
to Holland early in February. This was a delightful surprise and, when
it became official, it was very well received by everyone although we
were genuinely sorry to be leaving the 8th Army.

In our planning discussions with Charles Foulkes it was decided that
the Corps' move to Northwest Europe would be handled by the Administrative Staff assisted by the General Staff officer responsible for
movement control, Major Bob Hilborn. General Crerar had suggested
to Charles Foulkes that I and the other senior officers at the Headquarters who were on the operational side should leave Italy as soon as
possible so that we could liaise with Army Headquarters in Holland
and get the feel of things there and at 2nd Canadian Corps Headquarters which was about to become involved in a large scale operation
known as "Veritable." Brigadier "Sparky" Sparling had taken over
as Commander of Corps Artillery from John Plow, and Brigadier
Arthur Wrinch and taken over as Chief of Signals from Clarence
McKee. The three of us would fly from Rome to Marseiles and from
there drive north to Holland.

One of the big problems about the move of such a large number of
men, guns, tanks and vehicles was how to deny any knowledge of our
plans to the enemy. An elaborate cover plan was worked out which
would make it appear that our Corps was being withdrawn to central
Italy in order to rehearse our part in the great offensive being planned
for early spring. The route taken by our convoys led south as far as Ortona before turning west and then north to the port of Leghorn from
which most of our men and transport would be shipped to Marseilles.
We would be covering three sides of a square and all identification patches and signs were removed. However, we left behind in the

mountains enough Signal personnel and equipment to simulate an active training programme. The Germans had an excellent interception service and had been able to identify some of our brigades and units by our accents and the voice pattern of certain commanders. Tapes were made of these voices which were played back at appropriate times in the ensuing weeks. Our deception arrangements were effective and it is recorded that the Germans did not know the exact whereabouts of our Corps in Italy until we were fully concentrated and about to go into action in Holland in mid-April.

Another problem was that during the months in Italy all our units had acquired additional vehicles which generally were used to gather extra rations and other comforts for the men. The order went out that only official vehicles and tanks on the establishment would be taken with us; the others would have to be disposed of and there were many British and Indian units who were delighted to take them off our hands. One of our armoured regiments asked if they could have special permission to take with them four extra tanks which they said had been 'fixed up' as command tanks. Charles Foulkes paid an unexpected visit to the regiment one morning and asked to see the four tanks. Somewhat embarrassed, the regimental commander led him over to four rather scruffy tanks which were grouped together and isolated from the rest of the units' Shermans. Charles' suspicions were aroused when on approaching them he heard faint 'clucking' sounds which greatly increased in volume when he hit the side of the first tank with his stick. Charles had a good sense of humour on these occasions but he wouldn't allow the regiment to retain their egg-laying tanks in each of which were about 50 hens duly supplementing the daily rations with fresh eggs.

Before leaving Italy mention should be made of a soldier who was at the Headquarters of our 1st Division for over three years. He was Corporal Dragg and he served in the General's Mess. He did not have ambitions in regard to rank; in fact he was almost embarrassed when he was promoted to Corporal. He was a devoted member of the Mess and I know that everyone who ate in the Mess will have only the fondest memories of unflappable Corporal Dragg.

During the final weeks in Italy, General Foulkes received many messages congratulating him and the troops of 1st Corps on their hard-fought and successful attacks across the many river lines that dominated the area of our advance. General Mark Clark, Commanding Allied Forces in Italy wrote "congratulations on the successful attacks by your troops - the operation was thoroughly planned and executed." General McCreery, commanding 8th Army, praised "the splendid fighting spirit and great skill" of the Corps and took the trouble to visit three or four of our companies which were deployed along the Senio River to wish them a Merry Christmas. I am not sure whether the men realized who he was at the time because Army Commanders are rarely seen amongst forward companies. Furthermore, jeeps with Generals' flags flying were not always welcome in the forward areas as they frequently drew down fire onto the unfortunate troops who lived there. But in this case the 25-foot high banks of the Senio River prevented the enemy from observing the Army Commander's jeep so his visit went off without incident. General McCreery had a pleasant and helpful personality and his cheery greetings were appreciated by those who recognized him.

Perhaps the greatest compliments paid to the troops of the 1st Canadian Corps came from the enemy whose recorded telephone conversations and war diaries fell into Allied hands. When a British Division which was being supported by tanks of our 1st Armoured Brigade succeeded in capturing its objective, German Intelligence officers reported that it must be a Canadian division because "only Canadians attack like that." On another occasion a German General remarked to his senior Commander, "One of these days the Canadian Corps is going to attack and then our centre will explode." Enemy records also tell us that when Canadians appeared in a sector the Germans would generally commit their best formations against us.

In total, 93,000 Canadians served in Italy; of these nearly 5,500 were killed and 19,500 were wounded because, as Col. Nicholson wrote in his official history, "The Canadians in Italy," "the men who wore on their shoulders the name of Canada were identified with the costliest struggles of the entire campaign."

During February, the Canadian Corps left Italy with the 1st Armoured Brigade, commanded by Brigadier Bill Murphy, leading the way followed by the 5th Armoured Division; the tanks were loaded on railroad flat cars and the trucks moved in convoys to Leghorn and

Naples. The 1st Division remained in action until the latter part of February when the 3rd Brigade, commanded by Brig. Paulo Bernatchez, handed over our final positions in the evening of the 27th to the 8th Indian Division.

Meanwhile Sparky Sparling, Arthur Wrinch and I piled our equipment into a couple of jeeps and headed south for Rome. We were to spend a night there before flying to Marseilles where staff cars were waiting to take us the 700 miles to Holland. I reached headquarters, 1st Canadian Army, late in the evening of the second day and reported to General Foulkes who had flown direct from Rome. He had had a session with General Crerar and after passing on whatever instructons he had received from Harry Crerar, went on a well-deserved five days leave in England. General Crerar and his headquarters were extremely busy at that time as· Operation ''Veritable'' was underway.

This operation to clear the Germans from the west bank of the Rhine was the largest ever planned by 1st Canadian Army and involved an initial assault by five divisions followed by two more; but one the most important considerations in the planning was to disguise from the enemy that an attack was coming in that area at all and that five British divisions would be taking part in the assault. Special precautions were taken to make the enemy believe the attack would be made further south; and to cover the concentration of so many divisions in a comparatively small area, the most elaborate programmes wee initiated to maintain a smoke screen at all hours across the front and flank for five miles. 'Smoke' groups, employing many hundreds of men, were formed to ensure the screens effectiveness. A special office was set up employing as many as 1,600 men to control traffic into and through the build-up area. As the enemy had blown the dikes on the WAAL River and flooded many square miles of low lying farm land, our 3rd Divison which had to move through the floods were given over 100 'buffaloes' to assist them. Preparations everywhere were on a vast scale and it was evident to us from Italy that the Italian theatre had enjoyed a much lower priority for equipment than North-West Europe.

I went forward to call on General Simonds at his 2nd Corps headquarters. His Corps was about to go into action in an extension of Operation ''Veritable'' to be known as ''Blockbuster'' which would finally drive the enemy from the west bank of the Rhine in the Sector commanded by General Crerar. His only remark to me about the impending operation was his concern at the strength of many of the infantry battalions and the lack of reinforcements for them. I told him that we had had a somewhat similar problem but the closing of certain training and administrative establishments had produced a small bonus for us. On this visit I also saw Elliot Rodger who was Guy Simonds' Chief of Staff and Fin Clark, his Chief Signal Officer. They had come all the way from Normandy with the headquarters of 2nd Corps. By this time our staffs at the headquarters of both the 1st and 2nd Corps were very experienced and could take on almost anything. What would have seemed 'impossible' three years before, was handled as routine, although it might perhaps take a little more planning and supervision than more normal problems. ''Veritable'' and ''Blockbuster'' called for planning the moves of close to half a million men and the subsequent supply of munitions, food, fuel and medical supplies to keep them operational. It was a gigantic task in which the headquarters of 1st Canadian Army took the lead.

Our headquarters became operational again on the 15th March with only one division (the British 49th Division) under our command but with a multitude of different plans for our future battles. Political and military considerations began to conflict; for example, was the feeding of the starving Dutch people more important than the destruction of the German forces within Germany itself? ''No,'' said Montgomery, ''I need every soldier to concentrate on Germany but once that is finished we can turn to the liberation of the Dutch people.'' That is what he said in March so, of course, we started to think and plan for operations in northwest Germany. Slowly, as pressures grew for getting some relief for the Dutch people, the mood changed. We began to plan for various ways of crossing the Rhine and the Ijssel Rivers into West Holland.

Early in April, Montgomery issued new orders which clarified our tasks and directed our attention towards the liberation of the Netherlands, and in due course divisions assaulted Arnhem and Apeldoorn across the formidable Rhine and Ijssel Rivers. At that very time there was another change in our orders as the decision was taken on the highest levels that our attacks would not go beyond the German defences on the line of the River Grebbe. I can remember General

Foulkes' expression when he was told of this further change. He turned to me and said, "Jesus, George, I wouldn't be surprised if our next orders will be to vacate Arnhem and come back over the Rhine." My reply was that maybe we should all go back to Italy where we could be used to better purpose!

I continued to be impressed with Charles Foulkes' military decisions. The many plans we worked on were all based on sound common sense and I think his eventual orders to the commanders of our 1st and 5th Divisions and the British 49th Division were as well thought out and as well executed as any other battle plans of World War II.

The 49th Division had been in the thick of things from Normandy onwards and was a good steady division. Shortly after coming under our command it had a new General, Maj.-Gen. Rawlins, who had been the commander of Artillery in the hard worked 30th Corps of the British Army. I got the firm impression when we first started to deal with Rawlins that he was not happy to be under Canadian command. He was inclined to argue about matters I felt were of no consequence. Perhaps he was feeling his way since he was new to command of a division or perhaps he was being awkward in order to ensure that he wasn't pushed around by Foulkes. He was a big man, physically, and had obviously proven himself as an able commander of artillery so he did not need to be difficult. By the end of our operations in Holland he appeared to be more relaxed and I think was quite enjoying his stay with us. The 49th Division played an important role up to the line of the River Grebbe in the liberation of Holland and deserved a little more of the limelight than they got at the celebrations for the final liberation of northwest Holland in May.

The operation of 1st Corps, from 12 April when 1st Division crossed the Ijssel and the 49th British Division crossed the Neder Rhine, are described in great detail in the official history of the Canadian Army written by Colonel Charles Stacey entitled "The Victory Campaign." The highlight was the decision by General Foulkes to pass our 5th Armoured Division through the 49th Division in Arnhem and direct it north to the Ijsselmeer, thus cutting behind the enemy forces in Apeldoorn and isolating them from their main forces in the Grebbe Line. It was a classic role for an armoured division and the "Mighty Maroon Machine" under Bert Hoffmeister did its job thoroughly, causing the disintegration of the enemy resistance between the Ijssel and the Grebbe Line. The 1st Division quickly followed up the achievement of the 5th Armoured Division and soon was patrolling up to the defences along the Grebbe.

De Wereld Hotel, Wageningen, May 1945
Major Plessen, The Author,
General Reichelt, General Foulkes,
Prince Bernhard

16

The German Surrender

In early April, secret negotiations were being conducted with the German Reichskommissar for the Netherlands, Seyss-Inquart, in an effort to get food to the people of northwest Holland who, since the failure of our airborne landings at Arnhem in September 1944, had been reduced to a diet which was halfway to starvation. The outcome of these talks was that Seyss-Inquart was prepared to permit food to be brought into northwest Holland by certain routes provided we did not move beyond the main German defences along the River Grebbe. The plan was finally accepted and a series of meetings took place between friend and foe to work out the details of food shipments. Meanwhile we sent a message to all units in contact with the enemy that from 0800 hours, 28 April, they would cease any offensive action and the Germans were advised of this. Then began an extraordinary series of meetings with the enemy, culminating in their signing the Document of Surrender in Wageningen on 5 May 1945.

I attended all the meetings and can say that, initially, the Germans made it as difficult as possible for us to get firm agreements from them. They carefully avoided, for as long as possible, sending a representative to a meeting who had any real authority. At the first meeting on the 28th April, between General de Guingand, representing General Eisenhower, and Seyss-Inquart, the latter failed to appear;

instead, he sent two deputies neither of whom was authorized to agree to anything. A second meeting was, therefore, arranged for the 30th which Seyss-Inquart would attend and at which the Supreme Commander (General Eisenhower) would be represented by his Chief of Staff, General Bedell Smith. These meetings took place in the schoolhouse of a small but very tidy villge named Achteveld. Prior to the meeting on the 30th we had arranged for a direct telephone connection between the school house and General Eisenhower's headquarters in Rheims, France. This was a great achievement by our Signals personnel and called for the repair of civilian installations and the laying of miles of military cable but it worked. Before giving my impressions of the meeting on the 30th, I must digress for a moment and write about a man whom we, at Corps Headquarters, had met early in April and whom we all admired.

He was His Royal Highness Prince Bernhard of the Netherlands. Prince Bernhard was Commander in Chief of the Forces of the Interior - the Dutch Underground force of many thousands of loyal men and women which, over the years of occupation had, by cladestine means, kept Queen Wilhelmina and her Cabinet in London informed of events in Holland and had helped hundreds of Allied personnel to escape to Britain. It had also kept the flame of freedom alive in the hearts of the people. During the airborne landings near Arnhem in September 1944 very little use was made of the Dutch Underground as it was feared that they had been penetrated by the Germans, but we did not make that mistake again as we captured Arnhem and Appeldoorn. Everywhere our troops went they found representatives of the Forces of the Interior ready to guide them, give information about the enemy and hold ground to free our troops for further action. They were everywhere and were of great value, and the man controlling and encouraging them was Prince Bernhard who brought his Headquarters Staff to join our Corps Headquarters.

On the morning of the 30th April, General Foulkes and I arrived in the village of Achteveld in good time for the meeting. We were followed shortly after by General Bedell Smith who had flown in from General Eisenhower's Headquarters in France. We noticed that as we gathered in front of the school many of the villagers had their faces pressed to the windows wondering, no doubt, what on earth was going on. They had seen the German delegation move into the school with the much hated Seyss-Inquart in the lead and now they were watching us and wondering who we were with our different uniforms and varied shoulder flashes.

Suddenly, a large black open Mercedes-Benz roared into the village with the large special registration, R.K.1, on the front. This was the well-known car and identification of the Reichskommissar Seyss-Inquart - the most hated man in Holland. But behind the wheel, and wearing the uniform of a Dutch General, was Prince Bernhard. As he stepped out of the car and walked towards us every window was flung open and out came hundreds of yards of Orange bunting and Dutch flags. It was one of the most moving incidents I have ever witnessed. Here was their Prince - they recognized him immediately - and he was driving the Reichskommisar's car!

Prince Bernhard walked slowly down the street waving and saluting whilst the villagers called to him and thanked him. I am sure we all had tears in our eyes as we turned and walked into the school. Thirty years later, in 1975, I was privileged to accompany Prince Bernhard to a parade commemorating the Liberation and German surrender, and he remembered then, with great emotion, his greeting from the people of Achteveld.

I only attended the first few minutes of the meeting of the 30th with Seyss-Inquart because General Foulkes asked me to check on a problem raised by the Germans, but I was there long enough to appreciate what an unpleasant man Seyss-Inquart was. His eyes were pale blue and very cold, his blond hair was sparse, his lips were thin. He had a cruel face and I was reminded of the scene recorded on German film when he, an Austrian, officially handed over his country to a fellow Austrian, Adolf Hitler, after German troops had entered Vienna in March 1938. It was obvious that Seyss-Inquart could not be trusted; he alternated between a cold aloofness and an ingratiating warmth. He would "of course agree to our demands to feed the poor Dutch people and would make all arrangements for this. He would not ask Berlin for permission to do it because he knew it would be refused."

Seyss-Inquart was trying to place on record his deep feeling for the plight of the Dutch people. But he was stopped in his tracks at one point in the discussions when he was told to ensure that there was to be no more flooding of land by the Germans. He replied that he had always been against the flooding of land anyway and "rather than do that I would prefer to die." "You will," replied General Bedell Smith. He did - following the Nuremberg Trials.

The commander of the German Forces in northwest Holland was General Blaskowitz but he did not attend this meeting. At one point his deputy asked if the General was considered to be a 'war-criminal,' a term used by the Allies to indicate a man who would be tried for crimes against humanity. General Bedell Smith then took the trouble to phone Eisenhower's Headquarters and ask for a check on Blaskowitz's record. He was assured that Blaskowitz had a clean record and was not classified as a 'war-criminal.' This information was given officially to the Germans and I think it helped us in our negotiations of the next few days. At the conclusion of the meeting, General Foulkes requested a meeting with Blaskowitz or his deputy to work out a plan for convoys of Canadian vehicles to take food through the German defences for delivery to the Dutch underground who would distribute it. It was agreed that a meeting should take place the next morning at a restaurant-cum-service station which was inside the German lines and about one mile from Achteveld on the Amersfort Road. A Canadian soldier would advance from our lines at 10:00 a.m. carrying a white flag. Behind him the Canadian party would also advance on foot. We were assured there were no mines on that particular part of the road.

As we were saying 'au revoir' to the German group we had no idea that at that precise moment Hitler was saying his permanent farewells to members of his entourage before shooting himself. His suicide was announced to the world that afternoon and Admiral Doenitz was named his successor. When Seyss-Inquart heard the news he boarded a fast German "E" boat and escaped to Schleswig-Holstein where he hoped to contact either Doenitz or Himmler; he left General Blaskowitz in command. The death of Hitler released many senior officers of the German Forces from their personal oaths of loyalty to him as Fuehrer had, there is no doubt, it helped many of them to cooperate with us in ways that they might never had done had he lived.

Next morning, bright and early, we went by car to Achteveld for what we hoped would be an eventful meeting. I had arranged, at General Foulkes suggestion, for Brigadier Pat Bogert to join in the proceedings since it was his 2nd Brigade that occupied Achteveld and confronted the Grebbe Line defences to the west. At 10:00 a.m. exactly, one of our soldiers left the protection of the houses and walked towards the enemy carrying a large white flag which we were told was a sheet presented by one of the villagers—it was certainly big enough. About 50 yards behind came Pat Bogert and I, and about 100 yards behind us came Charles Foulkes, his ADC, and an interpreter. The road we marched along was flat and raised only a foot or so above the marshy ground that bordered it on each side. Our rendezvous with the Germans was about 1000 yards ahead and as we advanced we could see the beginnings of the German defences where the ground rose about 15 feet above the marshes. On each side of us, for the first three or four hundred yards, we could see our own soldiers, with helmets camouflaged with grass and reeds, lying on their groundsheets in an effort to keep dry.

Pat Bogert said they were the scouts and snipers of the Princess Patricia's Canadian Light Infantry. Our Intelligence had told us that the enemy in this part of the Grebbe Line was the 6th parachute Division - much reduced in strength but still a very effective formation. Pat and I joked as we went along and wondered whether some trigger-happy parachutist would try and seek immortality by bumping off a General and two brigadiers with a couple of bursts of his machine gun. But all went well and we arrived safely at the appointed rendezvous and were shortly joined by General Foulkes. There were three German officers to greet us, the senior of them being Major-General Plocher who commanded 6 Parachute Division.

Through our interpreter, General Foulkes told Plocher that at the meeting the day before Syess-Inquart had agreed that food could be taken through the German defences and that the purpose of our meeting today was to work out the details of how it was to be done. Plocher shattered us all by announcing that he had no authority to discuss those problems with us. He had just been told to meet us. At this point, Charles Foulkes became very angry and told the German that he and his superiors were fed up with the way the Germans imposed delay after delay in the feeding of the Dutch people and that Blaskowitz or someone with full authority must meet with him the next day or the German senior officers would pay the penalty of being branded as criminals. This had the desired effect. Plocher phoned Blaskowitz and the latter arranged that General Reichelt, his Chief of Staff, would meet with us the next day at a point just on our side of the Grebbe Line and west of the town of Wageningen, close to the Neder Rijn. Meanwhile, the very able Director of Supplies and Transport at our Headquarters, Colonel Curly McQueen, had organized everything so that twelve platoons, each of 30 trucks carrying 90 tons of food and medical supplies, would be ready to move into Holland at two hours notice, and continue on a twenty-four hour basis, if necessary.

The meeting place with General Reichelt, where we discussed details of the food convoys, was in a small wooden house painted dark green which lay about a mile from the western outskirts of Wageningen on the right of the road leading to Utrecht. General Reichelt cooperated fully with us and arrangements were made for telephone cable between the supply roadhead established by Curly McQueen (incidentally, he didn't have a hair on his head) and the delivery and distribution points west of Utrecht. Colonel McQueen's organization delivered over 15,000 tons of supplies over an eight day period which, with the rations being brought in by sea and dropped from the air, brought the much needed relief particularly to the people of Rotterdam and Amsterdam, the two largest cities, many of whose inhabitants were in dire straits.

At the meeting with Reichelt, General Foulkes said he also wanted to get convoys through on the road to the north connecting Appeldoorn and Utrecht. This was the area in which we had met Plocher the day before. However, Reichelt, who had been very cooperative up to that point, surprised us by saying that he did not have the authority to discuss this second route. He gave no reason but we thought at the time that it might be connected with certain reorganizations within the German forces in that particular part of the Grebbe defences. The Headquarters of their 25th Army was in Hilversum through which our convoys would have moved, and we realized that with the departure of Seyss-Inquart and the breakdown of political control, the military would probably be having problems. They feared the vengeance of the Dutch people and were trying to concentrate their forces as a means of self-protection, but, as events showed, the Dutch were really only interested in reprisals against members of the Dutch S.S. Division, the

Dutch people who had cooperated to their personal advantage with the German authorities, and against officials who had brought distress upon them. They did not appear to have strong feelings against the German soldier - they were just glad they were finally going.

On the 4th May we were informed that General Blaskowitz was prepared to surrender all German forces under his command. He had obviously received instructions to do so from Admiral Doenitz whose intermediaries were dealing with Field-Marshal Montgomery. Surrender was unconditional. It was, therefore, arranged that Reichelt would come to see us immediately in Wageningen to receive the terms of surrender and that on the following day, 5th May, General Blaskowitz would attend the official surrender ceremony in the "De Wereld" Hotel, Wageningen, where General Foulkes would accept his surrender.

The document of surrender had been prepared at Army Headquarters where I am sure a battery of lawyers, interpreters and Intelligence officers must have spent many hours in its preparation. It was much too long and baffled both ourselves and the Germans when Reichelt and his interpreter sat down to study it on the 4th in "De Wereld" Hotel. Paul Reichelt was a man of medium height, broad-shouldered and with what I would call a "trustworthy" face in the sense that there was nothing evil in it. He was a religious man - a good solid Bavarian - and the sort of man most people would trust. He was, of course, overwhelmed by the course of events and only his robust physique kept him from total exhaustion. After reading carefully the mass of "do's" and "don'ts" in the official documents he said he would work through the papers that night and appear with General Blaskowitz the following morning. He cautioned Charles Foulkes that some of the surrender terms might be beyond the control of Blaskowitz to obey, but he assured him that the will to obey the terms was paramount in Blaskowitz' mind and he had impressed this on his junior commanders. This meeting was only attended on our side by Charles Foulkes, Prince Bernhard, myself and two of our interpreters. Reichelt had with him an Austrian major who spoke excellent English. The Press did not attend this meeting.

Next morning the streets around "De Wereld" were teeming with our official Public Relations personnel, war artists and photographers and at the appointed hour Colonel-General Blaskowitz drove up in his command vehicle with General Reichelt. They, and their interpreters, were shown to their seats on one side of four small tables that had been joined together to form a large one. After a suitable pause during which time the 40 accredited P.R. and press representatives were able to get a good look at the German group from across the room, our party entered with General Charles Foulkes in the lead followed by Prince Bernhard. The German generals stood silently, bowed to General Foulkes and, having been told that the officer in the uniform of a Netherlands General was Prince Bernhard, they bowed in his direction. Charles Foulkes conducted the meeting well, he spoke clearly and directly to Blaskowitz who sat immediately opposite him. Charles had to read through the somewhat lengthy document of surrender and we amended certain parts of it at their request. For instance, paragraph 7 said that Blaskowitz would be held responsible "for the maintenance and safeguarding of all United Nations personnel in his area." "Who are the United Nations? How will I recognize them? How can I safeguard them if I have no arms?" Paragraph 7 was removed.

After about an hour it was obvious to General Foulkes that Blaskowitz was concerned at the number of instructions contained in the document, some of which he wanted to be sure he could carry out before signing it. Blaskowitz repeated that he acknowledged defeat, was quite prepared to surrender but wanted to be honest and not promise to do things that he could not do. It was therefore agreed that, having acknowledged surrender, he would be given two or three more hours to recheck with his commanders and staff any foreseeable problems. The German group then departed but before they went I told Reichelt that we would expect Blaskowitz to return at 4:00 p.m.

On the way to our Headquarters at Harskamp. I travelled with Charles Foulkes and, somewhat naturally, we talked about the personality of Blaskowitz. Charles said he quite liked the man and felt sorry for him as an individual. We joked about how we would have felt if the positions had been reversed and Charles was the one who was surrendering. Blaskowitz had retained a quiet dignity which must have been difficult after all he had been through. He had been one of the Army Commanders during the invasion of Poland in September 1939 but after a period of glory as one of the national heroes he had been dismissed by Hitler because he had refused to take part in the political extermination of the Polish people, particularly those of Jewish faith. He had remained unemployed until late 1943 when he was appointed to command German forces in the south of France. After the liberation of France in 1944 he ended up in Holland commanding 25th Army which he was now about to surrender to us. He had been a good soldier who had stood by his principles, and had been dismissed for doing so. We were glad he had not been condemned as a 'war criminal.' As we talked, I asked Charles if he wanted the Press to attend the actual signing ceremony which we were planning for 4:00 p.m. I recommended that they should not be admitted - they had all the photographs and copy they would need and I felt that Blaskowitz had been a pretty fair enemy - why humiliate him even more by allowing anyone to take pictures of him signing his whole life away. Charles did not need any persuading because he felt as strongly as I did about it. He decided that he, Prince Bernhard and I, with our interpreters, would be the only people present; and to make sure that we would be alone we changed the rendezvous from the ''De Wereld'' Hotel to the school next door and put a guard on the door so that no one could enter.

Shortly before 4:00 o'clock, we entered the schoolhouse and were joined by General Blaskowitz and his interpreter. There was some discussion about the terms of surrender. However, General Blaskowitz said he could now comply with the instructions as he had issued firm orders down to companies and he was sure they would be obeyed. He was prepared to sign. I filled in the date, time and place at the bottom of the documents and passed the five copies to Blaskowitz; after he had signed each copy, Charles Foulkes completed the formalities by accepting the surrender with his own signature. The time was 1603 hours. The date 5 May 1945.

Whilst we were anxious to move into northwest Holland and take full control, it was agreed that we would not cross the Grebbe Line until early morning of the 7th May. By that time, all German forces would be withdrawn from their defences. We had divided the area to be liberated into three main parts. The British 49 Division would take over the area Utrecht-Dordrecht; the 1st Canadian Division would take over Rotterdam-The Hague-Amsterdam and the coastal regions; the 5th Canadian Division would take over the north and eastern side of the

Ijssel Meer (better known to me as the Zuyder Zee). All went well as our troops moved in except for the commander of our Corps Artillery, Brigadier Sparky Sparling, who had a close shave when a trigger-happy member of the underground in Amsterdam sprayed his car with bullets by mistake. He thought it was a German vehicle.

The German divisions had been concentrated in different areas and were soon grouped into large camps where they were issued with the same rations as our own troops. The discipline amongst them was good and I think this may well have been due to a strong letter and order sent out to all officers and men by General Blaskowitz on the 6th May, the day after he had signed the document of surrender. His letter read:

"The German Army has been finally and completely defeated in battle, and has surrendered unconditionally to the U.S., Great Britain and the Soviet Union. The Army, Air Force and Navy will be disarmed and disbanded. The first requirement from everybody is CALM, ORDER and DISCIPLNE."

After the above introduction, the Order detailed a number of "do's" and "don'ts" and finally warned all subordinate commanders to tell their men of his letter and order, and also note that anyone who disobeyed the orders "is a Saboteur and will be treated as such." It was a strong letter and it had the desired effect. Three or four German soldiers who were caught stealing from their comrades were summarily shot - "pour encourager les autres."

Our Corps Headquarters moved from Harskamp on the 7th into our final location in Hilversum. General Foulkes and the members of his "A" Mess moved into the grounds of the Palace Hotel - a comfortable stone building of three floors which had been used to house senior visiting Germans. We used the dining room and lounge only, preferring to continue living in our caravans which were parked in the hotel gardens.

The welcome given to our troops as they went through cities, towns, villages and even past isolated houses in the countryside will never be forgotten. The Dutch poured out their hearts and their pent-up emotions and made it almost impossible for some of the convoys of trucks to get to their destination. To our men, who should have been a part of the celebrations as Northern Italy was being liberated, this welcome more than made up for the cold damp winter in the battle for the Senio and Ravenna. Clean streets, clean houses, blue eyes and pink cheeks were a most welcome change.

We had no sooner moved into Hilversum than we became involved in a variety of post-war problems. They included composition of the Pacific Force to fight alongside the Americans in the invasion of Japan, the need for the Occupation Force to remain in Germany for an indefinite period, the rehabilitation of men who had served for four and five years away from Canada, and the Canadian contribution to the Berlin Garrison; not the least of our worries was moving the German troops out of Holland and back to their own country. To expedite the latter, it was decided that all their troops would march out of Holland on side roads and along the north road that led across the top of the Zuyder Zee. In this way they would avoid passing through heavily populated areas and once on German territory would march, under British supervision, into camps for documentation and disbandment.

I went down to Blaskowitz' Headquarters to give them warning of our plans and also to have a look at their set-up. My opposite number was General Paul Reichelt and he was most interested in our plans to move them out of Holland. He said the men were anxious to make contact with their families as soon as possible; many had no idea if their wives, mothers, fathers, sweethearts were even alive as their mail system had broken down during the past few weeks. I was shocked when Paul Reichelt said he had not heard from his wife for two months. She lived in southern Germany. I told him to write a letter, put her address on the envelope and I would make sure she got it within a week. I cautioned him not to seal the envelope so that it could be examined by censors. One of our officers who was going on a liaison mission to Munich took the letter and delivered it to Frau Reichelt.

I was fascinated by the size and layout of the German Headquarters which was designed, I understood, as the headquarters in case of an invision from the sea. The complex was in a well-treed area of substantial houses occupied in peacetime by wealthy Dutch families. The families had been removed from a large part of the area and been replaced by officers and soldiers who had been ordered to maintain as normal a pattern of life in the houses as possible so that the area, roughly half-mile square, looked like the houses in the immediate vicinity.

The cars of the original owners were kept in the driveways and moved every now and again as if they were in normal use. Gardens were maintained as before. Civilian laundry was hung out to dry as before. New paths were not to be made between buildings since they would indicate military occupation. Every precaution was taken to make it look as if there had been no changes in the use of the area which might show up on Allied air photographs. In the centre of this complex and in a heavily treed area they had built an underground bunker which became the nerve centre of the whole headquarters. The roof of the bunker, with grass and bushes, exactly resembled the original path that led between the trees. The bunker was of concrete and the roof and walls were certainly three feet thick. It would take a heavy bomb to penetrate the roof. Reichelt told me that it had not been bombed until early in 1945 and on that occasion about thirty bombs fell all around the bunker just as he and other senior officers were running from their Officers' Mess in an adjoining house to take shelter in the bunker. However, not one of the bombs detonated!

Shortly after reaching Hilversum, we found we were in the centre of a round of parties given by the Dutch and also our own formations and units. Victory and peace was in the air and a great degree of thankfulness that we were there to enjoy it. The Dutch people never seemed to get tired of our victory parades or of the music of our bands, drums and pipers. One day, Sparky Sparling and I decided we would visit some of our units in the area of Rotterdam and The Hague. Since no restaurants were functioning we took with us sandwiches and chocolate bars from our own Mess and, having found a suitable place for lunch just outside Rotterdam, we stopped the car and reached for the sandwiches. In no time at all, and before we had started to eat, the faces of eight little children appeared in the windows. Their eyes seemed as large as saucers as they stared at the sandwiches and, needless to say, neither the driver, Sparky nor I had any lunch. The youngsters just devoured everything.

We felt a little ashamed that we took our rations for granted when little kids like these were still hungry; some of the smaller ones had never tasted chocolate. As the days went by all our units organized parties for the children in their neighbourhood and gave up the parcels of food and chocolate from families in Canada to provide gifts for their guests. I

am sure that many middle-aged men and women now living in The
Netherlands gained their first experience of Canadians when, as
children, they attended those parties.

With the assistance of the Dutch authorities we organized a day of
horse racing at the Hilversum track. About 20% of all money taken at
the tote was given to help the poorer and more needy families. In these
and other ways, the Canadian soldier became closely allied to the
Dutch people. We were grateful to them for making us feel so
welcome and we are grateful now that they still remember us with affection.

Before the defeat of Germany we had received strict orders from
Eisenhower's Headquarters that there was to be no fraternization
whatever with the German people. We were told that in contacting
German officials we were to keep them at arms' length and not to
acknowledge their salutes. I cannot personally think of a more stupid
way of antagonizing a people and of eventually inducing a lasting
hatred between friend and foe. It was as if the creators of the discarded
Morgenthau Plan, for the complete destruction of German industry and
the reduction of the German people to a race of rural serfs, were determined to get their ounce of flesh even if they could not get a pound. In
Winston Churchill's opinion Julius Caesar gained more by his
generous treatment of people than he did by defeating them in battles;
and in his history of the 2nd World War he states his conviction that in
war there should be resolution; in defeat, defiance; in victory,
magnanimity; and in peace, goodwill. If we had continued the
Eisenhower policy of ''no fraternization'' there would be very little
goodwill today and I doubt there would be peace.

Not many of us in the Canadian Army paid too much attention to
''no-fraternization'' when dealing with our opposite numbers in the
German Army. When all German forces had left Holland, Reichelt
came to see me with a letter from General Blaskowitz telling us oficial-
ly that apart from his own small staff at Headquarters, our part of
Holland was clear of his soldiers. I poured two glasses of Scotch and
we drank a toast to the future. I congratulated him on the efficient way
he had organized the withdrawal of the German Army. At this point he
handed me a small wooden cigar box which contained a minute
automatic pistol and a clip of nine bullets. He asked me to accept them

as a gift - he had nothing else to offer. He said that both Blaskowitz and he appreciated Charles Foulkes' attitude and the way we had treated the members of the Wehrmacht after the surrender. About fifteen years later, when I was attending a NATO Exercise in Paris I went forward to speak to General Hans Spiedel (who had been Chief of Staff to Field Marshal Rommel) and who was now commander of NATO Land Forces in Central Europe. Beside him was none other than Paul Reichelt, now a Corps Commander in the new German Army. We reminisced for a while and just before I left NATO in 1962 to return to Canada I sent him the small pistol in its wooden box as a reminder of our friendship.

After General Blaskowitz left our control he went back to General Crerar's Headquarters where he was treated well, given a tent of his own and allowed to retain his soldier servant who had been with him many years before the war. What happened next was to all of us quite disgraceful.

The Russians accused him of being a 'war criminal' in spite of his good record and General Bedell Smith's earlier assurance that he was not. Eisenhower's headquarters did nothing on his behalf; he was imprisoned along with S.S. generals and, a short time later, committed suicide. Why Supreme Headquarters bowed and scraped so much to the Russians I will never know. I was heartily ashamed.

General Plocher, who was the individual that General Charles Foulkes was so angry with at our meeting in the Grebbe Line at the end of April because he said he had no authority to agree to anything, commanded the 6th Parachute Division. After the surrender he asked if he could make one final address to his men in which he would stress the need to cooperate with us. He said he was sure he would get their full cooperation if, at the end of his address, he could tell his men that he had been given permission to lead them in a final "Heil Hitler" and Nazi salute, after which those salutations would be banned. He was permitted to do this; it was a small price to pay to ensure the goodwill of 3,500 very tough parachutists. I went along to hear him, accompanied by a British German-speaking officer who translated his words as he addressed the men. At the end he and his 3,500 men gave a final salute, stood still for perhaps 30 seconds and then broke off. The next time I saw Plocher was in Rome in 1961 when I, as Chairman of our

Joint Staff in London, signed an agreement on behalf of our Chiefs of Staff in Ottawa for the continued use of the facilities at Decimomanu in Sardinia. It was an Italian Air Force base used jointly by ourselves, the Italians and the Germans. The German representative was General Plocher who was obviously not interested in being reminded of our last meeting!

Our Corps Headquarters was to disband early in July and I was due back in Ottawa later that month. I did not look forward to saying good-bye to such a first class Army; one that expanded from almost nothing to one that maintained a quarter of a million men in action in Sicily, Italy, southern France and northwest Europe. One that had been acknowledged as "superior" by our enemies.

In 1939 we had been a civilian army marching off to war. We learn-ed to be infantrymen, tank men and artillery men the British way since we had little expertise in those fields. But in most other army opera-tions Canadians were already fairly expert.

For example, in matters of road transportation, we were far ahead of the British and so when our Army Service Corps started to operate in the U.K. in 1940 it was used in a civilian way without being too bound by military protocol. Our Signals and Engineers were in much the same position. In road building and airfield construction, our "Sap-pers" could get a job done in half the time of their British opposite numbers. They brought civilian techniques and equipment into military usage and made a great contribution in doing so. If our Signal Corps had realized early in 1940 that our Army would expand in the way it did, I'm sure we would have developed and built radios that were Canadian designed at the start instead of relying so much on the British sets which we then 'modified' to suit us. Our civilian-soldiers made an important contribution that was not always appreciated at the time.

At the end of June I went to England for a few days leave; but before taking me to the airfield Corporal Barr, my driver; Louis Schellen-burg, my batman; and Private Monk who drove my caravan, came for a farewell drink. They were a great team.

Back in London I was told to attend at Buckingham Palace to be in-vested by the King with the C.B.E. (Commander of the Order of the British Empire). When I marched up to receive the Order the King looked at me for a moment and then said, "The last time we spoke you were a major-general. Why are you now a brigadier?' I told him that I had run into trouble with General Simonds in Normandy. ''Well,'' said the King, ''he would be an interesting man to have trouble with, I'm sure.'' With that he smiled and hung the ribbon and Order around my neck. I felt this was a fitting climax to my war.

The Author, Toronto, Ontario, May, 1963

Audrey and I at the Ball.
Versailles Palace, 1961

The Author and the Hon. Keiller MacKay,
Toronto, Ontario, 1962

Chief Harry Broad Throat (center) and the Author, Calgary, 1954

Dressed (reluctantly) as a Modern Major General, 1979

17

Ottawa And Washington

When I took up my appointment as Vice Quarter Master General in the fall of 1945 in Ottawa, it was a very different city to what it is today. It was truly the Capital where the government wielded great power on behalf of all Canadians, both at home and abroad.

The Prime Minister was Mackenzie King, a mild and meek looking man but one whom his coleagues always addressed as "Sir." He had brought into his Cabinet a strong team - men such as C.D. Howe, Louis St. Laurent, Douglas Abbott, Ilsley, and Colonel James Ralston until he was replaced by McNaughton. There were also Chubby Power and Colin Gibson who were successively Ministers of Air, and Angus Macdonald, Minister of the Navy. These were dedicated men who had a real sense of purpose in the war years and I think that a great majority of Canadians felt at that time they were being well governed.

Economically, we were the fourth most powerful nation. We had sent hundreds of thousands of guns, vehicles, tanks, aircraft and other military equipment to Russia and China, and to the nations of Europe as they were freed from Nazi domination. Our Armed Forces, almost all volunteers, had made an outstanding contribution to the war in Europe, the Atlantic and the Mediterranean. Financially the country was sound and, although personal income tax had been high during the war, it had been paid.

The Civil Service, which had expanded to about 250,00, was being reduced rapidly to the projected peacetime requirement of about 160,000. English, which had been the wartime language of the Allies, dominated meetings although a high proportion of our civil servants, who were Ottawans by birth, could speak both languages with equal facility and without a trace of an accent in either French or English. The quality of senior civil servants was in keeping with the strength of the Cabinet whom they served.

As a soldier who had been out of touch with civil servants for nearly six years I was greatly impressed by their ability, sense of responsibility and the long hours they worked without benefit of overtime. Salaries in those days were low. As a Brigadier I received just over $7,200 a year. A General who retired in 1945 after 30 years' service received a pension of $400 a month to which he had contributed about 6% of his pay throughout his service. In the Armed Services low salaries were partly compensated by the various messes to which we belonged according to our rank. They were really small clubs and we all paid monthly dues for the privilege of belonging to them. In those days this was the only 'extra' available to us. We never received any additional allowance for entertaining whether or not we were ordered to look after visitors; neither did we receive any funds towards refurbishing new quarters when we were moved from one place to another. Inevitably, from time to time, there was a certain amount of grumbling but, generally, we were proud of being in one of the Armed Services. What a pity the word 'Service' has disappeared and been replaced by the word 'Force.' The older word reminded us always that we 'served' the people of Canada.

Army Headquarters was headed by the Chief of the General Staff who should really have been called "Chief of Staff" because under him were three main branches, one being the General Staff and the other two those of the Adjutant-General and the Quarter-Master-General.

The General Staff (G.S.) was headed by the Vice-Chief G.S. and responsible for operations, intelligence, training, plans and overall Army policy. The Adjutant-General (A.G.) was responsible for recruiting, personnel administration, pay, promotions up to the rank of Major, the Chief reserving all higher ranks for his own approval; he was also responsible for morale and the Medical and Dental Services.

The Quarter-Master-General (QMG), Major-General Hugh Young, was responsible for all storage including explosives and ammunition, maintenance, rationing, catering and cooking, accommodation including provision of barracks and family housing, construction, and movement of personnel and supplies by sea, rail and road. As Vice QMG I was the QMG's understudy and responsible for seeing that his policies and orders were carried out.

The main priorities in 1945 and 1946 were getting the troops back from overseas, moving them to their home towns where their families were waiting to greet them, disposing of the many camps, buildings and exhibition grounds which had been built for wartime purposes and were no longer required, and providing accommodation for the new peacetime Army; finally, the placing into mothballs, from our wartime production, of mobilization stores to equip a Corps of approximately 60,000 men in case of future emergency.

One of the biggest problems was providing accommodation for the married families of returning service men. There were several ugly incidents across the country when men, who had been demobilized, tried to take the law into their own hands and seize vacant properties. An interesting example occurred in Ottawa when a young ex-RCAF officer named Hanratty led a group of discontented and homeless wives, seized one of the large wartime buildings one Sunday morning, and moved their families in—lock, stock and barrel. The Government was in a quandary; if it took action against the squatters there might be a howl of protest from veterans organizations; if it did nothing it would appear to be condoning the takeover which might snowball into takeovers of other military properties throughout the country. The Prime Minister decided to do something about it and announced that a senior Army Officer was being appointed to ''look into the matter.''

The next Friday Charles Foulkes, who was the Chief of the Army, told me that I was to put together as powerful a team as possible of representatives from Government and the City and come up with a solution. I asked the Mayor to attend a meeting in my office on the Saturday morning and arranged with senior representatives of the Government departments concerned also to attend. A building close to the one occupied by the Hanratty group was, in fact, surplus to future Government requirements and so we all felt that it would be in the interest of the Government if, by pooling our resources, we could convert the building at reasonable cost to take in about 80 families of veterans. Although the suites would not be large and some toilet facilities might have to be shared, the accommodation would be satisfactory on a temporary basis. The City would manage the project and charge suitable rents to offset maintenance costs. It seemed a sensible solution which might be copied in other cities in which the Government had surplus accommodation.

With the agreement of those present, our proposals were drawn up and by Sunday evening we had the completed document, together with copies, ready for submission to Charles Foulkes first thing the following day. At noon Foulkes sent for me. I thought I was about to be congratulated on producing such an agreed solution. Instead, Charles Foulkes said with a smile, "Jesus, George, you have certainly put the cat amongst the canaries—the Minister is mad and wants to see you!" Charles accompanied me to the Minister's office. Douglas Abbott had taken over as Minister a few weeks before from McNaughton and he came quickly to the point. "Brigadier - the Prime Minister doesn't want a solution to the problem - he just wants you and your Committee to study it!" He went on to say that my proposals were sound and made sense but if the Government were to accept them the people would ask why we didn't do it before Hanratty forced us into it.

By continuing to report that the problem was being studied the Government hoped it might disappear or at least be replaced by something more vital to public interest. This form of political logic was new to me and I was not impressed. I think it would have been better to eat a little humble pie and provide housing for eighty veterans and their families.

After a few months it was obvious that, with all the uncertainties about the strengths and locations of the future regular Army, it would be difficult to get approval for permanent married quarters to be built except in one or two specific places such as, for example, Camp Borden. At the same time, it was clear we would have to do something if we were to retain the type of officer and non-commissioned officer that we wanted. Individuals who had spent four or five years away from their families were not going to remain in the Army if it meant further separation. At that time we had hundreds of Army huts of all shapes and sizes and one of my best achievements whilst Vice Q.M.G. was to obtain approval to allow nearly one thousand families to move into vacant huts and for the families themselves to make whatever alterations were necessary for their privacy. We gave each family a few hundred dollars worth of lumber, plywood and paint; then, with whatever assistance they could get from our engineers and maintenance units, they divided up the huts to give each family private access to toilets and wash facilities. Within a month many hundreds of makeshift quarters had been hammered together and painted a variety of colours. Heating systems were already installed in all huts and continued to provide the necessary warmth. Each occupant paid a small rent to offset the continuing maintenance.

Many of our militia regiments which had given great service during the war found on their return that the armouries in which they were to be based were either too small or quite unsuitable. I remember examining one that had been used as a cattle-barn for thirty years and the smell of urine was almost overpowering. Hugh Young had had a great deal to do with the militia in the 1930's and always felt that the community in which a militia unit was located should take much more interest in it than they had in the past. He felt that one way to accomplish this might be to build new armouries that would also be used as community centres. We decided that the Sault would be a good place for such an armoury for the Lake Superior Regiment which had distinguished itself in Northwest Europe in World War II. Building went ahead as planned, and, long after I had left the job of Vice Q.M.G., the new Minister, Brooke Claxton, accompanied the new Prime Minister, Louis St. Laurent, to the official opening. The Prime Minister duly cut the ribbon and declared it open. Claxton then told the P.M. that it was the first such armoury to be built to which St. Laurent replied, ''Then let it be the last.'' The cost was unpalatable in the piping days of peace.

In addition to being Chief of Staff of the Army, General Charles Foulkes was also chairman of the Chiefs of Staff Committee. One of the wisest moves he made was to establish the Defence Research Board as a fourth service to the Navy, Army and Air Force; and to appoint as its first chairman the distinguished scientist and administrator, Dr.

Omond Solandt who, in turn, attracted to the Board his eventual successor, Dr. Hartley Zimmerman, a Royal Military College graduate. The members of the Board helped us through the early years of computer systems and analysis and became an integral part of our war games and future planning.

Another wise move made by Charles Foulkes at that time was to get agreement that we should establish Mobilization stocks in case they were needed. Many hundreds of tanks, guns and trucks, together with thousands of smaller weapons and equipments, were stored carefully in special depots.

Field Marshal Viscount Montgomery paid his first visit to Canada in August 1946. He was then the Chief of the Imperial General Staff of the British Army and was due to visit Washington as the guest of General Eisenhower after ten days with us.

Monty had a very warm feeling for the Canadian soldier whom he always described as "quite magnificent" although he did not have quite the same regard for all our Generals! On this visit he presented a number of us with autographed copies of his two volumes of World War II, "Alamein to the Sangro" and "Normandy to the Baltic." There was no doubt that Monty was in excellent spirits and, while I spent only a few minutes with him on that occasion, he repeated a story about the "independence" of the Canadian soldier. At one time in Italy a new brand of cigarettes called "Victory V" appeared with the rations of 8th Army. We were told that they were made in Egypt but just what the Egyptians used for tobacco was anyone's guess. If you wanted to reduce numbers in a confined space all you had to do was light a "Victory V" and you were soon alone. Monty never smoked, and few smoked in his presence, so he had no idea they were so awful. Nor did he appreciate that we, in the Canadian Corps, had our own supply of excellent Canadian cigarettes, such as Macdonald's and Sweet Caps. When driving amongst troops, Monty would always stand up and wave to them and on many occasions throw several packets of Victory V's from the car. On one occasion he was passing a group of Canadian soldiers who were sitting by the side of the road. He stopped the car and threw them several packets of the Victory V's. Said Monty in telling the story, "And do you know, they threw them right back at me! No British soldier would have done that!"

I did not realize at the time of his visit how embroiled Monty was with the future of US-UK-Canada defence relations. But I recall distinctly his strongly expressed views that not only must we produce jointly-developed weapons but the British mania for producing the ultimate and expensive 'few' must give place to the North American system of producing very large quantities of 'good' weapons. Everything must be expendable and when equipments were damaged they should be replaced by new ones. ''Far too much time has been spent in the past in repairing things. In future, we must replace and not repair, ''he said.

By far the most important event of my life occurred on the 4th of October 1946 when Audrey Katherine Calhoun and I were married at St. Andrew's Church in Toronto by the Rev. Stuart Parker, a past Moderator of the Presbyterian Church in Canada. Accommodation in Ottawa was almost impossible to find but we were lucky to be able to take over the lower part of a house occupied by Col. and Mrs. Peter Bingham who were being posted elsewhere. Peter was my old friend from the Royal Canadian Regiment days and we still get together three or four times a year with other comrades from the Regiment.

A few months later General Foulkes asked if I would like to spend a year on a course at the National War College in Washington, D.C. I considered this would be an exciting change, particularly as I had not met many Americans during the war. We left for Washington in July 1947.

The National War College is situated in Fort McNair on a tongue of land that juts out on the northern side of the junction of the wide Potomac River and the lesser waters of the Anacostia. Originally it was the obvious site of a fort placed to deny passage to unfriendly shipping, but now the landscaping and general design of all the buildings and the frequent use of friendly red brick have transformed it into one of the most desirable locations in the U.S. capital. The tongue of land is about half a mile long and a quarter of a mile wide, the main War College building is at the point of the tongue. The roads to it run along each side in the form of a reversed 'U' leaving a wide carpet of green grass in the centre. Some delightful old married quarters, housing many very senior officers from the Pentagon, lay on the west side of the reversed 'U' road, together with the Officers Club. The east side was mostly taken up with administrative buildings. The whole atmosphere was of ordered and friendly efficiency.

Air Commodore (later Air Marshal) Larry Dunlap and Group Captain Bill Clements, both of the Royal Canadian Air Force, were the other two Canadians on the course. We were told we would be classed as 'observers'; we should wear civilian clothes at all times and, if challenged, say we were attached to the U.S. State Department.

On arrival, we found there were also three officers from the British Services, one of whom was Group Captain 'Zulu' Morris. Zulu became an Air Marshal years later and when he was knighted by the Queen we hoped he would retain the 'Zulu' but I'm afraid he is just plain Sir Douglas!

The Commandant of the College was Vice-Admiral Harry Hill, U.S. Navy. His deputies were Major-General 'Lem' Lemnitzer, U.S. Army and Brigadier-General Ted Landon, U.S. Air Force, both of whom were to go to the top of their professions before retiring. There was also a Deputy for Foreign Affairs, the Hon. Maynard Barnes of the State Department.

The year was taken up with studies of the political, economic and military problems facing the United States in the fast changing world of the late 1940's and the 1950's. The faculty included five outstanding civilians from the educational field, one of whom was Canadian born Dr. Wallace Sterling who later was President of Stanford University.

They were supported by fifteen officers from the Navy, Army, Air Force and Marine Corps. The student body was made up of a mixture of the U.S. Armed Forces, State Department, Foreign Service officers, and the U.S. Coast Guard. Together with us - the six observers - we totalled 112 students. The course lasted about ten months during which we visited a number of installations of the U.S. Army and Air Force and spent two nights aboard the new aircraft carrier, "Coral Sea."

The most important thing I gained from my year at the College was the friendship of so many Americans, many of whom went to the top in their professions. General Alfred Gruenther and General Lyman Lemnitzer were two of the staff whom I met during the year and each became, in later years, Supreme Commander of all NATO forces in Europe.

The student body produced a galaxy of stars in the 50's and 60's. Harry Felt became Commander-in-Chief of the U.S. Pacific Fleet, Chet Wood became a Vice-Admiral, George Mundy rose to three star rank in the Air Force, and in the Army, Bob Wood gained four stars; Jack Hinrichs and Emerson Cummings each became lieutenant-generals with three stars. On the diplomatic side I corresponded steadily with Charles Knox until his recent death. He left the College a few weeks before the end of the course to open the first U.S. Embassy in Tel Aviv.

Amongst the many great Americans who addressed the College was General George Marshall who was then Secretary of State under President Harry Truman. He reminded his predominantly American audience that prior to 1939 a very large part of the world had been under the control of Great Britain; Gibraltar, Malta, Suez, the Persian Gulf and Singapore were the pillars supporting an Empire, the brightest jewel of which was India. Whilst President Roosevelt had given the fullest possible support to Great Britain in her fight against the Nazis and Japanese, he, and many of his advisers, were not prepared to continue their help after the war if it meant supporting a form of colonialism they found distasteful. In fact, some of President Roosevelt's ambassadors had done their best during the 1930's to undermine Britain's position in India and elsewhere. For economic, political and other reasons the Labour Government of Britain was now divesting itself of her Imperial and Colonial possessions at a pace that would have bewildered even Mr. Roosevelt. The problem, General Marshal went on to say, was that the United States must fill the vacuum left by the British withdrawals at a time when her own Armed Forces had been reduced without thought to their future obligations. The U.S. must now support many of the Pillars of what had been British Imperial strategy. Western Europe must be strengthened through economic aid and encouraged to rebuild itself behind the shield of U.S. power. With the British withdrawal from Greece it was essential that stability and confidence be restored by an American presence. General Marshal went on to outline other problem areas in the world but I think the thing that impressed us most was that President Truman and he were determined to head off the difficulties by taking action before they became too great.

The Marshal Plan to put Europe on its feet and the Truman Doctrine to contain the Soviet Union in areas in which U.S. power could reach were, without doubt, two of the most courageous decisions of any U.S. Administration. The combination of the two made the North Atlantic Treaty Organization possible and, for a number of years, gave Canada a prominent position in the affairs of Europe.

It was to discuss the very early planning for NATO and cooperation between Canada, the U.S. and U.K. that Charles Foulkes paid a number of visits to Washington and it was on one of these that he told me that once my course was completed I would be taking over the duties of Brigadier on the General Staff in charge of Plans. As B.G.S. (Plans), two important Directors would report to me; Operations and Intelligence. I took over the job in September 1947.

Our two main tasks in those comparatively simple days were to plan the ground defence of Canada and prepare a mobilization plan in case we were again needed in Europe; but this time our job was to counter the aggressive moves of the Soviet Union who, by redrawing the boundaries of eastern Europe to give them direct access, were now threatening the existence of Czechoslovakia and Hungary in the same way they had engulfed Latvia, Lithuania and Estonia.

The decision of the Canadian government in 1946 was that the Regular Army would comprise one Brigade Group, the teeth of which would be one artillery regiment, two armoured regiments, and three infantry battalions. This was to be the 'ready' force in case of emergency but reinforcements and future buildup must come from the Reserve or Militia. It was soon realized that any 'ready' force must be trained in a parachute or airborne role to be effective and it was essential to train Engineer, Signal, Medical and other units as paratroopers so that they could play their normal part in ground operations. Of the total strength of 13,000 in the Regular Army over 50 % were trained as parachutists. It was far too small a force to have to deal with the millions of square miles of our Northland and, furthermore, it was spread in penny packets across the country with each packet under command of a different senior officer. There was obviously a need for coordination in our planning and also in our cooperation with the Royal Canadian Air Force who were the essential element in getting our troops to where they might be needed.

The DC3 or "Dakota" aircraft was then the workhorse of most Air Forces and it was agreed with our own RCAF that they would maintain a sufficient number of Dakotas to lift and drop a battalion group of about 500 parachutists. To maintain sufficient lift for the three battalions was not possible within the financial ceilings then being imposed.

The first joint exercise to practice our battle procedures took place in the Fort St. John and Peace River area in 1949. The Minister of National Defence was now Brooke Claxton, a man who was extremely sensitive to criticism of any kind. To gain some political points he invited the news media in large numbers to attend the Exercise. This was unfortunate because the 'Good Guys' (the Canadian Defenders) were rendered almost immobile by the 'Bad Guys' (the Russians) who carried out a surprise air attack the minute Exercise "Eagle" started and destroyed most of our Air Force on the ground.

The press and radio were quick to criticize the Canadian side's lack of preparedness and gave Brooke Claxton a roasting that he never forgot; furthermore, there was nobody he could blame since there was no one person in charge. What he could not understand was that the purpose of the exercise was to practice battle procedures and that the units taking part had profited greatly from it. All he could think of was that the 'Bad Guys' had beaten the 'Good Guys,' and the press had made much of it and placed the blame on him.

On his return to Ottawa he insisted that 'someone' in Army Headquarters should have the direct responsibility for planning the operations of our Parachute Battalions and for coordinating future exercises. This 'someone' would also be responsible for public relations and briefing of the Press.

So it came about that Charles Foulkes sent for me and told me that, in addition to my normal job, I was now "Commander Designate, Mobile Strike Force" with the full responsibility for planning in detail the defence of the Arctic. I was to assemble a very small headquarters of two or three officers and a couple of clerks. The Minister was going to announce the creation of the "Mobile Strike Force" in the near future so there was urgency in my preparing the small headquarters in order that we would be ready to answer questions from the press.

Fortunately, I was able to get an excellent trio of officers to set up the headquarters. Lt.-Col. Bob Keane, who had commanded the Lake Superior Regiment in 4th Armoured Division so well from Normandy to north Germany, became the Chief of Staff. He was assisted by Majors Stan Waters and Ken Campbell. Stan Waters, who had commanded a battalion in the joint U.S.-Canadian Special Service Force and had served with the Canadian parachute Battalion was a man of immense energy who went to the top position in the army of the present Unified Forces before retiring. Ken Campbell had served most of the war with Princess Louise Dragoon Guards in our 1st Division and later commanded a battalion of the Royal Canadian Regiment in Korea. The first thing we did was to sit down and look at the few detailed maps then available of the North West Territories. In 1949 that part of Canada was virtually unknown and the Innuit or Eskimo people continued to live as their ancestors had done for centuries.

There were a few small areas of mineral development near Great Slave and Great Bear Lakes but trapping was still the main means of support for the people centered on the small village of Yellowknife. The building by the U.S. Army of the highway from Whitehorse in the Yukon to Dawson Creek on the borders of B.C. and Alberta, had opened up the Yukon in a way that no one had dreamed possible. The Mackenzie River had also been affected as a result of the war with the building of an oil pipeline from Norman Wells to Whitehorse. But developers had not yet moved into the area and the construction of the DEW Line and other facilities by the Royal Canadian Air Force had not yet begun. It was still peaceful and unspoiled with the Eskimo living close to salt water and north of the tree line, and the Indian living south of it. Over-snow vehicles were still in their infancy. On the ground, movement was by dogteam and sled; in the air it was either the slow twin-engined Dakota, capable of landing on hastily prepared runways or the single-engined De Haviland "Beaver" which could land anywhere and fly from one gasoline cache to another.

We divided our north into two parts—one, the comparatively civilised Mackenzie River and the Yukon, and the second the vast area of barrens and inter-islands contained in the square Fort Churchill-Frobisher Bay-Resolute-Coppermine. With the willing help of the Royal Canadian Air Force, Stan Waters and Ken Campbell took off from Ottawa to report on the possibility, and the problems, of ground operations in their particular half of the Arctic. They were gone some weeks. The Defence Research Board under Dr. Ormond Solandt were vitally interested in our planning and were a great help in guiding our thoughts on the future requirements for clothing, weapons and vehicles to make Arctic operations practical.

It was obvious from the outset that any operations in our Arctic would have to be carried out in conjection with the U.S. Armed Forces. I, therefore, set out to visit the headquarters of the three U.S. Armies most affected. 1st U.S. Army, with headquarters in New York, was then commanded by General Bedell Smith whom I had met during the German surrender discussions in Holland in 1945. I next visited 5th Army in Chicago and 6th Army in San Francisco. In each case we received their full cooperation and these visits laid the groundwork for future Joint Exercises and discussions.

As the head Army Planner I was a member of the Joint Planning Committee which reported directly to our Chiefs of Staff. The Naval representative was Commodore Nelson Lay; Air-Commodore 'Brandy' Godwin represented the Air Force. We were a productive committee and established excellent relations with our opposite numbers in the Pentagon. It was at our meetings there that I became a firm friend of Al Gruenther - surely one of the most remarkable Americans of this century. He was acknowledged by Culbertson to be one of the finest bridge players in the world; he was praised by President Eisenhower, whom he succeeded as Supreme Allied Commander in NATO, as a man with an intellectual faculty which permitted him to listen to hours of discussion and then summarize it with great clarity and in the fewest number of words. But unlike others who may have that ability, Al Gruenther retained the details of the discussion in his brain and would, if necessary, repeat it months or years later. His mind could store important facts and details like a modern computer. With it all he had a warm and friendly manner. He died in 1983 after heading the American Red Cross for many years and, like many great men, gave much of the credit for his successes to his wife.

I recall a conversation with him in his office in the Pentagon in late '49 or early '50. The U.S. government realized that, following the withdrawal of Britain from India, the huge area of the Indian Ocean would no longer have quite the same importance to Britain. Should the

U.S. make formal agreements with the United Kingdom which would permit her to build extensive bases in such places as Aden, Socotra, Mauritius or perhaps the Seychelles Islands? With these bases she could dominate the Indian Ocean and stop the Russians from gaining too much influence. When he asked my opinion I said that, in the short term, a number of bases might be of value but that at the way the Labour Government in Britain was giving independence to all and sundry of her colonies and protectorates, I would not put too much faith in the future stability of some of them. I went on to say that if I were in his shoes, I would recommend the building of a large number of aircraft carriers and attendant warships and fleet-train supply ships to permit the stationing in the Indian Ocean of three or four such groups on a rotating basis. In the long run this would make friends, while the occupation of bases on someone else's land might eventually lead to bad feelings or even enmity.

Al Gruenther was interested in my views and said that it would probably be easier to get funds from the Congress to build the Navy than it would to build bases in some remote area. He reminded me of this conversation some eighteen years later when he was the Guest of Honour and speaker at the Naval Officers Association Dinner at the Royal York in Toronto.

One result of our discussions with our American counterparts was the setting up of an exercise called "Sweetbriar" planned for January/February 1950. It was to take place in Alaska and the Yukon and would involve a small force of one U.S. and one Canadian Infantry Battalion which would be given the task of recapturing ground that had been taken by the 'Bad Guys.' The battle was to rage between Whitehorse and a U.S. Air Force base in Alaska, passing through the superb landscape surrounding Kluane Lake over which twenty thousand foot Mount Logan rose majestically to the south, crowned by a plume of wind-driven snow.

Brooke Claxton was determined that "Sweetbriar" was going to be a great success to more than compensate for the debacle of "Eagle." He briefed me personally on what he wanted to come out of the exercise—"a good press and I don't care how you get it." He also briefed a number of news correspondents at a meeting in his home which I attended. It was arranged that I would accompany them on the flight from Ottawa to Whitehorse. They were an interesting and stimulating group who appreciated the opportunity of 'reading through' our planning documents which were, of course, Top Secret.

The representative of the New York Times was Hanson Baldwin, one of the most famous correspondents of the time. He had been with the U.S. Navy, retiring as a captain, and this was his first opportunity to study the units of our army and air force under operational conditions. He had nothing but praise for the Princess Patricia's Canadian Light Infantry (PPCLI) and the way the men conducted themselves under adverse conditions. However, he was not at all impressed with the infantry battalion of the U.S. Army, some members of which had never before been north of sunny Alabama and who were justifiably scared of the cold. In the last days of the exercise the temperature dropped to 50⁰ below Zero Fahrenheit - a condition that makes inhaling the smoke of a cigarette an unpleasant experience. Breathing must be done through the nose and one's physical exertions must be reduced to compensate. Climatic inversions caused each vehicle to raise a condensation cloud behind it that resembled thick fog and prevented the movement of convoys. On landing or take-off, each aircraft left a similar condensation cloud which had to lift before the next aircraft could be brought in. The air was too 'thin' on two mornings to permit the employment of paratroops. These, and other conditions, made the press realize the difficulties of operations in the cold of the Yukon and Alaska; later exercises on the barrens of the North West Territories let them see that, by comparison, Yukon cold is child's play compared to the windchill and driven snow-crystals of the barrens.

Exercise "Sweetbriar" was successful; our army and air force units got a good press, as did Brooke Claxton. So all was right with the world, but it was soon to change.

In the summer of 1950 North Korea, heavily supported by Communist China, invaded the Republic of South Korea. President Truman stood firm, the United Nations formally denounced the invasion, and, in the absence of the Russian delegates, voted to send a force to South Korea under the United Nations' flag. The Canadian government immediately authorized our contribution of three destroyers, a brigade group and a squadron of transport aircraft to the U.N. Force. From the army point of view, the decision was taken that we could not aford to send our parachute battalions - instead, we would raise the brigade group by making each unit duplicate itself overnight by taking in large numbers of recruits and training them as quickly as possible for war. We hoped that we would attract, amongst the recruits, a high proportion of World War II veterans. To encourage these veterans, many of whom had joined the militia reserve force, Charles Foulkes decided to give the command of the brigade and the battalions of infantry to officers who had distinguished themselves in World War II and were now civilians. John Rockingham was given command of the brigade (numbered 25th Brigade); Gordon Corbould, also of British Columbia, took command of the new 2nd Battalion, The Royal Canadian Regiment; Jim Stone took command of the 2nd PPCLI and Jimmy Dextraze took over the 2nd Royal Vingt-deuxième Régiment—the famous "Van Doos." Charles Foulkes was criticized for bringing back these officers instead of appointing those who had remained in the Regular Army.

At the outset of the Korean crisis I was given a new job, Director General of Army Personnel (DGAP). In this, I was responsible for the promotion of majors to lieutenant-colonel, and for recommending to General Charles Foulkes the names of officers for promotion to colonel and brigadier.

In my new capacity, I told Charles Foulkes that a number of regular officers were unhappy at being passed over for command of the new battalions. His reply was that with the new NATO, which was in process of being set up in Europe, we would soon be required to produce another two brigades and we would need all our Regular officers to raise and train them. Also we had to encourage the militia and other World War II veterans as we would need their help again in raising the brigades for NATO.

Charles Foulkes had an excellent team in his 'outer office,' the head of which was Major Barry Tackaberry. "Tack," as he was known, was a tower of strength to Charles and did not hesitate to correct him, or anyone else for that matter, if he felt we were doing something wrong. Sgt.-Maj. Lisowski and Sgt. Scott, both outstanding supervisors and clerks, headed the clerical staff. Frank Lisowski later became a lieutenant-colonel and Scotty a captain. Major-General Howard Graham was the Vice Chief of the General Staff, his military assistant was Major Jeffry Williams.* They were all good friends of mine.

It was soon becoming obvious that with the increasing tempo of consultations in Washington and in Europe, it was not possible for Charles Foulkes to be both Chairman of the Chiefs of Staff Committee and Chief of the General Staff of the Army (CGS). Too much of his time was taken up with national and international problems to allow him to be an effective CGS. But who would succeed him?

The most obvious choice was General Guy Simonds - the man whom General Crerar had warned the government about and who had been passed over for the job back in 1945. Guy had since spent over three years with the British Imperial Defence College in London where he was Chief Instructor and had then taken over our National Defence college in Kingston, Ontario. The government really had no option, there was no one else with anything like his qualifications. Early in 1951 General Simonds was appointed CGS. Charles Foulkes became a full-time Chairman of the Chiefs of Staff and in due course was given his promotion to full general.

I do not think there has been any doubt in the minds of those who served in the 1950's that Guy Simonds proved to be the most effective CGS the Army has ever had. He got on well with politicians on military matters although Mike Pearson was, I think, a little jealous of his grasp of international problems and the many personal contacts he had made whilst at the British Imperial Defence College. As Chief Instructor of that establishment, Guy had met every world leader and been privileged to discuss their problems with them. As Commandant of our National Defence College he had again travelled round the world, making the same high-level contacts and renewing old friendships in a way that embarrassed many senior officials in the Department of External Affairs.

Brooke Claxton, having known the value of the mobilization plans made prior to 1939, agreed to the production of such plans in 1951 after General Simonds had impressed on him the need for them shortly after he took over as CGS. I mention this item of forward planning because, as Director General of Army Personnel, I was asked by General Simonds to give him accurate figures of the number of staff

*Author of ''Byng of Vimy'', 1984

officers required to man the projected peace-time Army of 50,000 and also the number required to man a full Corps in the event of mobilization.

Having produced the figures for him, he told me that the Staff College in Kingston was operating at only about 50% of capacity. He wanted it to be given high priority and a full-time Commandant who had commanded a brigade during World War II. I produced the list of officers who had that qualification which included my own. He looked over the list and then asked me if I would like to be the lucky one. He told me he wanted the number of students raised from 50 to 100, and I could increase the number of instructors and staff to handle the load. Then he said, with a grin, "And since you are DGAP, you can take your pick of the best instructors!" I did.

The Author, Prince Claus of the Netherlands,
Hans Teengs-Gerritsen, Holland, May, 1985

18

Life And Death Of An Army

A Staff College is as essential to an Army as the combat soldier. It is where selected officers are trained to serve the soldiers in their Regiments and Corps, according to a common doctrine.

When I took command of the Staff College at Fort Frontenac, Kingston, Ontario, in April 1951 great changes were in the offing. The next course, due to start in January, was to be double the size of the existing one and a major construction programme was already in hand.

Guy Simonds realized, more than most officers, the need for a staff college with adequate facilities. He had planned extensive changes to the Officers' Mess to give it a capacity of 200 instead of a crowded 60 and alterations were to be made to the NCO's Mess which, although in a temporary building, was to be redecorated and refurnished. Furthermore, the National Defence College was also at Fort Frontenac and shared the Officers' Mess with the Staff College.

The class of 1952 had 96 students and 20 instructors. Col. Bill Anderson, who had been Chief Instructor in 1951, was succeeded by Col. George Leech, an officer from the Royal Canadian Corps of Signals, who had wide experience of communications at the divisional level during World War II.

From the outset the standard was high and set a model for each succeeding class. The quality of instruction attracted students from the

Commonwealth and the newly formed North Atlantic Treaty Organization. There were two instructors from the U.S. Forces - one from the U.S. Army and the other from the Marines; in addition, we had an instructor from the British Army. It was a galaxy of talent and once the students realised that they were there to enjoy themselves as well as work, they worked harder than ever.

As the first post-war, full-time Commandant, I was given "Barriefield House" as our official home. This old stone house, located in the village of the same name, was originally built in about 1828 for Commodore Barrie of the Royal Navy whose command included the docks and slipways in Navy Bay. Between World Wars I and II, it was the official home of the senior staff officer at the Royal Military College but, like most buildings of its kind, very little had been spent on its maintenance or improvement in the period 1940-1950. To Audrey and me it was our first 'official' home and we set about making it suitable for entertaining and housing distinguished guests. The provision of all furnishings was our responsibility and Audrey's search of the Kingston area's antique stores provided many attractive items which we possess today.

Among our many distinguished visitors was Camilien Houde, an unattractive-looking but dynamic personality and I could see why he had so much support from Montrealers when he was Mayor of that city. He was particularly interested in the history of Fort Frontenac and I showed him over the excavations of one of the earliest walls of the original fort. Looking around the buildings which are mostly of grey limestone, he said, with a twinkle in his eye, "I spent a lot of time looking at grey stone walls during the War but I really do like them." He had been sent to prison early in the war for publicly advising French speaking Canadians not to enlist in the Armed Forces.

I had hoped to get David Niven to come and talk to us one Friday about the value of film in Army training. In his letter of regret he wrote that he was opening in a new play in Dallas that week and "in spite of my playing the lead we are hoping the show will play all week."

Our most unusual speaker was a well-known British author of books on military subjects. He had served in the First World War, retired with junior rank shortly thereafter, and became a prolific writer on strategy, tactics and administration as well as being a critic of every successful general. For some reason the Minister, Brooke Claxton, felt that this knowledgeable celebrity would be able to advise him on the future role and strength of the Canadian Army. Claxton was having a problem at the time because he could not summon up enough argument to offset the plans put forward by General Guy Simonds for the future of the Canadian Army. Having risen to the rank of Sergeant-Major in the first war, Claxton considered himself well qualified in matters connected with the raising of armies. But Simonds was winning all the arguments. He needed outside support. He sent an invitation to the British author asking him to come to Ottawa. In due course the visitor arrived. He was to spend Monday and Tuesday with Brooke Claxton, Wednesday with Simonds, then come to Kingston on Wednesday evening, spend Thursday addressing the Staff College and on Friday speak to the National Defence College. We all looked forward to his visit.

On the Monday evening I had a call from General Simonds who told me that there was a change of plans. He did not give me any reason for the change but I was puzzled by an undertone of amusement in his voice. The great lecturer would arrive at the Staff College on Tuesday morning instead of Wednesday evening and he asked me to look after him for the rest of the week. In a way I was glad because I was due to leave for Europe early on the Thursday morning so we rescheduled his talk to the Staff College for the Wednesday. Our guest duly arrived and after lunch retired to his room above the Mess. As usual, with all visiting lecturers, we placed bottles of rye, scotch and gin in their rooms together with the usual mixes.

Following dinner the speaker asked if he might have a bottle of scotch and one of gin sent to his room. I was surprised at the request because I assumed that liquor would have been there already. I apologized and arranged for some to be sent up immediately. Meanwhile, we sat around and had a couple of drinks discussing with the speaker some of his books which we had read hurriedly the night before. He was garrulous, chatting happily on a wide variety of subjects.

His lecture in the morning was a disaster. He rambled from one subject to another, rarely finished a sentence and was, at times, almost incoherent. He took a great many quaffs of water from the carafe which was available to all speakers. When he staggered to the end of his remarks he asked if there were any questions. There were none, as very few of us had understood what he had been saying. I later found that he had consumed both bottles of scotch in his room and had poured the gin into the water carafe from which he drank so thirstily when 'addressing' us.

I phoned General Simonds that afternoon and was relieved to hear that the visitor had put on the same performance with the Minister who quickly tired of his ramblings. As Guy Simonds said on the phone, when apologizing to me for unloading the speaker on us in the way he had, "I'm sorry, George, but maybe it's the best thing that could ever have happened. From now on I think my relations with the Minister will be much improved!"

A Staff College is a valuable experimental establishment to try out new theories, and should be used as such. The environment lends itself to frank and knowledgeable discussion. The staff is highly qualified, the students are the pick of the younger officers of the Army, and come from all Corps. Between the two groups there is a wealth of experience which should be harnessed to the future thinking of the army. We were able to conduct two large scale exercises on the future of land warfare in the event that atomic bombs were used. At that time very few such weapons of mass destruction were available and life on the battlefield was still possible provided commanders appreciated the drastic changes required in the pattern of the battle.

Early in March 1954, General Simonds told me that I would be moving in May to Edmonton to be Chief of Staff at Western Command and also to command the 2nd Canadian Infantry Brigade which had its headquarters in that city. My replacement at the Staff College was to be Brigadier Pat Bogert who had commanded both a battalion and a brigade with distinction in the war and had also been the General Staff Officer I at 1st Divisional Headquarters. His knowledge of both Command and Staff was unrivalled and I was delighted at his appointment.

The Headquarters of Western Command was located on the Kingsway, a fine wide road which, when it was first built, led nowhere except to the northeast. It was used by the American flyer, Wiley Post, as a runway during his round-the-world flight; and, later, as part of the Royal route during the visit of the King and Queen in 1939. Our headquarters was in a series of temporary wartime hutments, part of an extensive development which followed the building of what was then the city airport. North-West Air Command of the RCAF was in an adjoining area.

The Army's Western Command included British Columbia, Alberta and the Yukon. It also had a watching brief over the Mackenzie River, the tributaries of which rose in B.C. and Alberta. The General Officer Commanding (GOC) was Major-General Chris Vokes whom I had first met in early 1941 at the headquarters of our 1st Division. That headquarters, which had been disbanded after World War II, was about to be reactivated and I think that Chris vokes hoped to be appointed to its command. With our commitment to NATO of a full infantry division, General Simonds had received authority to organize the headquarters and all the services required for a division.

Christ Vokes, with his past experience, would have been the ideal commander to start it up, but Guy Simonds decided to promote Brigadier John Rockingham and make him the GOC. "Rocky," as we called him, was one of the most courageous and inspiring commanding officers of a battalion in the Canadian Army of the Second World War. He had commanded a brigade in North-West Europe and later the first brigade that was sent to Korea in 1950. There was no one who knew more about fighting than Rocky but he had little idea of how to organize and work with his staff. He always wanted to do everything himself and did not appear to have much confidence in even the senior officers at the headquarters. This was unfortunate because most of them had been instructors at the Staff College and were well known to me. After a while the staff settled down under the guidance of such strong characters as Rad Radley-Walters and Strome Galloway, and all was well.

My Brigade Headquarters in Edmonton was, quite rightly, a small one since we were operational for only about six months of the year but Chris Vokes kept us busy in the interim, working on a variety of tactical problems. I was fortunate to have Major Vince Lilley as my brigade major who had an outstanding record as an infantry combat soldier in World War II and in Korea. Vince remained cool and practical at all times and was a pleasure to work with. In late August our small headquarters flew east to take part in General John Rockingham's first Divisional Exercise. This was set by General

Howard Graham who then commanded Central Command with Headquarters in Oakville, 20 miles west of Toronto. It was designed to test
the headquarters of the Division and its Brigades together with a
number of regimental headquarters. Brigadier Jean Allard, who later
became Chief of Defence Staff, was commanding a brigade from the
east. It went off well and it was following this exercise that the troops
were of great value during Hurricane "Hazel" when they did so much
to calm and steady the people of Toronto and neighbouring communities.

In December I went to Fort Churchill to direct Exercise "Bulldog
II." The plan involved a small enemy force landing near Baker Lake at
the north end of Hudson's Bay and subsequently capturing an important radio station nearby. An airborne battalion of The Royal Canadian
Regiment, supported by elements of artillery, were detailed to recapture the radio station and destroy the enemy. Fort Churchill was to be
the base from which the Canadian airborne force would fly in order to
carry out their tasks. Unfortunately, the weather, which had permitted
the 'enemy' to land, turned completely sour and prevented any further
airborne landings for several days. Very strong winds interfered with
any plans for a paradrop on most days and, on others, severe icing conditions prevented transport aircraft from taking off. In many ways it
was to us a great disappointment. However, as I explained to the
representatives of the press, we would not have learned as many
lessons if the weather had been perfect and the landing of our
paratroops had gone off as planned. The Exercise would have been
over in 48 hours. As it was, we had to consider and practice other ways
of getting at the enemy, and both the Army and the RCAF found the
Exercise to be a much greater challenge than we had planned.

The members of the press took an objective view of the exercise and
gave the men taking part full credit for their ability to live and move
under the worst possible conditions. On one occasion, with a blizzard
blowing a wind-chill factor of 40 below Zero Fahrenheit and limiting
visibility to ten feet, a platoon of the RCR led by Lt. Dan Loomis
demonstrated their skills by marching accurately, with the aid of com-
passes, a distance of three miles into the teeth of the blizzard. Each
soldier held on to the equipment of the man in front - that was the limit
of visibility. Direction was maintained by Dan Loomis with his

compass; he was in the lead with, immediately behind him, an NCO or Private whose job it was to count the number of paces taken. When it reached 100 they halted and recorded it as 60 yards. This slight pause allowed the line of men to close up and slowly they moved across the icy flat tundra racking up each measure of 60 yards. Loomis knew that after 29 or 30 such halts he would have gone about a mile and that each mile would take over an hour of effort. In the centre of the platoon three sleds were being pulled, each by two men and each tied head to tail with the other. An NCO brought up the rear of the line of men as they disappeared into the blizzard of ice, their parkas drawn tight over their heads and faces leaving perhaps a half inch slit for a field of vision which was darkened further by their snow-goggles. To expose one's flesh for as little as ten minutes could result in a gangrene which could effect the rest of the body.

After seeing this platoon move off I joined a small group of correspondents who were trying out the arctic ration issued to all troops. It contained over 5,000 calories per day and, when prepared away from the wind or in a snow house, was quite palateable. To reduce weight, most of the items were dessicated and in the form of a powder; all that was required to produce a quite pleasant plate of beef, potatoes and vegetables was a little moisture and the canned heat that was included in the ration. Unfortunately, the wind-chill was so great when we heated up our plate of 'meat and veg' that only about one-third of the plate became unfrozen. So, by moving the plate around the heat, we ate first the meat, then, after a pause, the patato; and after another pause, the 'veg.' It took quite a bit off the glamour of the event.

On the one occasion when I spoke at any length with Mr. Diefenbaker he asked me what I thought should be the future of our military effort. I told him that for two reasons we should put all our energies into the Arctic. First, to establish a strong national presence of perhaps 5,000 naval, army and airforce personnel and second, to provide a firm base from which private enterprise could explore and develop the surrounding seas and islands. It has always struck me as absurd that the Soviet Union has a larger population living, and gainfully employed, in their Arctic than we have in the whole of Canada. Admittedly their early developments may have been pushed forward by the sweated labour of thousands of political prisoners but new large cities have been built, great hydro-electric projects produce the needed power, and young people are encouraged to move there and play a part in the future development of the area. We should do the same.

When the Radar and Doppler stations of the Mid Canada Warning Line were established, their location and construction were done without much consideration to their impact on small isolated communities of the Inuit people. I visited one such site in the late 1950's at the mouth of the Great Whale River where it empties into Hudson's Bay. Where there had been three families of Inuit, living in their aboriginal, simple and happy way, there were now a number of dirty looking huts made from what looked like the sides of discarded crates. Lolling around the outside of the huts were a number of young men dressed as if they were resting from a construction job in Toronto. But they were the young Inuit who had been employed in the construction of the Radar Station, paid the same wage driving a bulldozer as an operator in Toronto, and were now out of a job and whose whole lifestyle had seemed irreparably destroyed. I am sure that this scene was repeated elsewhere amongst isolated communities.

In towns such as Inuvik, the impact of modern methods has not had quite the same effect. There the local Inuit were used in new construction and trained in the maintenance of new projects and there is a continuing need for their skills. Cambridge Bay, at the southern end of Victoria Island, and Frobisher, at the southern end of Baffin Island, were airfields created to serve the north and around them have sprung small communities. The native population of all the northern islands is very small indeed - perhaps a total of 1,500 in an area of 750,000 square miles. Their rights could easily be protected in the large scale development of the Arctic Islands that I had in mind and thought was a part of Mr. Diefenbaker's "Dream of the North" of which he spoke so strongly. Before Christmas, Chris Vokes told me that I was to take over the command of British Columbia Area and shortly after, Audrey and I drove west through the deep snow of the Rockies into the mild and welcome weather of Vancouver.

During the fifteen years from 1951-65 the Canadian Army, both Regular and Reserve, reached the highest levels of organizational and operational efficiency. It became the object of study and analysis by some of our NATO partners.

The man responsible for raising the Army to that standard was the Chief of the General Staff, General Guy Simonds. When he took over that job in early 1951 we had completed the recruiting of a Brigade for Korea but he realized that with our commitments to NATO and to Korea, we would have to increase the size of our small regular army from the original 13,000 to over 50,000 and this must be done in a period of two years and without the benefit of a national emergency. He reorganized Army Headquarters to make it essentially the centre for policy and planning. Wherever possible, the other functions were decentralized to the five Army Commands who were encouraged to assist in the recruiting and training of both officers and men. Funds that had been tightly controlled by Ottawa were now to be spent and accounted for by Commands according to agreed policy. Responsibility and power were decentralized to Commands who, in turn, decentralized as much as possible to their subordinate commanders. The effect was electric; it was no longer necessary to get the approval of the highest authority to carry out some low level manoeuvre. Initiative was encouraged at all levels and was rewarded.

General Simonds appreciated only too well that if this new Army was to maintain its efficiency it must have barracks and married quarters and the amenities to go with them since Army camps are generally located away from urban centres. Training areas were extended, where possible, and new ones purchased which would permit the training of a complete division of twenty thousand men with all the many hundreds of tanks, guns and vehicles that go to make up such a force.

Few people realize that the very successful DeHavilland "Caribou" short takeoff and landing aircraft was partly the brainchild of Simonds. He wanted a 'flying truck' to supplement the normal wheeled transport system. It must have the unsophisticated controls of a light aircraft and be capable of deliverying a 2½ ton load without the benefit of a prepared runway. It must be able to land in, and take off from, a normal grass field. Russ Bannock of DeHavilland cooperated fully with us. So did the U.S. Army.

However, since the policy of the Department of National Defence at that time classified the 'flying truck' as an 'aircraft' it was passed to the Royal Canadian Air Force for development. There it became so sophisticated, refined and expensive that we, in the Army, cold not afford it. It was no longer a simple 'flying truck.' The U.S. Forces, which had funded a fair amount of the development costs, bought 200 which were used to good advantage in the early days in Vietnam.

Perhaps Simonds' greatest achievement was bringing together the Regular Army and the Militia, which was renamed the Reserve Army. He relied heavily on the Reserve Army to make up the first of the NATO Brigades and, when creating new regular regiments, he associated them closely by name with well established and strong militia units. In addition, he introduced into the Army Council, which up till then had comprised the CGS, VCGS, Adjutant-General and Quarter-Master-General, a fifth official member to be known as "Major-General, Militia." A distinguished militia veteran from British Columbia, Major-General Harry Letson, was the first to hold that appointment.

Men who were now civilians, but who had reached high rank during World War II, were invited to attend special study periods designed to bring out the changes in tactical doctrine. In these and many other ways Simonds had succeeded in making us into a professional Army and it was into this atmosphere that I stepped when I arrived in Vancouver on New Year's Day 1955 to become the Commander, British Columbia Area. I was to be responsible for the effectiveness and welfare of over 2,000 regular soldiers, 5,000 militiamen and several thousand cadets.

At that time Canadians, generally, were defence conscious. We had been through World War II and Korea when our Navy, Army and Air Force had been our best ambassadors. In the late 40's and 50's the Army was called on frequently to take full control in communities threatened by floods or other catastrophies. The discipline and steadiness of the Army units which helped in the floods in Winnipeg in 1948 and, later, in the Fraser Valley and at Creston, did much to restore good order and lessen the tensions of those most affected which might, without the presence of the hard working soldiers, have led to a breakdown of authority. The Army's role when Hurricane "Hazel" hit Toronto in September 1954 was even more critical; bridges were swept away and communication broke down completely. Regular and Reserve soldiers became the links between communities, and Army

Engineers built Bailey bridges in record time to restore essential traffic.

On these occasions, and many others when the soldier was called on in emergencies, the public felt they were getting their money's worth; the Army was not just blasting off guns and learning about war, it was using its skills and discipline in aid of the Civil Power and it was effective. It also got a great deal of good publicity which I believe is essential to its existence in peacetime.

One of the problems in the life of the military is that the soldier seldom meets the civilian. He is posted to a camp that is some distance from the cities and towns that are the habitat of 90% of civilians. I feel strongly that the soldier must go out of his way to meet civilians, not only to keep abreast of what they are doing and how they feel, but also to show them how effective the military are at their job. I was determined to keep the Army in front of the public as much as possible without having to rely on disasters to do it.

With the full cooperation of the Royal Canadian Navy based at Esquimalt and the Royal Canadian Air Force I was able to put on a series of Tattoos and demonstrations that were seen by many thousands. On one occasion the Navy deployed the cruiser H.M.C.S. Ontario and four destroyers to carry a regular battalion in a simulated assault across the beaches of English Bay. We had landing-craft in those days and the sight of them being lowered from their mother-ships, moving towards the beaches covered by the guns of the fleet to be greeted by the chatter of machine guns and the rumble of defending tanks, was a never to be forgotten sight. We used only blank ammunition and simulated explosions but we had lots of them. If the people of Vancouver could not see what was going on they could certainly hear it.

Since Prince George and Prince Rupert rarely saw the new peacetime Army I arranged for a demonstration group of infantry of the Queen's Own Rifles together with a strong squadron from the Royal Canadian Engineer Regiment in Chilliwack to show the flag and put on a number of displays in those towns and neighbouring communities. The best part of that adventure was that the people in each town took our soldiers into their homes as guests because hotels, to look after such a large group, were non-existent at that time.

In Vernon we improved the accommodation for 1,000 young cadets who would concentrate there each summer from both B.C. and Alberta; and we asked the people of Vernon to get to know the cadets and encourage them by attending our parades. As a 'thank you' we put on a Tattoo in 1956 that was the talk of the Okanagan for many years.

In all this work I was supported by a first-class staff led by Majors "Huck" Trimble* and George Sharp. The Honorary Colonels of Militia Regiments were the leaders of industry, forestry and the professions.

In addition, we had capable and experienced officers commanding our Militia groups. It was easy to get things done with so much goodwill behind me. General Vokes, who was the General to whom I was responsible, decentralized authority to me. "Do a good job but don't spend a penny more than your budget" were his instructions.

In September 1956 I left for Ottawa to take over the appointment of Vice Chief of the General Staff. General Howard Graham had taken over from Guy Simonds. He continued, basically, the same pattern of command and control, decentralizing as much authority as possible to Commands across the country, but Graham felt it was important that we should establish closer relations with the U.S. Army.

During Simonds' five years as Chief, liaison had been very close with the British Army. It had been Simonds' decision to place our NATO Brigade Group under British command and in many ways this made sense at the time since our equipment was largely of U.K. design, although manufactured in Canada. Simonds was also happier dealing with his British counterparts than with those in the U.S.; he knew them personally from previous service. General Graham, however, felt that the Brigade Group in NATO was really the tip of the iceberg; what should be our real concern was the defence of Canada and this called for closer liaison with the U.S. He and I visited the Pentagon where I was able to introduce him to a number of Generals whom I had met during my War College and planning years including "Lem" Lemnitzer who was their Vice Chief of Staff, and Courtland Schuyler soon to become Chief of Staff at Supreme Headquarters in NATO.

As a result of these meetings we sent 150 officers to be trained to fly helicopters and the same number of technicians to become experts in

* Colonel Trimble - Chief of Security at U.N. Headquarters in New York for many years.

their maintenance. This was done without cost to us and, later, as an additional bonus we were offered 30 medium Sikorsky 'choppers' free, so that we could train our Brigades in their use on the modern battlefield. I went to see the Deputy Minister, Frank Miller, to tell him of this windfall. He had been in the RCAF and I assumed he would have some understanding of the requirements for 'choppers' in the Army but on financial grounds he would not permit us to accept them - he could not see the need for them. It was at this period that the Army began to refer to Frank Miller as "Mr. No"; he never seemed to approve of anything!

Shortly after taking over as Vice Chief, war erupted in the Middle East over control of the Suez Canal. Under pressure, Britain, France and Israel finally withdrew their forces and, when peace was finally declared, Canada played the leading role in establishing a peace-keeping United Nations Force. We immediately offered an infantry battalion as our contribution. The Queen's Own Rifles were named and hasty preparations were made for the battalion to be taken to Egypt in the aircraft carrier H.M.C.S. Bonaventure. However, President Nasser of Egypt objected to our sending a battalion with the title of "Queen's Own" - it would remind his countrymen too much of the British connection! So Canada changed its contribution to one of supplying headquarters and administrative units of Royal Canadian Signal Corps, Royal Canadian Army Service Corps, Royal Canadian Ordnance Corps, Royal Canadian Electrical and Mechanical Engineers and a squadron of Royal Canadian Dragoons. Quel différence!

In 1957, with a change in government, General George Pearkes became Minister of National Defence. Initially, there were few changes in policy as a triumphant Diefenbaker officially approved the use of nuclear weapons in NATO and our full participation in the new North American Air Defence Command (NORAD).

After I paid a visit to our Brigade in Europe General Graham agreed to increase our tank strength there from one squadron to a full Regiment of three squadrons. He also agreed to a very large increase in the strength and mobility of scout platoons in infantry battalions to provide commanders with better intelligence of what was going on around them now that their areas of responsibility were increasing. In addition, we got agreement for the Reconnaissance Squadron to be equipped with a number of light helicopters to be piloted by Army officers whose whole previous training had been in observation of ground and recognition of enemy units.

We produced a pamphlet outlining the operations of a Corps on the atomic battlefield. A few of our senior officers felt this was a waste of time as they did not believe 'atomics' would be used but I have always felt that if you prepare and make plans to cope with a disaster it will probably not happen. The pamphlet was largely produced by Colonel Strome Galloway; it was provisional and designed to encourage discussion. It was the first of its kind and dealt in some detail with the operational and administrative problems of operating on wide fronts and in great depth. Our theory was that Divisions and Brigades must operate like fleets at sea; concentrations larger than a battalion were to be avoided; helicopters, amphibious tanks and armoured personnel carriers (APC), would make concentrations at bridges a thing of the past. The whole battlefield would be fluid. The pamphlet was studied with great interest by General Spiedel and other German Generals in NATO. Early in 1958 George Pearkes and our Chiefs of Staff attended a cloth model briefing of this new type of warfare. Pearkes' reaction was "it makes you think, doesn't it."

Efforts to get some form of standardization of our warmaking equipments had been going on for some years between the US, UK and ourselves. However, the need for mass production of existing equipments for the Korean war and the rebuilding of the NATO Armies upset earlier thinking. My opposite numbers in our discussions on standardization were General Dick Hull who later became the Chief of Defence Staff of the British Services, and General Jim Gavin who was later sent by President Kennedy to be the U.S. Ambassador to France. I could not have wished for two more knowledgeable and practical people with whom to work. Although we could never quite agree on particular equipments for joint production, we exchanged information on research and our discussions formed the basis of many standardization agreements reached in NATO in later years. General Gavin paid several visits to Canada at the time as he was committed to the development of the Caribou aircraft at DeHavilland. He also wanted to introduce into the U.S. Army our system in which a soldier did his recruit training at the training depot of a Regiment and, after graduating, would remain with that regiment for most of his service. This gave the soldier something tangible to which he could pledge his loyalty. Furthermore, our battalions were generally associated by name with a city or town, which gave the soldier additional pride.

Jim Gavin had been one of the best divisional commanders in World War II. He remembered the importance of morale and pride to his soldiers during the many months that he had commanded the 82nd Airborne Division in action. He wanted to spread loyalty, pride and the 'airborne' discipline throughout the peace-time U.S. Army. His story* of U.S. involvement in North Africa and Europe in World War II and the detailed story of the operations of his 82nd Airborne Division should be studied by all officers who aspire to high command.

Stemming from our contacts with the U.S. Army, a large number of our officers and senior non-comissioned officers were able to witness the explosions of low yield atomic warheads in the desert about 120 miles from Las Vegas. We gained from our experiences in the desert but lost our shirts in the casinos of Las Vegas.

In May 1958 I was told that in July I would be taking over the job of Chairman, Canadian Joint Staff in London, England (C.J.S.L.) and also be the National Military Representative (NMR) at Supreme Headquarters, Allied Powers in Europe (SHAPE) in Paris. Brigadier Jean Allard was to take over from me as Vice C.G.S. with a promotion to Major-General.

By this time our family had grown to four with the arrival of our daughter Kate in 1952 and our son George three years later. The next four years in London and Paris proved to be exciting ones for us all.

As Chairman of the Joint Staff and the National Military Representative in Paris I reported directly to the Chief of Defence Staff (C.D.S.) in Ottawa—at that time, General Charles Foulkes. As his representative I had access in London to the British Chief of Defence Staff, Admiral of the Fleet Earl Mountbatten; I was also the defence adviser to our High Commissioner in the U.K., the Hon. George Drew. In Paris I was responsible to General Norstad, the Supreme Allied Commander whose Deputy was Field Marshal Viscount Montgomery and whose Chief of Staff was my old friend of Washington

*"On to Berlin," James M. Gavin, Viking Press, New York, and Penguin Books, Canada, 1978.

days, General Courtland Schuyler. Also, in Paris I was the defence adviser to our Ambassador to NATO, the Hon. Dana Wilgress. He was succeeded by the Hon. Jules Leger—our future Governor-General. Quite a galaxy of stars!

In London we were fortunate to find a comfortable house which, after being badly bombed, had been rebuilt with two equally good heating systems—natural gas and electricity. We maintained the house at 70⁰ in winter which often caused some embarrassment when guests arrived for dinner. In London, at that time, few houses had adequate central heating and heavy underwear was the order of the day when attending formal dinner parties. On three or four occasions we were asked by our delighted guests if they might use a spare bedroom to remove their underwear before dinner!

In 1959 when George Pearkes was Minister of National Defence, he visited England to discuss defence matters. The U.K. was very anxious to sell us a ground-to-air missile which they told us was accurate 99 times out of a hundred. We understood that they were planning to equip their forces in NATO with the system.

Arrangements were made for our Minister and me to fly to the testing ground in Wales with Duncan Sandys, who was Minister of Defence in the U.K., and Lord Mountbatten.

We flew in two aircraft - Pearkes and Sandys in one, and Mountbatten and myself in the other. I had a feeling that Mountbatten didn't quite trust Sandys, because amongst other remarks, he said to me quietly, "I wonder what they are talking about now. Please, George, let me into their secrets if your Minister tells you what they discussed."

Eventually we arrived at the firing site on the coast. The sky was overcast, but we could hear the sound of a Drone, which we were assured was flying at about 6,000 feet and controlled from a point nearby. In order to impress us, there would be two missiles fired and there would be a second Drone to replace the one knocked down by Missile No. 1. The great moment came. SWOOSH! went the missile. We listened for the explosive impact. Nothing happened except that the Drone kept flying.

Duncan Sandys was most upset and sent for the officer giving the demonstration and grilled him for five minutes. The second missile must hit the target and no fooling. Mountbatten did not appear too distressed.

The original Drone approached. Up went the second missile. We held our breath. Nothing happened. After a long pause, we heard the voice of the officer giving the demonstration, as he, thinking the loudspeaker had been turned off, exploded with "another fucking miss". Quick as a ferret, Sandys turned to Mountbatten and asked, "what was that he said?" The calm reply was "he said 'it was another unlucky miss,' Minister, that's all".

We returned to London with a very subdued Sandys. George Pearkes said that he had enjoyed the day and the nice sea breezes. When we were alone in his hotel he laughed and said, "well, that saved us a few million dollars."

Our High Commission The Hon. George Drew had excellent relations with the British Government of Harold Macmillan and was able to pick up important items of special interest to our own government which I am sure would not have been possible under different circumstances. One morning Mr. Drew told me that at a small private dinner party the previous evening he had overheard two senior Cabinet Ministers discussing "long range plans" and, in the course of their talk, he had heard them saying that they were "glad that Mountbatten had attended." George Drew wanted to know if I had heard anything about "long range plans" in my contacts with British defence officials. I had not, but told him I would try and learn more about it. Between us we were able to find out that special meetings were going on at Cabinet level which were attended, on occasion, by the Chiefs of Staff, although we were not able to discover the purpose of the meetings. But we had enough information to make it appear that we knew much more, and it was not long before Mr. Macmillan sent a senior official to see George Drew. I attended the meeting. Briefly, Macmillan and a special group of Cabinet Ministers were planning in great secrecy the course to be followed politically, economically and in defence during the next 10 years by the United Kingdon. The official gave us details but the important thing from my point of view was that the Chiefs of Staff were being consulted in those significant matters. I reported on the military details to the Chief of Defence Staff in Ottawa. George Drew sent the full details to Mr. Diefenbaker in the hope that he would follow Mr. Macmillan's lead.

At a reception in London's superb Guildhall, following a meeting of Commonwealth Prime Ministers, Mr. Diefenbaker took me aside and told me that I had been considered by him and certain members of Cabinet as a successor to General Foulkes who had recently retired as Chief of Defence Staff. He said they had selected "Mr. Miller" for the job because of his wide experience in the Department as Deputy Minister but he wanted me to know that I was next to the top. I started to thank him for having such confidence in me but he broke in by asking me just what I would want of him as Prime Minister had I been Chief of Defence Staff. I remembered the recent British experience and said that I would recommend that Canada set up a Cabinet planning committee to look into our future defence requirements and that the Chiefs of Staff attend the committee meetings. Their presence would not undermine the authority of the Minister of Defence instead, it would make the final recommendations of the Committee much more acceptable—whatever the result—since they had taken part in it and would have to implement its future policy.

I think Mr. Diefenbaker listened to what I was saying although he was not always a good listener. I liked him personally in spite of his egotism. Audrey and I had attended a Ball in Ottawa in February 1957 with the Diefenbakers and George and Blytha Pearkes and, although it was said that Diefenbaker was not too happy amongst military people, he was certainly in good form that night. That was the occasion when he asked me what the role of the Army should be and I told him that we should be up in the high Arctic.

As I thought later about Mr. Diefenbaker's remarks at the Guildhall I was sorry that he and the Cabinet had not chosen Air Marshal Hugh Campbell to be Chief of Defence Staff. He had a strong personality, was practical and had a positive approach to problems. Things would have been different, with him as Chief, when the roof fell in with Hellyerisation in 1964/1965.

I was sorry to see Charles Foulkes leave although he had been far too long as Chairman of the Chiefs of Staff Committee. After 15 years in the job he was becoming almost an institution—almost a separate organization within the Defence establishment. Having known him at his best, I did not like to see him going gradually down hill. He was becoming too political and too confident at a time when others were losing confidence in him. His opinions did not carry much weight with senior members of our External Affairs Department and I think that General Norstad felt that he was not always being honest and frank in his dealings with him. The British felt that he had become "a man for all seasons" and his visits to the U.K. became fewer and less productive.

In the early 1950's one of the problems in our dealings with some senior officers of the British Army was that they had very little idea of the way Canadian customs and thought differed from their own. They had not had an opportunity to visit Canada so assumed that, as we had the same Queen, wore somewhat similar uniforms and spoke, with variations, the same language, we must be the same kind of people. I must admit that some of our senior representatives in the United Kingdon gave them good reason for thinking tht way. Ralph Campney, our Minister of National Defence in 1956, told me at that time that on a trip to London he went to visit our Canadian Defence Liaison Staff and thought at first he was in the wrong building because there to greet him were three elegant dark suited men complete with bowler hats and leaning on furled unbrellas!

On one occasion I had arranged for the Chief of the Canadian Army, General Findlay Clark, to meet his opposite number in the British Army, General Frank Festing, to discuss an armoured personnel carrier being developed in Canada. Festing cancelled the meeting with only one hour's notice and without apology. When I told Admiral Mountbatten about this he was most upset and, after apologizing to General Clark, arranged for him to meet Festing's eventual successor during the following week.

Another British general of the old fashioned type with whom we had a problem was Dudley Ward. He was then commanding NATO forces in Northern Army Group which comprised, amongst others, German, British and Canadian soldiers. Our Canadian Brigade of about 6,500 men was under the command of the British who had reduced their army contribution at that time to about 30,000 from an original 65,000. In spite of these reductions, however, the British still retained the same large contingent of generals and senior officers on the staff of Northern Army Group. Since there were no Canadians holding senior positions on that staff, and since we, numerically, represented 20% of the fighting strength of the British contingent, I told him that I was now officially requesting that we should have at least one Brigadier and a Lieut.-Colonel on the staff of Northern Army Group.

Dudley Ward had a ruddy complexion but by the time I had finished speaking his face was a deep purple. He could hardly speak for a moment but then blurted out "George, are you suggesting that I should replace British officers for Canadian for political purposes?" I replied, as quietly as I could, that the only reason why he and so many other British officers in Northern Army Group had their jobs was political. The German forces in Northern Army Group outnumbered the British—they should have many of the dominant positions but, for political reasons only, they were being kept out of them. The Dutch, Danish and Belgian people would not, at that time, accept an overall German commander—that's why he, Dudley Ward, had the job! I don't think he ever forgave me for my remarks and it is a great pity that I felt they were necessary.

The British Army of today is quite different. The "colonial" attitude, which so angered the old Dominions, is gone. Their senior officers now are in daily touch, and in competition with their opposite numbers in NATO and, man for man, I think they are far more alert and knowledgeable than most of their forbears of the 1930's.

In addition, the British soldier has changed for the better—perhaps even more than his officer. The social pattern in Britain is so different now, there is a much greater exchange of ideas between classes. Wealth is more evenly distributed, individuals are more self-reliant and, in spite of the exhortations of some union bosses, competition is encouraged and rewarded. Young men, who before 1940 would not have had many opportunities to get ahead, are now being encouraged to strike out on their own. All these changes produce a recruit who is better able to handle modern weapons, enjoys the rivalry of competing with his NATO allied, is learning to be a better and more alert soldier with each tour in Northern Ireland, much as he may dislike taking part in its problems.

When I first went to Paris in the summer of 1958, meetings of the NATO council were held once a week and were fairly quiet affairs. By the time I left in 1962, we were meeting as many as four times each week in lively session. The change was partly due to De Gaulle's takeover of France, the growing power of West Germany, the increasing strength and reequipment of the Soviet forces and Kruschev's intemperate threats to blow us to bits. Behind the scenes there was much discussion about the control of nuclear weapons and the storage of their warheads.

I did not know whether Jules Léger really enjoyed his time as head of our NATO delegation. Jules was a man of peace, a truly gentle man who did not enjoy confrontations and was not at all at home in a robust military atmosphere. He once remarked to me that a diplomat looked at a problem quite differently to a military man. He said soldiers work on a given problem, examine all conditions as they exist at the time and then come up with a plan. After it is approved it is filed away as Plan A. If the conditions change they come up with another plan and file it away as Plan B. In External Affairs we never come up with a plan because the conditions affecting our problems change every hour. We come up with a number of considerations that may influence a final decision but we never make a detailed plan.

Certainly in matters pertaining to External Affairs and Foreign Policy Jules was without peer. On one occasion Howard Green, our Minister for External Affairs, called into conference in Paris all our Ambassadors in Europe. Also attending was Doug Harkness, our Minister of Defence, and Frank Miller the Chief of Defence Staff. At the meeting Howard Green shook me by denigrating NATO and all that it stood for, implying that we were a bunch of warmongers wasting taxpayers' money which could be better spent feeding the poor of 3rd world countries. He went on to say that Canada's foreign policy was going to change; in future it would be to get to know and love and help the small countries of the world. I was getting extremely irritated. Doug Harkness and Frank Miller cautioned me to cool down, when Jules Léger stood up. Addressing the Minister, I recall his saying that he did not wish to interpose on the discussion but he wanted to caution the Minister, because he had experience in these matters, that a policy based on loving everyone is not a foreign policy. He then sat down. I wanted to call for three cheers. Those few words had quite an effect on Howard Green.

Jules' quiet sense of humour, his vivacious and attractive wife Gaby, and their love of France helped him to endure his NATO posting. When he left he was succeeded by George Ignatieff with whom I had worked in London where he was Deputy to George Drew. How true it is that great men generally have wonderful wives; Gabrielle Léger and Alison Ignatieff fitted that description.

Whilst the political side of NATO was housed in the heart of Paris, the military headquarters of the Supreme Commander was in the country, about ten miles north-west of the city. Each country in NATO, except Iceland, was represented on the staff of Supreme Headquarters. Because of the size and efficiency of our Air Division, Canada had the position of Deputy Chief of Staff to General Norstad; it was filled, when I was there, by Air Marshal Larry Dunlap, a highly qualified airman and a great friend.

Supreme Headquarters was an operational headquarters in every sense and General Norstad was charged with many critical responsibilities. He could never let his guard down because the Russians played a number of tricks to test his reactions. One very serious incident, which could have led to the isolation of West Berlin, occurred when the Russians suddenly announced that the long established and agreed "air corridor" from West Germany to Berlin would be closed indefinitely because they would be firing rockets and anti-aircraft guns throughout the corridor.

To accept this "ukase" from the Kremlin would have been the beginning of endless discussions to find an alternative route. Instead, the decision was taken to ignore it and Plan "A", as Jules Léger would have called it, was put into affect. The British Airways flight that normally left West Germany for Berlin took off on time the next morning but it had no passengers; its crew were Royal Air Force and it carried cameras to record Russian reactions. As it entered the "prohibited" corridor it was accompanied by six fighters - two American, two British, two French. Other fighter aircraft were alerted in case of emergency.

The Russians did not interfere with the passage of the British Airways flight or the accompanying fighters, although they made all sorts of noises with anti-aircraft guns just outside the previously agreed corridor. Their bluff was called and normal traffic was resumed.

Field Marshal Montgomery used to hold a special study session each year to which he invited all Admirals, Generals and Air Marshals in NATO and the Chiefs of Staff of each country. Perhaps two or three hundred of us would attend and of course we all knew that there would be ''no smoking''—that was one of his rules. Another was that there would be ''no coughing'' and to ensure that those attending would have a means of suppressing their coughs he would have one of his aides push a large trolley around the audience containing as much as forty or fifty pounds of peppermint candies. We were expected to help ourselves. On one occasion Admiral Mountbatten waited until everyone had taken a few and then advanced across the floor and started ostentaciously to fill the pockets of his naval uniform. When Monty saw what he was doing he called out ''Go ahead Dickie - help yourself.'' ''I am,'' replied Mountbatten, ''that's the only reason I came here!''

During my four years with NATO I was able to see our Army and RCAF units on several occasions. I also visited Portsmouth when H.M.C.S. Bonaventure and four St. Laurent class destroyers of our Navy were taking part in NATO exercises. I have never been so proud of our Armed Services as I was during those years. They were well equipped, morale was high, discipline was good and there was a mood of confidence. The R.C.A.F. squadrons were winning trophies in air to air firing competitions and beating all comers including German and American. Their maintenance crews established records in the availability of aircraft. The Regiments in the Army Brigade were also winning all competitions that they entered. In fact, the 1st Battalion of the Canadian Guards, under Stu Graham and Willy Mulherin, won every competition one year that was open to them. They returned home with a truck full of trophies. Our three Services were our best ambassadors in NATO.

In June 1962 we returned to Canada and moved to Oakville. I was to take over the Army's Central Command there, comprising the whole of the Province of Ontario. At that time we had about 10,000 Regular Army and 21,000 Reserves or Militia in the command and also 43,000 cadets. We had the resources of material and transport to be able to make training fairly realistic.

One big problem in this important command was to keep the Army in front of the people. Toronto was a very large city even then and had already overtaken Montreal as the financial centre of the country. Its newspapers devoted a lot of coverage to items of national importance but they did not seem to have much interest in local military matters. But this certainly changed when Jim McPhee, a former bomber pilot in World War II, became my public relations officer. At his suggestion we had an annual "Press Night" in our Mess at which we were able to interest a number of able reporters in our activities.

I knew this command was to be my last posting in the Army; I would reach the retirement age of 55 in 1965 which would complete 35 years of army life for me. I was thoroughly enjoying my job and I had a good hard-working staff headed by Colonel Bill Seamark who had been with the 1st Canadian Division when we went overseas in 1939.

A year after the Liberals came to power again in 1963, a "White Paper" on Defence was published by the Minister, Paul Hellyer, which highlighted the need for integration of many functions in the Services, with which many of us agreed in principle; but it also made it appear that our Chiefs of Staff and their committees were ineffectual and that some unified command structure was essential to replace them. From the number of times it is quoted in the 1964 White Paper, the report of a Royal Commission on Government Organization appears to have been the basis of Hellyer's ideas.

I did not read the full report of the Royal Commission and I do not know if anyone on the Commission had any real knowledge of our Chiefs of Staff system but I have a strong feeling that Grant Glassco, who headed the Commission, got most of his information about the failure of the Chiefs of Staff system from none other than General Charles Foulkes who, in my opinion, had been the reason for the failure of the system. As Chief of Defence Staff, Charles Foulkes had the necessary authority to chair our effective Chiefs of Staff committee but he no longer had the ability to do it. He had not always been honest in his dealings with them and so they had lost confidence in him.

For Charles to blame the failure of the system on the inter-service rivalries of the Chiefs was unforgiveable to me because I had attended a number of their meetings when I was Vice Chief of the Army and it was becoming obvious that the weakness was in the Chairman himself.

Paul Hellyer lived in Toronto so I used to see him occasionally when he could get away from Ottawa. Although I could not agree with his plans to replace the Chiefs of Staff, I was very interested in his proposals to give top priority to reequip the Army as a Mobile Force, provide an adequate air and sea lift for it and purchase tactical aircraft to support it. It seemed to me that we were going to produce a smaller version of the U.S. Marine Corps which Paul Hellyer confirmed in conversations I had with him later. I told him I would support him if that was his intention. This would mean that in war our navy, army and airforce would be operating together instead of being kept apart as we were in World War II. The appointment of General Jean Allard as ''Chief of Operational Readiness' to build up the new force strengthened my belief that Hellyer knew what he wanted.

In November 1964 the Chief of Defence Staff, Air Chief Marshal Frank Miller, summoned all Admirals, Generals and Air Marshals to his office. We assumed we would be given further details of the plans for integration.

Instead, Mr. Hellyer strode in, sat down and addressed us as if we were a group of immigrants. My recollection is that he said the government had been elected by the people a year earlier, partly because of its announced plans to reorganise the Defence Forces. He said he was now speaking as a representative of those people and as a Minister of the Government. He told us that the government had decided to proceed immediately to the full unification of the navy, army and airforce, and we would become one force, with one uniform and one salute. He asked if we had any questions.

There was stunned silence for a moment and Admiral Bill Landymore said he would like to talk to his sailors about the proposed changes before asking any questions.

I recall Hellyer replying that he was not asking the Admiral to discuss the matter with anyone. He said that his plan for unification was going into effect immediately. He suggested that if any of us did not approve, we were to write our name and rank on a piece of paper and put it on his desk; we would be relieved of our commands and retired the next day. He then got up and left.

We all looked at Frank Miller and Geoff Walsh, who was now Vice Chief of Defence Staff, hoping for an explanation of Hellyer's outburst. Frank Miller tried to reassure us by saying that things were under control and that he would keep matters on an even keel. But from that moment I really began to have doubts about Miller's and Walsh's ability to do anything. They were pawns in the game - given the highest positions but without any real authority. It was following this meeting that I was told by Bill Landymore about the way Admiral Jeffry Brock had been fired by Hellyer in August. Frank Miller had been present on that occasion and must have realized that he was serving a very unstable minister. Yet, here he was telling us that he would not let things get out of hand. I was losing confidence already in the new look. Strangely enough, although physically we were fairly close to Ottawa, we in Central Command had very little idea of the chaotic conditions that prevailed there. Perhaps I should have realized what was happening when General Bernatchez - surely the best French-Canadian ever to become a General while in the Army - wrote to me in the summer of 1964 and told me he was retiring from the Army. He wrote ''I hope you won't think of me as a rat leaving a sinking ship, but I cannot take it any longer.''

In the spring of 1965 a group of influential men in Toronto, who had been in the Services during the war, led a crusade against unification. They were shocked that I supported Hellyer although they appreciated that as a serving officer I could not openly defy him.

Before I retired, the Militia officers of Toronto, Brampton and Oshawa Garrison presented me with a magnificent leather-bound set of Winston Churchill's History of World War II and his History of the English Speaking Peoples. General Guy Simonds attended the presentation and afterwards I had a letter of appreciation from him in which he thanked me for keeping everything going full blast in Ontario even though things were falling apart in Ottawa. Simonds was Honorary Colonel of two regiments in Toronto, so he realized only too well the way things were going.

I retired in June 1965 after three years in Central Command which I believe were profitable to both the Regular Army and Militia. We had not let the reorganization in Ottawa affect our training programmes, although some of the directives emanating from the new unified staff were quite incomprehensible. I had one letter signed by an Admiral dealing with the training of private soldiers; when I phoned him to get clarification he admitted that he had no idea what the letter was about when he had signed it. Obviously, changes were being made for the sake of change.

But the incident that disturbed me most occurred at my final parade at the Canadian National Exhibition when 18 bands, in full dress, marched and counter-marched in my honour. Paul Hellyer attended the parade and told me that he had been able to get the promise of their full support from three senior officers of the Royal Canadian Air Force; Sharp, Reyno and Carpenter. I told him I did not know Sharp but neither Reyno nor Carpenter had any knowledge of how the Army operated or of its requirements; and that I had a poor opinion of Carpenter. I said that I hope they would never be in a position of authority over soldiers. He did not reply. It was obvious that Hellyer was buying loyalty with promotions and I was sorry to see friends of mine climb on the bandwagon and join the circus in Ottawa.

Once I had officially retired I began to hear about the scramble for power at National Defence Headquarters. I realized that Hellyer's plans for a tri-service force-in-being along the lines of the U.S. Marines, outlined in his White Paper of 1964 and in conversation with me, had been discarded. I then wrote a personal letter to the Prime Minister, Mike Pearson, asking him if he realized what was happening to the Armed Services; and suggesting that, if he and his cabinet were so convinced that unification was the right step, it would be sensible to bring about the changes in an orderly, planned, sequence based on a 5 or 10 year programme. This would give time for each move to be assessed intelligently before proceeding to the next. His reply stated that he valued my advice.

Bob Winters, who was a member of Mr. Pearson's cabinet had told me that the cabinet would not allow Hellyer to go too far. I heard subsequently from him that when Mr. Pearson questioned Hellyer on his plans he said flatly that he knew what he was doing and that he would resign from the Liberal Party unless he was allowed to go ahead with his reorganization. Rather than divide the Party, Pearson backed down.

Thus, in a short period of a year and a half I witnessed the dismemberment of one of the most efficient and cost-effective small armies that had been created in peacetime. No longer did anyone in Ottawa have the direct responsibility for the efficiency of the Army. The General Staff and the commanders it served were removed; the three administrative Corps that had served the Army so well and of which we were so proud disappeared, the Service Corps that fed and moved us, the Electrical and Mechanical Engineers that repaired us, the Ordnance Corps that housed our stores and ammunition. All were gone. Camps, training areas, storage depots were disposed of. Six first class infantry battalions and an armoured regiment were disbanded; all Regimental depots were closed. One General even proposed that the infantry and armoured Regiments that remained should be forced to give up their names, of which they were proud, and be given numbers instead. It was change for the sake of change.

Promotions were handed out to gain support for the changes. During World War II we had a total of three Chiefs of Staff of three star rank in Ottawa responsible for over 750,000 sailors, soldiers and airman - today, there are five in that city responsible for only 75,000. In the Army in 1964 we had a ratio of one officer to thirteen other ranks - today, as part of the unified force it is one officer to five. There are now more Warrant Officers and Non-Commissioned Officers than there are Privates. I could go on and on with examples of wasteful use of personnel resources but I think that one of the most destructive changes made from an Army point of view was to destroy the initiative of junior commanders by centralizing authority to the new "geographic" commands. Training Command was established in Winnipeg and it had to authorize the smallest items across the whole country before any action could be taken. Fortunately this system was changed when later the authorities found it would not work.

In 1974 I was appointed Colonel Commandant of Royal Canadian Infantry Corps. In many respects this is an honorary title since the individual receives no pay but it gave me an opportunity to visit a number of regular and militia infantry units. I also attended conferences of the Infantry Association, a group of serving and retired officers who are dedicated to the future welfare and efficiency of the Infantry Corps. On a visit to our Brigade Group in Germany I was shocked to see that the strength of the infantry companies was about one half of what they should have been. This was particularly serious since we only had two battalions of infantry in the Brigade instead of three.

From a helicopter I observed one company taking part in a training exercise. I counted only 42 men instead of at least 100. I was assured that the 42 I had seen were the complete company - no one was absent. On my return to Canada I wrote a strong letter to the Chief of Defence Staff and, since he said he could do nothing, I went to see the Minister who was the Hon. Barney Danson. Barney had been in the Queen's Own when they landed on D-Day in Normandy and had been severely wounded, so I knew I would be dealing with a man who realized the importance of maintaining the strength of infantry units. When he landed in Normandy his company was about 120 strong - by the end of the first day it had been reduced to about 70. I asked him how he would like to command a company going into its first battle with only 42.

He was shocked when I gave him the accurate strengths of all our infantry battalions with most of them at about 55% of requirements. I also reminded him that the Brigades in Canada had not been exercised since 1964 and that, since unification, no one had been permitted to prepare a mobilization plan in case of emergency. Barney Danson admitted he could not make any changes as Prime Minister Trudeau had ordered the reduction of our NATO ''commitment'' to one half of its effective strength in 1968 and was not interested.

When ''unification'' was mentioned to Sir Winston Churchill he said he wanted none of it. He was reported as saying the end result would be ''a sludge of amalgam.'' How right he was.

In the United States and in Britain they retained their Chiefs of Staff and the three services. The change they made in the U.K. was to make the individual services into training and administrative organizations. Their duty now is to train their officers and men and group them into operational units. Once the unit is operational, its deployment is the responsibility of the Chief of Defence Staff who, of course, is assisted by the Chiefs of the three services; but the individual service must continue to provide for and administer its operational units. Command is exercised by the Chief of Defence Staff through a ''unified'' command structure in which a soldier, sailor or airman commands all the forces in his command. For the Falklands operation an Admiral was the overall commander throughout - he had a small unified headquarters and reported directly to the Chief of Defence Staff. I understand that the U.S. Forces operate in much the same way. If Canada had adopted that same policy it would have saved us the humiliation of our present military impotence.

Dedication of the "Surrender Room", Wageningen, Holland, 1975
Hans Teengs-Gerritsen, The Author, Prince Bernhard

19

Tomorrow's Leaders

Two years after I retired, the Duke of Edinburgh appointed me President of his Award scheme in Canada. In was honoured and delighted to accept. His Royal Highness had long felt that, due to the increasing pace and technical complexity of life, youngsters were having difficulty in focusing on and attaining achieveable goals. For my part, as a soldier, I had always been among young people, enjoyed their company and admired their youthful energy so that I now welcomed the opportunity to serve in this constructive programme.

The Duke of Edinburgh's Award is not a team project; its aim is to help the individual. The idea is that a youngster, boy or girl, aided by an adult, selects a project of interest in each of the four sections of the programme: Service, Expedition and Exploration, Skills and Physical Fitness. Under Service, for instance, a youngster has the choice of life saving, first aid, home nursing, care of animals, mountain rescue, helping those who are deaf, dumb and blind, and other similar activities. Having selected one of them, the youngster and the adult set an attainable standard which must be achieved in a prescribed period. It is a challenge from Prince Philip to individual youngsters to measure themselves, not against each other but against standards set for them—to make the effort and to stay with it.

There are three levels of challenge—bronze, silver and gold—and the Award is designed for the average person. The standards are within reach of the great majority of young people. It is a test of character and, throughout the years, I have been impressed at the change of outlook in youngsters who have progressed through each of the three Award categories. Perhaps shy and withdrawn at first, they have emerged confident and skilled. The disabled, crippled and deaf also take part and gain even more from the programme than those not disadvantaged because their sense of accomplishment is greater.

In 1963 Vacy Ash, then President of Shell Canada, was appointed by Prince Philip as first president in Canada. He was followed two years later by Trumbull Warren who was President of RHEEM. When I took over in 1967 George Manson, a retired Commander of the Royal Canadian Navy, was our only full time worker, and as usual in projects of this kind, we had very little money but a great deal of enthusiasm. George Manson travelled across Canada spreading the word and trying to interest adults in various towns in becoming the catalysts around whom the Award would develop. He met with considerable success but I felt that a personal visit from Prince Philip was needed to create the momentum necessary for the success of the project. In the fall of 1969 he flew his aircraft across the Atlantic and we met him at St. John, New Brunswick. This was the beginning of a tour during which he devoted two weeks to visiting schools and groups in eleven communities from New Brunswick to British Columbia.

Fortunately General Jimmy Dextraze, and others in the Armed Forces, realized the value of the Award in the development of youth and lent us their support. Their most important assistance came from Lieut.-Colonel Jim McPhee who headed our public relations programme. Jim had been with me in Vancouver and Oakville and had the confidence of the press wherever he went. By the end of the tour he had also gained the confidence of Prince Philip to such an extent that he was made responsible for public relations on many subsequent visits of Her Majesty the Queen and His Royal Highness.

The best display by young people in the Award programme was staged in Peterborough, Ontario, where 7,000 parents and friends crowded the bleachers in a local arena and the youngsters exhibited their achievements on the floor. One group of three girls had done their exploration by horseback through Algonquin Park and the rugged

Haliburton Hills. They had made a model of their journey to show Prince Philip and had a detailed diary with photographs to indicate the difficult terrain they had traversed; to cap it all, they had their ponies in the arena with them. Another Award winner, this time a boy, had built a bicycle out of bits and pieces he had found on a dump; on it he had mounted a small engine which gave the bike a speed of about 10 m.p.h. Prince Philip had the crowd cheering as he drove the bike around the arena. There were about 50 other exhibits; each proudly displayed by a youngster who had reached a bronze, silver or gold standard. Prince Philip was very impressed by the young people and the quality of their achievements. He said it was the best display he had seen.

A few days later, after a number of other visits, we left Calgary early for Cranbrook, B.C., the airport for Kimberley. Unfortunately it had been snowing for several hours so there was some doubt about whether we would be able to land. Prince Philip, who was flying his aircraft, was determined to try and make it as we knew, from phone calls the evening before, that the whole town of Kimberley was keyed up and waiting. It was still snowing hard, with zero visibility as we flew over Crankbrook, so Prince Philip circled the area for about half an hour, hoping for a break in the snow-clouds. Suddenly we heard a shout over the intercom, ''Hang on—there's a hole and I'm going down through it.'' Prince Philip had a tumultuous reception in Kimberley where, in spite of light snow, the drum majorettes in leotards and scanty costumes made way for him down the main street. It was a most enjoyable and rewarding visit.

In Vancouver and Victoria Prince Philip visited a number of schools including one for the deaf and another for retarded children. He was extremely moved by the achievements of these disadvantaged young people. I think they were the first schools of their kind that had taken up the Award, and the benefits of its challenge were very obvious.

The only unfortunate event on the tour occurred at the Vancouver Hall when Prince Philip called on the Mayor. After His Royal Highness signed the visitor's book, the Mayor, without any previous warning, asked Prince Philip if he would open a wing of the City Hall that had just been completed. Normally, because of tight schedules, this sort of request would have been turned down but Prince Philip agreed to do it when he was assured there would be no ceremony—just a ribbon to be cut.

It was raining when we stepped out into a courtyard. There, opposite, was an unfinished and unattractive extension to the City Hall. There was a problem with the ribbon ceremony because no one had any scissors and, whilst we waited in the rain, Prince Philip asked the Mayor what the extension was to be used for. The Mayor appeared very vague and said he really did not know. By this time Prince Philip was obviously annoyed at His Worship so, when the scissors were finally produced, he cut the ribbon, looked up at the extension and said, "Whatever you are going to be - consider yourself open." We left the City Hall immediately after.

The Award has gained momentum in the past fifteen years and close to one hundred thousand young Canadians have participated, the majority of whom have succeeded in reaching bronze, silver or gold standard. Around the world many hundreds of thousands of young people have taken part as the scheme has been adopted, not only in most Commonwealth countries but also, under different names, in countries such as the United States and Israel.

In 1968 I became interested in another project connected with youth which has since expanded to become known as the United World Colleges, of which "Pearson College of the Pacific" on Vancouver Island is one of several.

But in 1968 there was only one school in the system. It was called Atlantic College and was the brainchild of many eminent people including German born Dr. Kurt Hahn whose theories on the education of youth led to quarrels with Adolf Hitler and happily for Britain, to the founding in the 1930's of Gordonstoun School in Scotland and, in the early 1960's, of Atlantic College in Wales. On a visit to Paris, Kurt Hahn had been impressed by the degree of understanding reached at the N.A.T.O. Defence College between officers of countries which, only a few years before, had been at war or, even worse, had considered themselves superior to those from the smaller nations. How much more effective it would be, suggested Kurt Hahn, if the understanding could be encouraged in young people of 16 as a part of their education. So, Atlantic College was born with students from many of the countries of Europe and the Mediterranean area. The youngsters came from all classes of society to complete their last two years of high school prior to entering university. Initially a boys school, it soon changed to include girls.

Where possible students were given scholarships and amongst the school's earliest supporters were British Trade Unions and the educational authorities in the various counties and districts in Britain.

The first headmaster was a retired Admiral and Engineer, Desmond Hoare. He was a man who had an understanding of young people and a sympathetic approach to their problems. But he was shrewd, practical and consistent—qualities that were much in demand as he, the teachers and the boys worked out a curriculum together. It was a new type of school, designed to promote understanding between young people of different colours, races, creeds and wealth. It required a very high academic standard and, to develop the character of the students, it had an outdoor programme that challenged the resolution of each individual. Competitive sports were not a part of the curriculum as they tended to produce "gladiators"; instead, stress was placed on the individual taking part in activities such as cliff rescue, mountain climbing and off-shore resue. If individuals were not suited to such exploits they went into forestry, land reclamation or social work.

Through the generosity of a Frenchman, Antoine Besse, the college was given St. Donat's Castle in South Wales, a medieval fortress rebuilt by Randolph Hearst for Marion Davies. Fortunately for us she did not like it and it was sold with all the modern improvements, including central heating.

The purpose of Atlantic College is to bring intelligent young people of different nations together in an environment in which they gain a better and more sympathetic understanding of many of the world's problems. They share everything—meals, rooms, studies and leisure time. Discussions of a country's problems are conducted, without rancour, both in and out of class. Sharing a room in one of the houses might be a Turk, a Nigerian, an Italian and a Canadian. In another, an Arab and an Israili sleep beside each other; they gain an understanding of the others' problems without necessarily agreeing with their policies.

Atlantic College now has 300 students; it was one of the first schools to introduce the International baccalaureate as the graduating examination, in keeping with the high academic standards required for entry.

In 1968 I joined a group who were planning to open a similar school in Canada. The originator of the idea was Dr. Cedric Sowby, Principal Emeritus of Upper Canada College; the President of our Committee was Senator Donald Cameron, the founder of the Banff School of Fine Arts. It was slow going at first because very few people had heard of Atlantic College or of its growing importance. But two events helped to change this. Earl Mountbatten had taken over the Chairmanship of the United World Colleges and Lester Pearson, who had just retired as Prime Minister, became most interested in the Canadian plan and accepted the position of Honourary Chairman of the committee. I was named its Executive Director. Funds began to trickle in and ideas were beginning to firm up.

Before his death Mike Pearson had persuaded Senator John Nicol of Vancouver to head the fund raising drive for the new school. After his death John Nicol took over the Chairmanship of the whole project and, with the agreement of the Pearson family, launched the very successful drive for funds which resulted in the College being built and named "Lester B. Pearson College of the Pacific."

There are an increasing number of schools operating under the banner of "United World Colleges." In addition to Atlantic College and our own Pearson of the Pacific there is the College of South East Asia in Singapore, the College of Southern Africa in Swaziland, the College of the Adriatic in Italy, the College of the American West in the U.S. and Simon Bolivar College in Venezuela.

It has been a rewarding experience to be so closely linked with a system that has turned out many hundreds of bright intelligent students who are now scattered around the world with a much better understanding of each other's problems. Many of them will doubtless become leaders in their own countries and it is to be hoped that when they rise to the top they will put into practice what they learned at one of the United World Colleges.

In October 1969 I was asked by Premier Robarts of Ontario to go as Commissioner of the Ontario Pavilion at the World's Fair, EXPO 70, opening in March at Osaka, Japan. This was a challenge which I was delighted to accept particularly as Audrey and our son and daughter could join me during the school holidays.

Canada had a total of four Pavilions at EXPO 70. The Canadian one was a brilliant combination of wood, water and mirrors and was officially judged to be the most attractive at EXPO. The B.C. Pavilion was also attractive but in a smaller way. Its main feature was a grouping of over fifty giant Douglas fir logs arranged and stepped up like the organ pipes in a church. The tallest was over 200 feet and the shortest about 4 feet; it was quite spectacular and attracted the attention of millions of Japnese visitors.

By comparison the exteriors of the Ontario and Quebec Pavilions were dull, making use largely of concrete and steel in a country that was then the second largest steel producer in the world. The Japanese were not impressed. I don't think the architect of the Ontario Pavilion could have studied the Japanese mentality. Wood and water are two of the most important elements in the minds of most of them. How much better it would have been to design a building of plywoods and laminated beams enclosing a large scale reproduction of Niagara Falls accompanied by the tumultuous roar of the falls themselves.

We showed a good film of Ontarians at play on a 120 foot wide screen but by far the best "exhibits" we had were the 48 young hosts, hostesses and members of the Ontario Provincial Police (O.P.P.) who were on our staff. We had 16 of each and they were outstanding. The hosts and hostesses were given special instruction in Japanese for six months before EXPO so that they were able to talk with the people and get to know them. They were a lively group and were the envy of other Pavilions.

The 16 members of the O.P.P. were all well over 6 feet in height, had also been coached in Japanese and were great favourites with the millions of camera buffs who visited the Pavilion.

If I had designed the Ontario Pavilion I would have included a restaurant. I know they absorb a lot of energy and mean a lot of extra work but I think they are worth it. New Zealand had a small Pavilion with a restaurant; it had a menu limited primarily to their famous lamb but it was always packed and gave that country a special place at EXPO.

When it was all over and it came time to pull down every building in accordance with normal EXPO agreements, Ontario had to pay over $150 thousand to have ours removed; our steel and concrete had little wreckers value. On the other hand B.C. received a handsome sum from the wreckers for their valuable timber—as were other Pavilions that were primarily of wood.

One further point of interest. The Japanese had to clear a huge area of bamboo swamp to create the site for EXPO 70; land is a very precious thing to them. For our EXPO 67, with more land to spare than any other country, we solemnly filled in a large area of the St. Lawrence River! Japan's EXPO was planned and built by hard-headed business men—they made an official profit of $180 million. God knows who planned our EXPO 67 but they were certainly not business men—we lost $280 million!

EXPO 70 had taken me away from my work with United World Colleges for almost a year; however, in October 1970, on my return I had a letter from Lord Mountbatten concerning our future activities. He was playing a very active role in our affairs and was anxious to promote the fullest cooperation between the U.S. and Canada. He wanted me to be the catalyst in both countries.

President Nixon had offered to help and a dinner had been arranged at the White House in November to which he had invited about one hundred of the most influential men in the United States. We were to be represented by Senator Cameron, Dr. William Gibson of Vancouver, Colonel Bob Houston and myself.

Shortly before leaving for Washington to attend the gathering, Premier Robarts offered me the Chairmanship of the Liquor Control Board of Ontario, of which I would be Chief Executive Officer. Audrey and I felt I could not refuse; it would give me a challenging few years at a fair salary when expenses for the education of our children would be at their highest.

On the following morning I accepted, and shortly afterwards John Robarts asked me to go and see him. He surprised me by saying that he knew very little about the way the Board operated. When he had taken over as Premier one of the first things he had done was to take the Chairmanship of the Board out of politics; he had appointed to that job the retiring Chairman of I.B.C. Mr. Shepherd. Prior to Shepherd the Chairman had always been a senior politican and member of the Provincial Cabinet. Shepherd had done a good job for eight years but his health had broken down and he was anxious to retire.

John Robarts went on to say that if I had any problems that might reflect on the Board or on the Government I was to call him personally—no matter what hour of the day or night. "I want to hear about it from you—and not be confronted with it by someone else." He told me not to allow politics to interfere with the operation of the Board—"if a politician puts any pressure on you, give me his name and I'll deal with him." They were comforting words from a great man. I was to take over on 1 December 1970.

My problem now was to let Mountbatten know that I would have to give up my working interest in United World Colleges. I decided to tell him in Washington after the President's dinner—it was only a week away—but I was not looking forward to telling him. He had been boosting my name to all his friends and he was so anxious to get on now that we had a good team. I changed planes in New York and climbed on board the one bound for Washington. As I was going forward to my seat I heard a shout "George - come and sit here with me. I want to introduce you to my friends." I was introduced to "Bo" Polk who told me he had just raised fifteen million dollars on behalf of some university, and to Mr. Dewey who had been defeated by Harry Truman in the race for the Presidencey in 1948. I felt awful as Mountbatten regaled us with his plans and told his friends what I was going to do in Canada. I didn't summon up the courage to tell him even after the dinner; instead I wrote him a letter apologizing for not having been frank with him, and had an understanding reply saying that from a family point of view he didn't blame me—he would have done the same.

When I arrived at the Liquor Control Board early in December I was delighted to find that the Board was one in name only since the only two people who were officially a part of it were myself and Jack Harris. Jack was Vice Chairman whose particular job was to handle most of the problems that had political overtones and he was very good at it. He had been a Conservative member of the Legislature for some years; he had been at Dieppe in 1942, been wounded and finally rescued after floating around in the Channel.

I want to write about my five and one half year stay with the L.C.B.O. to outline briefly its strengths and its weaknesses as I saw them. To tell the full story of our operations and my experiences would fill a book by itself.

Shortly after taking over I was able to get clarification of an important question from Mr. Robarts. What is the main purpose of the Liquor Control Board? Is it to raise money for the treasury or is it to satisfy the public? I spoke to him on the phone; he said that in about 1942 profit from the Board represented over 20% of the Provincial budget; it was then considered an important source of funds. However, it now only represented about 3½%—so in his opinion a satisfied public was now the top priority. We went ahead on that basis.

The General Manager was Jim Abra who had been with the Board in a variety of jobs for about 25 years. Jim knew everything there was to know about the operations of our different departments and his judgment was sound. I think his greatest strength was the respect in which he was held by all our Managers. They trusted him to be frank with them and he was.

To me our supervisors and the managers of our stores were a strong group. Many of them were veterans of World War II or Korea who had had to make decisions when they were very young and this had helped them when they were in positions of authority. We encouraged them to take part in community projects in their areas in order to gain the confidence of their public; one became mayor of a large town, others headed fund raising drives for United Way and other charities.

Another strength was the addition by my predecessor of a number of chartered accountants to the staff at Head Office. They maintained an effective in-store year round audit and also helped in the introduction and operation of an efficient computer system.

The division at Head Office which we called Product Control was a particularly good one which we expanded greatly. It was responsible for checking the quality of all products we were buying or planning to buy. We provided our chemists with all the latest laboratory equipments in order that they could do their job efficiently.

We also had an efficient system for the tasting and selection of wines; however occasionally I had to remind our committee that we were the only marketplace for liquors and wines. When agents took the trouble to visit Europe to select wines that they felt were good, or different enough, to be listed by us we should bend over backwards to give them a chance.

Our main weakness was our monolithic structure. Once employees joined us they would generally remain until they had earned maximum pension, and, of course, there was no other branch of government to which they could be transferred to improve their position or gain more experience. We were the only marketplace in the government handling our kind of product and the opportunities for an employee to get to Head Office were not great. Our staff there was small and with nowhere for them to go they might remain in the same position for fifteen years; far too long for continued efficiency and also a block against the promotion of others.

During my years with the Board we increased the number of our stores from about 290 to over 500. We established a Rare Wine and Spirit Division which brought in wines and spirits in limited supply for the benefit of those who appreciated their particular qualities. We recruited and trained a number of employees to be wine consultants—giving them the advantage of visits to the wine producing areas of Europe. We equipped 25 large trailers as mobile Liquor Stores so that they could be moved from place to place to respond to seasonal activities.

In my first two years we doubled the number of imported wines by listing an additional 500 brands. This was done primarily to satisfy the demands of an increasingly travel conscious and knowledgeable public but it had an important side effect. The grape growers of Ontario had a strangle-hold on the majority of wine makers of that Province. In order to protect the grape growers the Government would not permit the wineries to import any foreign grapes for the production of wine. They could only use grapes grown in Ontario; and since the common purple Labrusca grape gave a good yield and a fair price many grape growers were content to grow nothing but Labrusca. This grape does not produce good wine and gave most earlier Ontario wines a bad name. In desperation the wineries often used this grape in the production of sweet sherry-type wines, some of which were not palatable except to those on the verge of becoming alcoholics.

Fortunately a small number of wineries, including Brights , and Jordans which owned tracts of land capable of growing good grapes, experimented in the 40's and 50's with a hybrid vine by grafting good European cuttings onto Labrusca roots. The results were encouraging and fortunately for me these experiments were beginning to bear fruit when we started to import increasing numbers of foreign wines.

Brights and Jordans began to produce better quality wines; Inniskilling Wines, a new company which controlled its own supply of grapes, went into limited production of excellent wines. The Grape Growers Association saw the writing on the wall but, still protected by the Government, they stupidly raised the price of their grapes above that of good Californian ones. It made no sense—particularly as the Government allowed 20,000 tons of California grapes each year to be imported duty free by the Torontonians of Italian descent so that they could process the grapes and make their own wine! They could have the grapes but the wineries could not. It seemed to me that the wine drinkers of Ontario were the hostages of a handful of grape growers. It was dirty politics and I'm happy to say that shortly after I left the Board in 1976 the wineries got their first break and were allowed to import some foreign wines for blending.

In May of 1975 and 1985 I was invited officially by the authorities in Holland to attend the 30th and 40th anniversaries of their liberation from the Nazi yoke. On each occasion religious services and the laying of a wreath by the Queen at the National Cenotaph in Amsterdam have been the highlight of their celebrations. At these ceremonies they thanked God for their liberation and remembered the courageous men and women of the Resistance and the Armed Forces who had died in their struggle for freedom.

It was at other ceremonies and parades that the people of Holland remembered the part played by Canadians in those momentous weeks leading to the German surrender.

On these occasions the normally staid and calm Dutch people release their emotions with laughter and tears of joy in just the same way they did when our soldiers moved into their towns and villages in 1945. It is an experience that the thousands of our veterans who have taken part will never forget. It is like a second home-coming to be their house guests; to meet such kindness and such a warm welcome from young and old after so many years, and then to visit the Canadian cemetaries in which our dead are buried and find each grave adorned with flowers laid there by Dutch children whose families makes a point of tending each grave; it makes each one of us veterans realize more than anything else, the value that the Dutch people set on their freedom. That is what our soldiers gave back to them after five years of Nazi domination when freedom of speech, freedom of movement—in fact every, freedom which we enjoy in a democracy—was denied them. It was during this period that the Resistance (or Forces of the Interior as it was officially called) was formed and it was my privilege in both 1975 and 1985 to meet a number of the men and women who had survived the ordeal of being hunted by the Gestapo and others who, once caught, were imprisoned under terrible conditions in concentration camps such as Dachau. Only the strong could survive the treatment they had to endure. Many were executed by firing squads on what is now hallowed ground amongst the sand dunes near the Hague.

On one inspiring leader of the Resistance who survived over two years in Dachau is Hans Teengs Gerritsen whom I met in 1975. He introduced me then to others who had kept the flame of freedom alive; P.C. Maleipaard of Hilversum, a giant of a man who was known as "the Horse"; Ries Ville - the "Rat of Rotterdman" because he hid in the sewers of that city. I will always remember them. The Horse died recently but the Rat was once again at the celebrations in Wageningen in 1985.

Prince Bernhard took the salute at the parade in 1975 and it was interesting to me to see him moving amongst the veterans of the Resistance. In 1945, as their overall Commander, he had welcomed them as each part of Holland was liberated. The climax of these welcomes must have been when the Dutch survivors of Dachau, liberated by the U.S. Army and provided by them with a German bus for transportation, drove back to Holland with Hans Teengs Gerritsen at the wheel. I wish I had been there to witness it.

Unfortunately Prince Bernhard could not attend the 1985 celebrations as he was in hospital recovering from major surgery, however his daughter Princess Margriet took his place on the reviewing stand. She was born in Ottawa during World War II and so had a special place in the hearts of our veterans. That night Hans Teengs Gerritsen and his friends of the Resistance gave a dinner for 900 veterans and their wives as a "thank you for giving us back our freedom."

It seems to me that it is only when freedom has been denied, and then regained, that it is fully appreciated. We, in Canada, have not been invaded for 170 years—we have not had our towns and villages destroyed in war; we have never had our freedoms denied to us. In fact we should be the happiest and most united of peoples and yet we tend to do everything we can to disunite ourselves. The Provinces have gained strength at the expense of the Federal authority—in fact "authority" at any level is constantly being challenged by dissatisfied groups aided by lawyers who want to profit financially or through publicity. On the surface no one seems content with anything. The news media, desperately looking for something controversial to fill in time or "copy," will create a problem by inuendo or supposition in order to grab a headline or start a telephone hot-line. Governments are voted in with handsome majorities only to be told by opinion polls six months later that they no longer enjoy the confidence of the people! Almost everything a successful man, or woman, company or institution does is suspect and has to be investigated; there must be something rotten somewhere that will bring them down. Whilst I don't believe for one moment that people believe the stories that are fed them through the media, I am very concerned that the gradual erosion of confidence in our institutions and in our fellow men and women will produce a nation of sceptics and doubters. We need a National Purpose; a catalyst that will give us all a common resolve.

There is no doubt that the two World Wars gave Canadians a real sense of pride and accomplishment. In 1945 we were a united people and had become a very important country in spite of a population of only 12 million. Our actions and opinions were greatly respected in the world; we attracted a million immigrants. But it must not take another war to bring us together.

Our history books tell us that the completion of the railroad in 1885 gave a great sense of national pride and accomplishment to Canadians at the time. It brought the West firmly into Confederation and a flood of immigrants into the country. I believe that, in the same way that the railroads focussed the attention of Canadians a hundred years ago, the opening up and exploration of our Arctic could be the catalyst that would give Canadians a great sense of national achievement. I think the Armed Forces must take the lead in establishing bases in the High Arctic together with the R.C.M.P. They represent the Federal authority which is so necessary to establish soveriegnty and law and order. In order to interest all young Canadians in joining the move to the North I would establish a form of national service to be known as "Arctic

Service'' for which all young people of 18 and 19 years of age would be eligible. This would have to be a form of military service in order to instil the necessary desciplines for survival and movement. The fittest of these young people would go into the High Arctic—the others would be support groups on the mainland of the North West Territories. After 6 months of training and then 12 months of achievement in the Arctic, the individual could be rewarded with special credits for university entrance or a bonus for those going into business.

In our retirement here in Victoria we keep in touch with young people in a variety of ways. Although jobs are the first things they want and 90% of them will go out of their ways to find one, what they need just as much is leadership and inspiration. It is time that our men and women in their forties and fifties gave it to them. Go North, young Canada, go North!

INDEX

THE RANK ACCORDED TO INDIVIDUALS IS THE SENIOR
ONE REACHED IN THE TEXT OF THESE MEMOIRS.

INDEX

INDEX

INDEX

INDEX

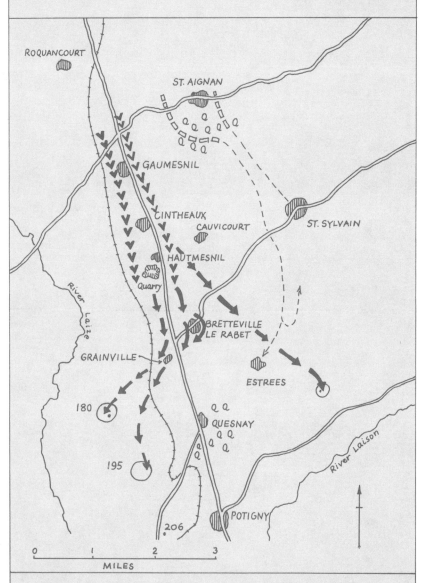

TOTALIZE PHASE 2 8-9 AUGUST

ROQUANCOURT

ST. AIGNAN

GAUMESNIL

CINTHEAUX
CAUVICOURT
ST. SYLVAIN

HAUTMESNIL

River Laize

Quarry

BRETTEVILLE
LE RABET

GRAINVILLE

ESTREES

180

QUESNAY

River Laison

195

206 POTIGNY

0 1 2 3
MILES

4 CANADIAN ARMOURED DIVISION   1 POLISH ARMOURED DIVISION
8·August > > > > > > > > > >   8· August □ □ □ □ □ □ □
9·August ➔ ➔ ➔ ➔ ➔ ➔   9 August – – – – – – ➔